Race, Space, and the Law

RACE,

SPACE,

and the

LAW

Unmapping a White Settler Society

edited by
Sherene H. Razack

Between the Lines, Toronto

Race, Space, and the Law

First published in Canada in 2002 by
Between the Lines
720 Bathurst Street, Suite #404
Toronto, Ontario
M5S 2R4

National Library of Canada Cataloguing in Publication Data

Main entry under title:

   Race, space, and the law : unmapping a white settler society

Includes bibliographical references.
ISBN 1-896357-59-8

1. Segregation—Canada—History. 2. Race discrimination—Canada—History.
3. Canada—Colonization. I. Razack, Sherene

FC104.R313 2002   305.8'0971   C2002-900111-0
F1035.A1R33 2002

Cover and text design by David Vereschagin, Quadrat Communications

Printed in Canada

Between the Lines gratefully acknowledges assistance for its publishing activities from the Canada Council for the Arts, the Ontario Arts Council, and the Government of Canada through the Book Publishing Industry Development Program.

This book is dedicated to the memory of all those who have endured the loss of loved ones through racial violence, and who have suffered through their loss a second time when the law and society refused to name it so.

Permissions

The publisher gratefully acknowledges the *Canadian Journal of Law and Society* for granting permission to reproduce revised versions of chapters 2, 3, 4, 5, 6, 8, and 9, which originally appeared in volume 15,2 (2000) of the *Journal*.

CONTENTS

ACKNOWLEDGEMENTS

This collection began as a special issue of the *Canadian Journal of Law and Society*. We owe a debt of gratitude to the editor Ruth Murbach and to all the anonymous reviewers whose comments helped to make the chapters better. The authors wish to thank their family and friends for endless hours of support. Paul Eprile of Between the Lines displayed an unflagging enthusiasm for the collection as did Beth McAuley who painstakingly edited and greatly improved the book. We thank them both. The majority of the contributors produced their work in the department of Sociology and Equity Studies in Education (SESE) of the Ontario Institute for Studies in Education of the University of Toronto. We are grateful to all those in SESE who enriched our scholarship. The production of this book was supported by a grant from the Social Sciences and Humanities Research Council and we thank them. Finally, these chapters owe a great deal to the people whose lives are discussed here. It is our hope that this book contributes to the ending of racial violence in the lives of Aboriginal peoples and people of colour.

Sherene H. Razack
Toronto
January, 2002

When Place Becomes Race

Sherene H. Razack

In 1983, commenting on section 97 (b) of the *Indian Act*, which made it an offence for a person to be intoxicated on an Indian reserve, a judge of the Manitoba Court of Appeal commented that its logic was both spatial and racial: "Place becomes race," he concluded succinctly of the now repealed section.[1] This book explores *how* place becomes race through the law. The authors examine drinking establishments, parks, slums, classrooms, urban spaces of prostitution, provincial parliaments, the location of mosques, and national borders, exploring how such spaces are organized to sustain unequal social relations and how these relations shape spaces. To highlight our specific interest in how the constitution of spaces reproduces racial hierarchies, we examine the spatial and legal practices required in the making and maintaining of a white settler society.

A white settler society is one established by Europeans on non-European soil. Its origins lie in the dispossession and near extermination of Indigenous populations by the conquering Europeans. As it evolves, a white settler society continues to be structured by a racial hierarchy. In the national mythologies of such societies, it is believed that white people came first and that it is they who principally developed the land; Aboriginal peoples are presumed to be mostly dead or assimilated. European settlers thus *become* the original inhabitants and the group most entitled to the fruits of citizenship. A quintessential feature of white settler mythologies is, therefore, the disavowal of conquest, genocide, slavery, and the exploitation of the labour of peoples of colour. In North America, it is still the case that European conquest and colonization are often denied, largely through the fantasy that North America was peacefully settled and not colonized.

For example, delivering the prestigious Massey lectures for the year 2000, the well-known Canadian scholar Michael Ignatieff takes to task Aboriginal leader Ovide Mercredi and Aboriginal scholar and judge Mary Ellen Turpel for using the term "settler-colonials" when referring to the Europeans who colonized Canada: "To speak this way, as if settlement were merely a form of imperial domination, is to withhold recognition of the right of the majority to settle and use the land we both share." In this view, violent colonization simply did not happen:

> Throughout centuries of collaboration between newcomers and aboriginal nations, Native peoples have always accepted, with varying degrees of willingness, the fact that being first possessors of the land is not the only source of legitimacy for its use. Those who came later have acquired legitimacy by their labours; by putting the soil under cultivation; by uncovering its natural resources; by building great cities and linking them together with railways, highways, and now fibre-optic networks and the Internet. To point out the legitimacy of non-aboriginal settlement in Canada is not to make a declaration about anyone's superiority or inferiority, but simply to assert that each has a fair claim to the land and that it must be shared.[2]

Mythologies or national stories are about a nation's origins and history. They enable citizens to think of themselves as part of a community, defining who belongs and who does not belong to the nation. The story of the land as shared and as developed by enterprising settlers is manifestly a racial story. Through claims to reciprocity and equality, the story produces European settlers as the bearers of civilization while simultaneously trapping Aboriginal people in the pre-modern, that is, before civilization has occurred. Anne McClintock has described this characterization of Indigenous populations as one which condemns them to anachronistic space and time.[3] If Aboriginal peoples are consigned forever to an earlier space and time, people of colour are scripted as late arrivals, coming to the shores of North America long after much of the development has occurred. In this way, slavery, indentureship, and labour exploitation—for example, the Chinese who built the railway or the Sikhs who worked in the lumber industry in nineteenth-century Canada—are all handily forgotten in an official national story of European enterprise.

The national mythologies of white settler societies are deeply spatialized stories. Although the spatial story that is told varies from one time to another, at each stage the story installs Europeans as entitled to the land, a claim that is codified in law. In the first phase of conquest, we see the relationship between law, race, and space in the well-known legal doctrine of *terra nullius*, or empty, uninhabited lands. As Dara Culhane has shown in the case of British colonialism, already inhabited nations "were simply legally *deemed to be uninhabited* if the people were not Christian, not agricultural, not commercial, not 'sufficiently evolved' or simply in the way." In land claim cases launched by Aboriginal nations in Canada, Culhane points out, when Aboriginal people "say today that they have had to go to court to prove they exist, they are speaking not just poetically, but also *literally*."[4]

When more European settlers arrive and the settler colony becomes a nation, a second installment of the national story begins to be told. In Canada, this is the story of the "empty land" developed by hardy and enterprising European settlers. In our national anthem, Canadians sing about Canada as the "True North Strong and Free," an arctic land unsullied by conquest. This land, as both Carl Berger and Robert Shields have shown, is imagined as populated by white men of grit, a robust Northern race pitting themselves against the harshness of the climate. "These images," Carl Berger points out, "denote not merely geographical location or climactic condition but the combination of both, moulding racial character."[5]

The imagined rugged independence and self-reliance of the European settlers are qualities that are considered to give birth to a greater commitment to liberty and democracy. If Northern peoples are identified with strength and liberty, then Southern peoples are viewed as the opposite: degenerate, effeminate, and associated with tyranny.[6] Racialized populations seldom appear on the settler landscape as other than this racial shadow; when they do, as David Goldberg writes, they are "rendered transparent . . . merely part of the natural environment, to be cleared from the landscape—urban and rural—like debris."[7] In the Canada of the national mythology, there are vast expanses of open, snow-covered land, forests, lakes, and the occasional voyageur (trapper) or his modern-day counterpart in a canoe. So compelling is this spatial vision of pristine wilderness that a contemporary advertising campaign for Stanfield's underwear is able to proclaim: a Canadian is someone who knows how to make love in a canoe.

In the 1990s there is a third, equally spatialized development of the national story. The land, once empty and later populated by hardy settlers, is now besieged and crowded by Third World refugees and migrants who are drawn to Canada by the legendary niceness of European Canadians, their well-known commitment to democracy,[8] and the bounty of their land. The "crowds" at the border threaten the calm, ordered spaces of the original inhabitants. A specific geographical imagination is clearly traceable in the story of origins told in anti-immigration rhetoric, operating as metaphor but also enabling material practices such as the increased policing of the border and of bodies of colour.

The September 11, 2001 terrorist attacks on the World Trade Center in New York City and on the Pentagon in Washington (attacks in which over three thousand people lost their lives) have deeply intensified the policing of bodies of colour. Like the United States, Canada has proposed an *Anti-Terrorism Act*[9] that will give sweeping powers to police to identify, prosecute, convict, and punish suspected terrorists. With terrorist activity broadly defined, a person can be arrested without a warrant and detained for more than twenty-four hours solely on the basis that the police have suspicions of terrorist activity. Already many men of Arab descent or who are Arab looking have been detained indefinitely, often in solitary confinement. The incarceration of Japanese Canadians in camps during the Second World War, discussed by Mona Oikawa in chapter 3, readily comes to mind.

With its purpose to give the state a chance to sort out who is a terrorist and who is not, the *Anti-Terrorism Act* draws inspiration from a number of existing and proposed changes to Canada's *Immigration Act* that established a two-tier structure of citizenship. For example, the Act penalizes Convention refugees without documents (in contravention of the United Nations 1951 Convention and the 1967 Protocol Relating to the Status of Refugees) and requires them to wait three years before enjoying the benefits of full citizenship. Politicians justify the penalty on the grounds that the original inhabitants have a legitimate right to defend themselves from the massive influx of foreign bodies who possess few of the values of honesty, decency, and democracy of their "hosts." Refugees, it is argued, must be given time to learn respect for Canadian culture, and original citizens must be given time to know who they can trust.[10]

To contest white people's primary claim to the land and to the nation requires making visible Aboriginal nations whose lands were stolen and whose communities remain imperilled. It entails including in the national story those bodies of colour whose labour also developed this land but who are not its first occupants. It is to reveal, in other words, the racialized structure of citizenship that characterizes contemporary Canada. The contributors to this book propose to undertake this by unmapping the primary claim. "To unmap," Richard Phillips notes, is not only to denaturalize geography by asking how spaces come to be but also "to undermine world views that rest upon it."[11] Just as mapping colonized lands enabled Europeans to imagine and legally claim that they had discovered and therefore owned the lands of the "New World," unmapping is intended to undermine the idea of white settler innocence (the notion that European settlers merely settled and developed the land) and to uncover the ideologies and practices of conquest and domination.

In unmapping, there is an important relationship between identity and space. What is being imagined or projected on to specific spaces and bodies, and what is being enacted there? Who do white citizens know themselves to be and how much does an identity of dominance rely upon keeping racial Others firmly *in place*? How are people kept in their place? And, finally, how does place become race? We ask these questions here in the fervent belief that white settler societies can transcend their bloody beginnings and contemporary inequalities by remembering and confronting the racial hierarchies that structure our lives.

In tracking dominance spatially, this book joins in the virtual explosion of books in the 1990s that pay attention to the material and symbolic constitution of actual spaces. It is perhaps true, as some have speculated, that the popularity of spatial theory has something to do (ironically) with the colonial mastery that maps and concrete spaces provide.[12] We feel in control and anchored in something real when we can think and talk about a specific street, town, or region.[13] Spatial theory lends itself to so much "specificity," I tell my graduate class on Race, Space and Citizenship, seizing the opportunity to encourage theory grounded in an empirical base. But the attraction to the concrete is also bound up with the hope that we can pin down something about racialization processes that are directly *experienced* as spatial. When police drop Aboriginal people outside the city limits leaving them to freeze to death, or stop young Black men on the streets or in malls, when the eyes of shop clerks follow bodies of colour, presuming them to be illicit, when workplaces remain relentlessly white in the better paid jobs and fully "coloured" at the lower levels, when affluent areas of the city are all white and poorer areas are mostly of colour, we experience the spatiality of the racial order in which we live.

The geographical turn in critical theory may falsely reassure us that we have mapped how white supremacy works, yet it promises a stronger connection between everyday life and scholarship, and a closer connection to radical politics. The contributors hope that our engagement with spatial theory will yield insight into the multiple ways in which whites secure their dominance in settler societies. For the most part, we focus on the geographical spaces of Canada, inviting others who consider both Canadian and other geographies to examine the role of Canadian law in producing and sustaining a racial social order.

It must be said at the outset that our focus on racial formations is automatically a focus on class and gender hierarchies as well. Racial hierarchies come into existence through patriarchy and capitalism, each system of domination mutually constituting the other. The lure of a spatial approach is precisely the possibility of charting the simultaneous operation of multiple systems of domination. As Edward Soja explains in *Postmodern Geographies,* "the spatiality of social life is stubbornly simultaneous, but what we write down is successive because language is successive."[14] To consider, for example, the multiple systems that constitute spaces of prostitution, we must talk about the economic status of women in prostitution, the way in which areas of prostitution are marked as degenerate space that confirms the existence of white, respectable space, the sexual violence that brings so many young girls to prostitution, and so on. Yet, beginning with any one practice privileges a particular system and leaves the impression that it is that system that is pre-eminent. A spatial analysis can help us to see the operation of all the systems as they mutually constitute each other.

☐ Points of Entry: Space as an Object of Study

What an interdisciplinary collection on space such as this one gains from geography must be clarified from the start. The academic world is still largely discipline bound: geographers sometimes think they own the concepts associated with space, legal scholars guard the gates to the study of the law, and sociologists lay claim to social identities and social inequality as their own objects of study. The gate keeping is not merely a turf war, that is, a contest over who has the right to teach and write about whom and where. Rather, each discipline has approached its "proper" objects of study with specific questions in mind. Further, each has its own critical traditions. Borrowing from a variety of disciplines increases the risk that something of the depth of these scholarly projects will be lost. Geographers have not failed to express their concern that those of us eager to assume the language of geography sometimes end up taking as our "unexamined grounding a seemingly unproblematic, common sense notion of space as a container, a field, a simple emptiness in which all things are 'situated' or 'located.'"[15]

The risk, duly noted here, is that non-geographers are not well qualified to engage in spatial theory. While we acknowledge from the start a partial and incomplete access to each discipline, we deliberately reject the boundaries created by them. If there is anything we have learned about racial projects it is that they come into being and are sustained through a wide number of practices, both material and symbolic. The study of the creation of racial hierarchies demands nothing less than the tools of history, sociology, geography, education, and law, among other domains of knowledge. In an effort to delineate the interdisciplinary approach that is the basis of this book, I provide below an outline of the core ideas that have engaged the contributors, providing the reader with a kind of schematic guide to the starting points we each had in mind and offering an indication of the limits contained here.

☐ Space as a Social Product

To question how spaces come to be, and to trace what they produce as well as what produces them, is to unsettle familiar everyday notions. Space seems to us to be empty. Either we fill it with things (houses, monuments, bridges) or nature fills it with trees, a cold climate, and so on. Space, in this view, is innocent. A building is just a building, a forest just a forest. Urban space seems to evolve naturally. We think, for example, that Chinatowns simply emerged when Chinese people migrated in sufficient numbers to North America and decided to live together. Slums and wealthy suburbs seem to evolve naturally. In the same way that spaces appear to develop organically, so too the inhabitants of spaces seem to belong to them. If the slum or the housing project has a disproportionate number of Black or Aboriginal people, it is thought to be simply because such people lack the education and training to obtain the jobs, and thus the income, that would enable them to live in a wealthy suburb. Perhaps, we often reason, poor districts are simply occupied by recently arrived immigrants who will, in time, move up to more affluent spaces.

If we reject the view that spaces simply evolve, are filled up with things, and exist either prior to or separate from the subjects who imagine and use them, then we can travel along two theoretical routes. First, we can consider the materiality of space, for example, the fact that a large number of workers must be housed somewhere. The buildings in which they live, perhaps the rooming houses built by their wealthy bosses, become a particular kind of space which we might say was shaped by capitalism and the class system. Here space is the result of unequal economic relations. A second approach is to consider the symbolic meaning of spaces. The rooming houses of the workers mean something specific in our context. Perhaps they represent poverty to us and enable us to understand ourselves as located in a social system where status derives from one's position in the means of production.

By itself, each of these approaches to understanding space is limited, as Henri Lefebvre argues. A theory of space, he maintains, has to cut through the dominant notion of space as innocent and as more real "than the 'subject,' his thought and his desires [sic]," but it also had to avoid reducing space to the status of a "message" (what it can tell us about social relations) and the inhabiting of it to the status of a "reading" (deciphering the codes of social space and how we perform it).[16] To treat space this way is to remain on a purely descriptive level that does not show the dialectical relationship between spaces and bodies. It does not show how the symbolic and the material work through each other to constitute a space.

Lefebvre's project, as Eugene McCann observed, "was to write a history of space by relating certain representations of space to certain modes of production through time."[17] Lefebvre saw, for instance, that capitalism relied upon and produced what he called "abstract space," which, McCann notes, is commodified and bureaucratized space arranged in the interests of capital and produced as a concerted attempt to define the appropriate meaning of public space and what citizens can do in it. Lefebvre proposes the concept of social space, as indistinguishable from mental and physical space, and as containing the social relations of production and reproduction. In his widely cited formulation, Lefebvre identified three elements (perceived, conceived, and lived space) in the production of social space.

First, perceived space emerges out of spatial practices, the everyday routines and experiences that install specific social spaces. For example, the daily life of a tenant in a government sponsored housing project includes the rhythm of daily life (the buses one must take to work, the spaces through which one must walk), how people know themselves in it, as well as how they are known in it, and what the space accomplishes in relation to other spaces. Through these everyday routines, the space comes to perform something in the social order, permitting certain actions and prohibiting others. Spatial practices organize social life in specific ways. In the case of the housing project, it organizes, among other things, who will be able to walk in green spaces and who will not.

Second, conceived space entails representations of space, that is, how space is conceived by planners, architects, and so on. Here we might consider how the housing project was initially conceptualized, perhaps as a cleaning up of slums and a collecting of the poor into units that are centralized in the city but nonetheless peripheral to it.[18] Third, lived space is space "directly *lived* through its associated images and symbols, and hence the space of 'inhabitants' and 'users,' but also of some artists and perhaps of those, such as a few writers and philosophers who *describe* and aspire to do more than describe."[19] For the tenant, the housing project may be experienced as racialized space in which communities of colour both experience their marginal condition and resist it. Perhaps people gather on street corners to socialize, defying the containment offered by the buildings and imagining them instead as symbols of community. In lived space (representational space), the users of the space interpret perceived space (spatial practices), and conceived space (representations of space).

In her study of the homeless body, Samira Kawash offers a compelling example of how we might consider space as a social product by attending to the social hierarchies that sustain and are sustained by the idea of abstract public space. Drawing on Rosalyn Deutsche's analysis of how exclusions from public space are officially justified by representing the space as a unity that must be protected from conflict (in effect, Lefebvre's abstract space), Kawash discusses Deutsche's example of the padlocking after dark of a public park in New York. The padlocked park produces as illegitimate the homeless who might use the park to sleep, while neighbourhood groups in favour of the padlocking are produced as legitimate users and natural owners of public space.[20]

The homeless body is constituted as "the corporeal mark of the constitutive outside of the realm of the public."[21] That is, it is through this body that we know who is a citizen and who is not. Through its presence as a material body that occupies space, but as one that is consistently denied space through a series of violent evictions, the homeless body confirms what and who must be contained in order to secure society. The war on the homeless, evident in so many cities in the last few years (including the passage of restrictions on sleeping in public space, on begging, "bum-proof" bus shelters, and restrictions on "squeegee kids" in public space), must be seen as "the production of an abject body against which the public body of the citizen can stand."[22]

It is important to note how symbolic and material processes work together to produce these respectable and abjected bodies. When public toilets are systematically closed, the homeless have no choice but to perform bodily functions in public, a produced mark of degeneracy that only confirms who is respectable. The violent evictions that produce the homeless body are therefore a "constitutive violence"; they make possible subjects who are legitimate and those who are not.[23] Kawash's exploration of the production of the illegitimate homeless body makes it clear that the production of space is also the production of excluded and included bodies, an aspect of the production of space illustrated in the work of Michel Foucault.

☐ The Body in Space

It is from Michel Foucault that many of us learned to think about the production of subjects in space. In his work, we encounter the body marked as degenerate and its opposite, the bourgeois body marked as respectable. Foucault believed that space was fundamental in any exercise of power.[24] Foucault begins his analysis with the establishment in the seventeenth century of "enormous houses of confinement,"[25] of the Hôpital Général for housing the poor and the unemployed, the asylums for the insane, and extends it to prisons and schools to consider what was meant by the physical segregation of marginal populations, an exclusionary practice characteristic of the liberal state. He proposed that the bourgeois citizen of the state, the figure who replaced the earlier orders, distanced himself from the aristocracy and the lower orders of this earlier hierarchy by developing

and making maps with their scientific knowledge, and thus creating a European discourse about a non-European world,[33] Mohanram reflects on how the bricoleur, a pre-capitalist and pre-modern figure, is tied to place while the engineer, located within capitalism and modernity, has the freedom to roam. Noting the same two figures in Alfred Cosby's book *Ecological Imperialism,* where Europeans are described as shaping the environment of the Americas to their advantage, Mohanram comments that the European settler becomes the disembodied Universal Subject, "a subject who is able to take anyone's place." The Indigene, on the other hand, remains "immobile against the repeated onslaught of the settler."[34] For the settler, it is through movement from European to non-European space that he comes to know himself, a journey that materially and symbolically secures his dominance.

☐ Gender, Transgression, and Journeys Through Space

We know the black body by its immobility and the white body by its mobility. However, bodies are gendered and when we speak of subjects coming to know themselves in and through space, we are speaking of identity-making processes that are profoundly shaped by patriarchy. It is not only that men and women come to know themselves as dominant or subordinate in different ways. It is also that dominant masculinities and femininities exist symbiotically. In *Mapping Men and Empire*, Richard Phillips examines Victorian adventure stories showing, in the case of Robert Ballantyne's novels, how the journeys of male heroes through nineteenth-century Canada enable their coming to manhood through encounters with the rugged Canadian wilderness and its "wild Indians." Heroic boys learn the "rough life" and return home to women and civilization confirmed in their mastery and ready to assume the responsibilities of patriarchs. Careful to note that readers have agency when they enter into such fantasies, what Phillips nonetheless underlines is the process through which individuals gain a sense of self in and through space, by moving from civilized to liminal and back again to civilized space.

Liminal space is the border between civilized and primitive space, the space inhabited by savages whom civilized men vanquish on every turn. The subject who comes to know himself through such journeys first imagines his own space as civilized, in contrast to the space of the racial Other; second, he engages in transgression, which is a movement from respectable to degenerate space, a risky venture from which he returns unscathed; and third, he learns that he is in control of the journey through individual practices of domination. In the boys adventure stories, white masculinity is confirmed when the boy hero punches out an Indian who is cruel to dogs.[35] Here the young white boy comes to know himself as white and in control, and as possessing superior values, a knowledge gained through the bodies and spaces of the racial Other. He also learns his place through white girls and women who stand as the marker of home and civility.

As Radhika Mohanram observes, it is as "feminine women" that white women are co-opted into imperial ventures as keepers of the imperial hearth.[36] Thus for white girls, Phillips points out, confined to domestic and enclosed material space, journeys into liminal space and contact with the Other in adventure stories required a gender transgression. Paradoxically, refusing their gender-specific imperial role in the home and undertaking such an imperial journey enabled girls to understand themselves as part of the colonial project and as potential settlers.

The journeys through the metaphorical space of the adventure stories have their material expression. Young white boys and girls learned something of who they were through such stories and the stories promoted popular support for imperialism. Phillips is rightfully emphatic, however, in noting that the novels of colonial culture did not "cause" colonialism.[37] The novels suggest the relationship between space, identity, and racial domination, a relationship I describe as a racial journey into personhood. Today, the identity-making processes of such journeys are evident in women's participation in development work in the Third World, where, as development workers, women of the First World can know themselves as autonomous, competent, and good through their interactions with Third World peoples and their efforts to "help" them.[38] Their development activities fix the natives, confining them to their environment and mode of thought and making them available to be assisted into modernity.[39] We might also see a racial journey into personhood taking place when Northern peacekeepers leave their own "civilized" spaces determined to save Southern nations from their own chaos.[40]

The identity-making processes at work in journeys from respectable to degenerate space are multiple and gendered. The processes described above do not show what the spaces might mean to the subordinate person in the encounter, for example. How might the Indian in Ballantyne's Canadian adventure stories experience the encounter differently from the young white boys? To return to Kathleen Kirby's example of Samuel de Champlain, when Champlain is lost, the land is experienced as chaotic, wild, and untamed, something it would not have seemed to the Aboriginal nations whom Champlain encountered. As well, we cannot presume that subordinate peoples were merely dominated. There is a spatiality to their resistance, which we do not take up to any great extent in this book.

☐ Space and Interlocking Systems of Oppression

To interrogate bodies travelling in spaces is to engage in a complex historical mapping of spaces and bodies *in relation*, inevitably a tracking of multiple systems of domination and the ways in which they come into existence in and through each other. Spatial theorists have not generally used an interlocking approach. For example, in many anthologies devoted to gender and space,[41] woman remains an undifferentiated category with an occasional article on women of colour as a variation on the original model. That race, gender, and class hierarchies structure (rather than simply complicate) each other is not considered. For example, in their work on the segregation of large numbers of women into poorly paid jobs in Worcester, Massachusetts, Susan Hanson and Geraldine Pratt focus on the social and economic geographies of women's lives as compared with men's lives. They note that occupational segregation begins at home, that suburbs make it difficult to combine work and home, and that neighbourly networks facilitate participation in the workforce.[42] These patterns largely apply to white women, something the authors do not interrogate. More significantly, the patterns are themselves embedded in an economy in which, for example, Black women clean the houses of white suburban women. Had Hanson and Pratt considered how their locality was historically produced as a white space, exploring for instance how it comes to be that 70 per cent of the largely white working-class population has lived there for forty years, they might have seen how the gendered conditions they explore are profoundly shaped by a racial economy.

Similar erasures are evident in work on geography and disability. For example, in her review of the edited collection *Mind and Body Spaces: Geographies of Illness, Impairment and Disability*, Sheila Gill identifies what is elided when the category of analysis is an uncomplicated notion of disability. Articles in this collection discuss, among other topics, the ableism of nineteenth-century architecture theory, the spatial dimensions of the "mental deficiency" asylum, and the moral topography of intemperance yet pay no attention to the context of imperial expansion and colonialism. The result is that "mental deficiency" in nineteenth-century Canada is understood as largely unconnected to the eugenics movement and to the making of a white Canada. That a disproportionate number of new immigrants were confined to the asylums and a vigorous discourse about preserving the health of the white race was in place do not interrupt the text's central raceless narrative about "feeblemindedness."[43]

Race also strangely disappears in some geographical work on cities in spite of the fact that difference is a sustained feature of urban spaces and geographers have long paid attention to how the city is experienced differently.[44] Jane Jacobs explains how this erasure of race is most likely to happen. Many of the spatial features of cities, including gentrification, mega-developments, large malls, and heritage buildings are understood primarily as hallmarks of postmodernity. That is, it is clear that globalization has resulted in the growth of international cities in which financial activities are concentrated. Cities are characterized increasingly by a polarization of labour—young professionals in the information and financial sectors on one end and large pools of migrant labour in the service sector on the other. Inequalities are understood here as class inequalities, sometimes complicated by race (for example, the argument that people of colour are overrepresented in the lower levels of the labour market).

Such monocausal explanations, Jacobs argues, ignore the way that "postmodernity manufactures difference in service of its own consuming passions." Older racial orders are reshaped and revitalized in the new globalized conditions. To keep imperialism in sight, Jacobs recommends a closer attention to how spaces are mapped together. "Imperialism," she reminds us, "in whatever form, is a global process—it occurs across regions and nations—but even in its most marauding forms it necessarily takes hold in and through the local."[45] Her reminder is an important one, not only because it instructs us to explore how spaces are linked but also because it insists that we abandon monocausal explanations in favour of those that pay attention to interlocking systems of oppression.

Two steps mark our interlocking approach. First, we examine how the systems mutually constitute each other, an analysis aided by Jacobs's advice to map how spaces are linked. Second, we pursue how all the systems of domination operate at the local level, a task facilitated by attending to material and symbolic constitution of specific spaces. Our goal is to identify legal and social practices that reproduce racial hierarchies. For us, a spatial approach is one way, among others, to uncover processes of racialization. The concept we have all worked with is simply expressed by Radhika Mohanram: racial difference is also spatial difference.[46] Making the same point, David Goldberg writes: "Racisms become institutionally normalized in and through spatial configuration, just as social space is made to seem natural, a given, by being conceived and defined in racial terms."[47]

To denaturalize or unmap spaces, then, we begin by exploring space as a social product, uncovering how bodies are produced in spaces and how spaces produce bodies. This, in turn, entails an interrogation of how subjects come to know themselves in and through space and within multiple systems of domination. We draw on spatial theorists, including, but not limited to, Lefebvre, Foucault, and on a wide range of postcolonial scholars (Mohanram, Phillips, Kirby, and others). Additionally, each chapter draws on scholars who consider colonial space, city space, suburban space, institutional space, and so on. What ties the collection together, however, is the central idea of national space, in this instance, the space of a white settler society. Our concern is to tell the national story as a racial and spatial story, that is, as a series of efforts to segregate, contain, and thereby limit, the rights and opportunities of Aboriginal people and people of colour.

The book begins with an overview of the practices that facilitated the theft of land by white settlers on Canada's East Coast and what is now Ontario. Bonita Lawrence argues that although the strategies of land theft varied, from deliberately infecting Aboriginal populations with smallpox to destabilizing existing alliances among Indigenous nations, the violent dispossession of Aboriginal peoples has been relatively uninterrupted. Historians have written of this dispossession in ways that obscure the racial processes at work. Scholars often leave the impression that white settlement of the land occurred naturally and without considerable violence. Myths abound about Aboriginal peoples fighting too much among themselves to mount an effective resistance to the "traders" or being too ignorant of European relationships to land to successfully challenge Europeans. Lawrence rewrites the story from a critical Aboriginal perspective.

In chapter 2, Renisa Mawani explores the regulation of spaces of interracial contact at the end of the nineteenth century in British Columbia and shows how liquor provisions of the *Indian Act* were used to regulate the movements of mixed-race people. Wanting neither to swell the ranks of

Aboriginal people legally classified as status Indians nor to admit "half-breeds" to the privileges that white identity conferred, the state used the law to regulate contact between these groups. Their movements between white space and Indian space threatened a colonial project that was highly dependent on policing identity categories and ensuring that the boundaries between the reserve and white space remained secure.

Mawani's article is followed by Mona Oikawa's examination in chapter 3 of the effects of legislation enacting the spatial separation of Japanese-Canadian families and communities in 1941 and 1942, which resulted in the dispersal of twenty-two thousand Japanese Canadians from their homes on the West Coast. Oikawa's work is the first to connect diverse spatial practices of domination created by one law. Her analysis shows that the internment of Japanese Canadians was a national project of dispossession and displacement that did not end with the war and that provided white people with considerable material and symbolic advantages.

Chapter 4 introduces the contemporary period. Carol Schick analyzes the impact of teacher-training regulations on the Prairies that require students to take a course on multiculturalism. Schick argues that the regulations strengthened the university as a white elite space through producing white students as the managers of multicultural populations. White students confirmed their place as the rightful managers of Aboriginal people and reacted with hostility when an Aboriginal teacher, or Aboriginal texts on colonization and discrimination, threatened their sense of identity. The ivory tower, Schick concludes, is kept as a place where the rational subject is the subject who does not speak of racism; it is thus kept as a place where bodies of colour do not belong.

Chapter 5 takes us from the white university classroom to the streets of prostitution. In this chapter, I explore gendered racial violence and the continued colonization of Aboriginal people in the trial of two white university students for the murder of Pamela George, an Aboriginal woman working as a prostitute. I show that the enormity of what was done to her remained largely unacknowledged in the law. In chapter 6, Sheila Gill interrogates what lies behind the Manitoba legislature's ruling of the word "racist" as unparliamentary and the consequent expulsion from the House of a Cree member who raised issues relating to the oppression of his people. Connecting the Cree member's expulsion to the flooding of Cree lands, Gill shows the two-sidedness of law: on the one hand a blanket commitment to neutrality, where the word racism cannot be mentioned, and on the other, the passing of laws that flood Aboriginal lands and produce Aboriginal displacement.

That spatial regulation is about membership in the nation is explored in chapter 7. Engin Isin and Myer Siemiatycki examine the reasons why the Greater Toronto Area's city council rejects proposals by different Muslim communities to build mosques, then approves them in restricted ways. In this struggle over urban citizenship, Siemiatycki and Isin show how parking regulations are used to assert the dominant group's entitlement to space and how Muslim groups, cast as outsiders, contest their exclusion from public space through the building of mosques.

The eviction of one of Nova Scotia's oldest Black communities from Africville shows how municipal land-use regulations of the City of Halifax allowed white people to dismantle a one-hundred-year-old Black community in the 1970s. Today, the City of Halifax commemorates the site where Africville once stood, a commemoration Jennifer Nelson argues in chapter 8 that paradoxically enables white people to "forget" their violent acts of dispossession.

The last chapter by Sheryl Nestel traces how legislation enacting midwifery in the province of Ontario in the early 1990s was accompanied by regulations that discredited foreign-trained midwives and instituted attendance at a substantial number of births as a mandatory prerequisite for licensing. White midwives were better positioned than immigrant midwives to travel to the U.S. where they could obtain the necessary experience in birthing clinics along the U.S.–Mexico border. Thus Mexican women's bodies become the source of white women's experience in live births. Nestel terms this "midwifery tourism" and carefully maps the forces that bring both groups of women to the border clinics—an encounter that advantages Northern women over Mexican women.

These nine chapters, which cover two coasts of Canada, its Prairies, and the borders between Canada and the United States and the United States and Mexico, show us in intricate detail how the law is used to protect the interests of white people. Each author challenges the racelessness of law and the amnesia that allows white subjects to be produced as innocent, entitled, rational, and legitimate. We are encouraged to ask on what basis our emancipatory projects lie and are reminded not to forget history. The chain of events that begins with eviction and moves through "burials, denials, and complicities through time" must be resurrected. We must find ways to move beyond law's insistence on abstract individuals without histories. The tracing of the constitution of spaces through law and the mapping of the hierarchical social relations they create and sustain is one way of beginning. *Race, Space, and the Law* proposes some initial methodologies for this work of denaturalization, the work of asking how spacial divisions by race come into existence and are sustained.

CHAPTER 1

Rewriting Histories of the Land

Colonization and
Indigenous Resistance
in Eastern Canada

Bonita Lawrence

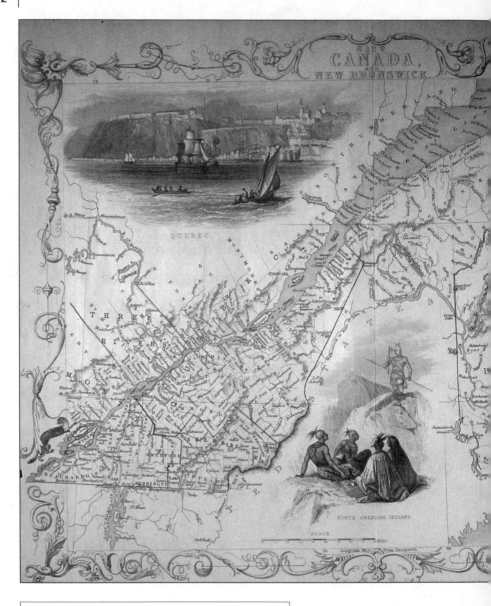

East Canada and New Brunswick, c.1845–51.

[JOHN RAPKIN, MAP MAKER. W.H. PUGSLEY MAP COLLECTION,

MCGILL DIGITAL LIBRARY PROJECT, MCGILL UNIVERSITY]

The claim to a national culture in the past does not only rehabilitate that nation and serve as a justification for the hope of a future national culture. In the sphere of socioaffective equilibrium, it is responsible for an important change in the native. Perhaps we have not sufficiently demonstrated that colonialism is not simply content to impose its rule upon the present and future of a dominated country. Colonialism is not merely satisfied with holding a people in its grip and emptying the native's brain of all form and content. By a kind of perverse logic, it turns to the past of an oppressed people, and distorts, disfigures, and destroys it.

—Frantz Fanon,
The Wretched of the Earth

Canadian national iden-

tity is deeply rooted in the notion of Canada as a vast northern wilderness, the possession of which makes Canadians unique and "pure" of character. Because of this, and in order for Canada to have a viable national identity, the histories of Indigenous nations,[1] in all their diversity and longevity, must be erased. Furthermore, in order to maintain Canadians' self-image as a fundamentally "decent" people innocent of any wrongdoing, the historical record of how the land was acquired—the forcible and relentless dispossession of Indigenous peoples, the theft of their territories, and the implementation of legislation and policies designed to effect their total disappearance as peoples—must also be erased. It has therefore been crucial that the survivors of this process be silenced—that Native people be deliberately denied a voice within national discourses.[2]

A crucial part of the silencing of Indigenous voices is the demand that Indigenous scholars attempting to write about their histories conform to academic discourses that have already staked a claim to expertise about our pasts—notably anthropology and history. For many Aboriginal scholars from Eastern Canada who seek information about the past, exploring the "seminal" works of contemporary non-Native "experts" is an exercise in alienation. It is impossible for Native people to see themselves in the unknown and unknowable shadowy figures portrayed on the peripheries of the white settlements of colonial Nova Scotia, New France, and Upper Canada, whose lives are deduced solely through archaeological evidence or the journals of those who sought to conquer, convert, defraud, or in any other way prosper off them. This results in the depiction of ancestors who resemble "stick figures"; noble savages, proud or wily, inevitably primitive. For the most part, Indigenous scholars engaged in academic writing about the past certainly have little interest in making the premises of such works central to their own writing—and yet the academic canon demands that they build their work on the back of these "authoritative" sources. We should be clear that contemporary white historians have often argued in defence of Aboriginal peoples, seeking to challenge the minor roles that Native people have traditionally been consigned in the (discursively created) "historical record." What is never envisioned, however, is that Indigenous communities should be seen as final arbiters of their own histories.

What is the cost for Native peoples, when these academic disciplines "own" our pasts? First of all, colonization is normalized. "Native history" becomes accounts of specific intervals of "contact," accounts which neutralize processes of genocide, which never mention racism, and which do not take as part of their purview the devastating and ongoing implications of the policies and processes that are so neutrally described. A second problem, which primarily affects Aboriginal peoples in Eastern Canada, is the longevity of colonization and the fact that some Indigenous peoples are considered by non-Native academics to be virtually extinct, to exist only in the pages of historical texts. In such a context, the living descendants of the Aboriginal peoples of Eastern Canada are all too seldom viewed as those who should play central roles in any writing about the histories of their ancestors.

Most important, however, is the power that is lost when non-Native "experts" define Indigenous peoples' pasts—the power that inheres when oppressed peoples choose the tools that they need to help them understand themselves and their histories:

> The development of theories by Indigenous scholars which attempt to explain our existence in contemporary society (as opposed to the "traditional" society constructed under modernism) has only just begun. Not all these theories claim to be derived from some "pure" sense of what it means to be Indigenous, nor do they claim to be theories which have been developed in a vacuum separated from any association with civil and human rights movements, other nationalist struggles, or other theoretical approaches. What is claimed, however, is that new ways of theorizing by Indigenous scholars are grounded in a real sense of, and sensitivity towards, what it means to be an Indigenous person. . . . Contained within this imperative is a sense of being able to determine priorities, to bring to the centre those issues of our own choosing, and to discuss them amongst ourselves.[3]

For Indigenous peoples, telling our histories involves recovering our own stories of the past and asserting the epistemological foundations that inform our stories of the past. It also involves documenting processes of colonization from the perspectives of those who experienced it. As a result, this chapter, as an attempt to decolonize the history of Eastern Canada, focuses on Indigenous communities' stories of land theft and dispossession, as well as the resistance that these communities manifested towards colonization. It relies primarily on the endeavours of Indigenous elders and scholars who are researching community histories to shape its parameters. Knowledge-carriers such as Donald Marshall Senior and Indigenous scholars who carry out research on behalf of Indigenous communities such as Daniel Paul, Sakej Henderson, and Georges Sioui are my primary sources. For broader overviews of the colonization process, I draw on the works of Aboriginal historians such as Olivia Dickason and Winona Stevenson. In some instances, I rely on non-Native scholars who have consulted Native elders, such as Peter Schmalz, or who have conducted research specifically *for* Indigenous communities involved in resisting colonization (where those communities retain control over ownership of the knowledge and how it is to be used), such as James Morrison. In instances where no other information is available, the detailed work of non-Native scholars such as Bruce Trigger and J. R. Miller is used to make connections between different events and to document regional processes. The issues at hand are whether the scholar in question is Indigenous and the extent to which the scholar documents the perspectives of Indigenous communities about their own pasts.

As history is currently written, from outside Indigenous perspectives, we cannot see colonization *as* colonization. We cannot grasp the overall picture of a focused, concerted process of invasion and land theft. Winona Stevenson has summarized how the "big picture" looks to Aboriginal peoples: "Mercantilists wanted our furs, missionaries wanted our souls, colonial governments, and later, Canada, wanted our lands."[4] And yet, this complex rendition of a global geopolitical process can obscure how these histories come together in the experiences of different Indigenous nations "on the ground." It also obscures the *processes* that enabled colonizers to acquire the land, and the *policies* that were put into place to control the peoples displaced from the land. As a decolonization history, the perspectives informing this work highlight Aboriginal communities' experiences of these colonial processes, while challenging a number of the myths that are crucial to Canadian nation-building, such as the notion that the colonization process was benign and through which Canada maintains its posture of being "innocent" of racism and genocide. Other myths about Native savagery and the benefits of European technologies are challenged by Native communities' accounts of their own histories and are explored below.

☐ ### Mercantile Colonialism: Trade and Warfare

The French and early British trade regimes in Canada did not feature the relentless slaughter and enslavement of Indigenous peoples that marked the Spanish conquest of much of "Latin" America. Nor did they possess the implacable determination to obtain Indigenous land for settlement by any means necessary that marked much of the British colonial period in New England. Thus the interval of mercantile colonialism in Canada has been portrayed as relatively innocuous. And yet, northeastern North America was invaded by hundreds of trade ships of different European nations engaged in a massive competition for markets; an invasion instrumental in destabilizing existing intertribal political alliances in eastern North America. It is impossible, for example, to discount the central role that competition for markets played in the large-scale intertribal warfare that appears to have developed, relatively anomalously, throughout the sixteenth, seventeenth, and eighteenth centuries in much of eastern Canada and northeastern United States. Oral history and archeological evidence demonstrate that these wars were unique in the history of these Indigenous nations.

It is important to take into consideration the extent to which the new commodities offered by the Europeans gave obvious material advantages to those nations who successfully controlled different trade routes. Inevitably, however, as communities became reliant on trade to obtain many of the necessities of life, access to trade routes became not only desirable but actually necessary for survival (particular as diseases began to decimate populations, as the animal life was affected, and as missionaries began to make inroads on traditional practices).[5] These pressures resulted in such extreme levels of competition between Indigenous nations that an escalation into continuous warfare was almost inevitable. For example, in the seventeenth century, the Mi'kmaq people of the Gaspé began killing Iroquoians who crossed into their trade territories. They also fought a trade war with the Abenaki in 1607.[6] Meanwhile, the Innu nation in the sixteenth century became embroiled in two different trade wars—the Naskapi fought the Inuit for access to furs in Labrador while the Montagnais fought the Iroquois for control of the rich Saguenay River route to James Bay and the Great Lakes.[7] But most profoundly, trade wars (in conjunction with the diseases accompanying the traders) decimated populations in what is now southern Ontario and Quebec.[8]

The nations of the Iroquois Confederacy, which waged much of this warfare for control of trade territories, were themselves devastated by the century-long struggle between Britain and France for control of the fur trade in the Great Lakes region. They were ultimately defeated by the Ojibway nation after a lengthy conflict that left "mounds of bones" at certain sites in southern Ontario. In 1701, the Iroquois signed a peace treaty with the Ojibway.[9] In the face of encroaching European trade, this treaty developed into a mutual non-aggression pact that, until the land was taken, was never violated.

Warfare and trade among Indigenous nations profoundly changed the ecology of the land and way of life for nations of many regions. Yet these should not be seen as evidence of Indigenous savagery or of a breakdown of Indigenous values;[10] rather, these profound changes, in part, resulted from the severe pressures caused by the intense competition of European powers during mercantile colonialism to depopulate entire regions of all fur-bearing animals.

Intertribal wars were also carried out for another reason, according to the oral traditions of many of the nations whose homelands were assaulted by these processes. According to Georges Sioui, warfare was also waged by many of the nations weakened by disease and trade warfare as a way to replenish their population base. Often, Indigenous nations adopted their captives:

> We used our alliance to the French to go and attack the English colonies to the south with the primary intent of capturing people, especially young and female, and ritually, through adoption, giving them a new life in our Nations. As it was, clanmothers and matriarchs had the principal say in these military undertakings; they had the primary responsibility of maintaining and restoring the integrity and composition of the societies which, as woman-leaders, they headed. White, and other, captives were given over to clanmothers who had organized war expeditions through approaching and commissioning war chiefs. The captives were then ritually and factually nationalized and, then, brought up and treated as full members of their adoptive social communities . . . some of our Aboriginal Nations survived almost only because of our traditional mother-centred thinking. Had we, at that time, had leaders formed in patriarchal colonial institutions, as is so often the case nowadays, many of our nations simply would not have survived beyond the eighteenth century.[11]

☐ Disease and Christianization in the Huron-Wendat Nation

Although French colonial policies focused primarily on the fur trade, under the terms of the Doctrine of Discovery, the monopolies they granted to different individuals in different regions included the mandatory presence of Christian missionaries.[12] The missionaries relied on trade wars (and the epidemics frequently preceding or accompanying them) to harvest converts from Indigenous populations physically devastated by mass death. Nowhere is this more obvious than among the Huron-Wendat people.

The Wendat, whom the Jesuits labelled "Huron," were the five confederated nations of the territory known as Wendake (now the Penetanguishene Peninsula jutting into Georgian Bay). It was made up of twenty-five towns, with a population that peaked at thirty thousand in the fifteenth century.[13] The Wendat relied both on agriculture and fishing, and until extensive contact with French traders began in 1609, they enjoyed remarkable health and an abundance of food.

Georges Sioui suggests that Wendat communities first came into contact with disease through the French, who were dealing with large groupings of Wendat living together as agricultural people. It was not until 1634, however, when the Jesuits, who had visited in 1626, returned to set up a mission that the Wendat encountered a continuous wave of epidemics, which culminated in the virulent smallpox epidemic of 1640 that cut their population in half.[14] So many elders and youths died in the epidemics that the Wendat began to experience serious problems in maintaining their traditional livelihoods and grew extremely dependent on French trade for survival. The epidemics also had a catastrophic effect on the Wendat worldview. The psychological shock of such an extreme loss of life was experienced as sorcery, as the introduction of a malevolent power into the Wendat universe.[15]

It was into this weakened population that the Jesuits managed to insinuate themselves, using their influence in France to have French traders withdrawn and replaced by Jesuit lay employees. The Jesuits sought to impress the Huron with their technological superiority and allowed their traders to sell certain goods, particularly guns, only to Christian converts.[16] As the number of Christian converts grew in response to such virtual blackmail, the Jesuits gradually obtained enough power in the communities to forbid the practising of Wendat spiritual rituals. In response, a traditionalist Wendat faction developed in an attempt to resist the Jesuits and, indeed, any dealings with the French. Instead, they proposed a trading pact with the Iroquois but were unable to obtain sufficient influence to achieve this. Despite the growing power of the Jesuits, the mission could not protect the Christian Wendat against attacks by Seneca and Mohawk war parties in the winter of 1648 and the spring of 1649. The Confederacy was shattered and the Wendat abandoned their villages, dying of starvation and exposure by the thousands.

About six hundred destitute survivors followed the Jesuits back to Quebec, forming a community at Loretteville, which still exists today. A large number were captured by the Iroquois and adopted into the Seneca, Onondaga, and Cayuga nations. Others joined traditional allies and migrated to Ohio in the United States, where they acquired land as "Wyandot" people. In the 1830s, the Wyandot were forcibly relocated from Ohio to Kansas as part of the U.S. government's "clearing" of Eastern Native peoples from the land. Many lost their tribal status in Kansas, but a small group of Wyandot acquired a reserve in northeastern Oklahoma where they continue to live today. A small number of Wendat remained in Ontario and maintained two reserves in the Windsor region. In the early nineteenth century, both reserves were ceded and sold by the Crown. A small acreage remained and was occupied by a group known as the Anderdon band. This band, consisting of the remaining forty-one Wendat families in Ontario, were enfranchised under the *Indian Act* in 1881, at which point they officially ceased to exist as "Indians." Their land base was divided up into individual allotments. Despite the loss of a collective land base and "Indian" status, the descendants of the forty-one families in Windsor still consider themselves Wendat.[17]

Georges Sioui is a member of the Loretteville Huron-Wendat band. He reflects on his people's experience of Jesuit conversion and how central missionaries were to the economic order of colonial agendas:

> Throughout history, the process of conversion has been a process of subversion and destruction. All over the world, in whatever climate, missionaries have considered disease and death as particularly effective means of undermining the pride of circular-thinking peoples . . . and impoverishing them, thereby making them submit to the socio-economic order of the invader. Impoverishment is the natural outcome of disunity, which is hastened by the poverty brought on by disease. Brebeuf [the Jesuit who established a mission among the Wendat known as Huronia] foresaw an abundant harvest of souls following the disastrous epidemic that cut down thousands of Wendats. . . . Such a harvest could only be realized among a people who walked in constant fear of death and the spectre of annihilation. By 1636, the Jesuit missionaries were already conscious of wielding almost absolute power over Wendat leaders. At the end of the Feast of the Dead that he attended, Brebeuf publicly refused a present from the hands of the great chief of the Attignawantans (and possi-

bly of the entire Wendat confederacy). *The only acceptable gift was the abandonment of their culture by all the savages.*[18]

It is clear, when we explore what happened at Wendake, that the confluence of disease, dependency on trade, and the missionary crusade weakened the Wendat people so drastically that attacks by the Seneca and Mohawk were sufficient to shatter their Confederacy beyond repair. It is also clear that the presence of the missionaries played a significant role in narrowing the options of Confederacy members and that later legislation, such as enfranchisement policies, caused further dispersal and dissolution. All of these processes were part and parcel of the colonial strategies to assert and formalize European presence and authority on the land.

From the perspective of the Huron-Wendat people, the destabilization that mercantilism brought was in many respects almost as deadly a process for Indigenous societies as the actual land acquisition project that followed it. Indeed, when land acquisition is not marked by direct military force, mercantile trade is usually the preliminary step.

Huron-Wendat history that emphasizes the destabilization of mercantilism directly challenges the notion that the large-scale warfare between Native peoples during colonization was a function of savagery or a total breakdown of Native values. Rather, it can be understood as an effort to survive in the face of the massive pressures of European trade interests and from the need to repopulate nations devastated by disease and invasion. Perhaps more important, this history challenges the ubiquitous notion that the small nations devastated by colonization have ceased to exist. As Sioui demonstrates, the Huron are more than a tragic remnant of history:

> from the Native's point of view, the persistence of essential values is more important than change, just as from the non-Native point of view, it has always been more interesting to shore up the myth of the disappearances of the Amerindian. . . . An examination of the Amerindian philosophical tradition will show the persistence, vivacity, and universality of the essential values proper to America . . . if history is to be sensitive to society's needs, it must also study and reveal to the dominant society what is salutary, instead of continuing to talk about "primitive" cultures that are dead and dying. . . . In short, Amerindians think that while they have changed, like everything in the world, they are still themselves.[19]

The catastrophic changes that the Huron-Wendat have undergone are perhaps less important than the fact that they have survived as a people, and that their worldview has changed but remains fundamentally Wendat. These myths of savagery and of a "loss of culture" form an essential part of contemporary settler ideology—a justification for the denial of restitution for colonization, the backlash against Aboriginal harvesting rights, and policies of repression against Native communities. Through exploring Huron-Wendat history informed by their own realities, a culture regarded as "dead" by the mainstream speaks to us about its contemporary world.

☐ The Mi'kmaq: Diplomacy and Armed Resistance

Not all nations faced the Wendat experience of Christianization. The Mi'kmaq nation was perhaps unique in the way it used Christianity as a source of resistance to colonization in the earliest years of contact with Europeans.

Mi'kmaki, "the land of friendship," covers present-day Newfoundland, St-Pierre and Miquelon, Nova Scotia, New Brunswick, the Magdalen Islands, and the Gaspé Peninsula. It is the territory of the Mi'kmaq, which means "the allied people." The Mi'kmaq nation became centralized during a fourteenth-century war with the Iroquois Confederacy. Since then it has been led by the Sante Mawiomi, the Grand Council, and has been divided into seven regions, each with its Sakamaws or chiefs. It is part of the Wabanaki Confederacy, which includes the Mi'kmaq, the Abenakis in Quebec, the Maliseets in western New Brunswick, and the Passamaquoddies and Penobscots in New England.[20] The Wabanaki Confederacy is only one of seven Confederacies, the others being the Wampagnoag, Pennacook, Wappinger, Powhattan, Nanticoki, and Leanape. These Confederacies represent the thirteen surviving Indigenous nations along the Eastern seaboard which have asserted their sovereignty over the entire Maritime and New England regions of Canada and the United States.[21]

The Mi'kmaq people were the first Native people in North America to encounter Europeans, and were aware of the political implications of contact. The French entered their territory in earnest in the sixteenth century and had set up small maritime colonies by the early seventeenth century. Knowledge of the genocide of Indigenous peoples in the Caribbean and Mexico by the Spanish travelled along the extensive trade networks that existed across North America at the time and reached the Mi'kmaq by the mid-sixteenth century. In response to this information, and to the spread of disease that increased with greater contact, the Mi'kmaq avoided the French coastal settlements and consolidated their relationships with other Eastern nations of the Wabanaki Confederacy.[22] However, Messamouet, a Mi'kmaw[23] scholar and prophet who had travelled to France and learned of how the Europeans conceptualized law and sovereignty, developed another option known as the "Beautiful Trail," which would involve the Mi'kmaq nation negotiating an alliance with the Holy See in Rome.

When the French began their colonial ventures into North America, the Catholic monarchs of Europe were in a power struggle over sovereignty issues with the Holy Roman Empire, which had been instrumental in consolidating independent European tribal groups into nations governed by the Holy See.[24] The discovery of the existence of the Americas by explorers such as Columbus amplified the power struggle between the Holy See and the ascendant monarchs of Europe over the question of whose authority would prevail in these "discovered" lands—that of the nations of Europe or the Church?

By building an alliance with the Holy See, the Mi'kmaq nation sought recognition as a sovereign body among the European nations. In this way, Mi'kmaki could resist the authority of the French Crown. In 1610, Grand Chief Membertou initiated an alliance with the Holy See by negotiating a Concordat that recognized Mi'kmaki as an independent Catholic Republic. As a public treaty with the Holy See, the Concordat had the force of international law, canon law, and civil law. Its primary effect was to protect the Mi'kmaq from French authority "on the ground." The process, however, initiated a gradual centralization of authority in the Mawiomi— prior to the Concordat, Mi'kmaw families were organized into regional self-governing units; under the Concordat, the Mawiomi attained political authority for the Mi'kmaq nation. The terms of the Concordat also gave individual Mi'kmaw people the freedom to choose or reject Catholicism. Priests under the authority of the Holy See, rather than those under the French Crown, baptized each family and its extended family from one hunting district to the next within Mi'kmaki territory. Within twenty years, most Mi'kmaw families had been baptized. As well, the alliance granted the Church access to Mi'kmaki where it could build churches and promised Mi'kmaki protection from the Holy See against all other European monarchies. Under the Concordat and alliance, the Mawiomi maintained a theocracy which synthesized Catholic and Mi'kmaq spirituality and maintained Mi'kmaq independence from the French Crown.[25]

In 1648, the Treaty of Westphalia ended the Holy See's rule over European monarchies. The treaty's settlement of territorial claims placed some lands under the control of nation-states and others under the control of the Holy See: Mi'kmaki "reverted" to Mi'kmaq control and all protections ceased to exist.

Unfortunately for the Mi'kmaq, the French were not the only colonial power to invade their world. What the British sought was not furs and missions but land where they could build colonies for their surplus populations. The colonies they developed along the Atlantic seaboard, therefore, practised open extermination against the Indigenous peoples around them. Once they had taught the English colonists how to survive in the new land, Indigenous peoples were deemed superfluous at best, and an impediment to settlement at worst. Despite the fact that massive outbreaks of illness had already decimated the populations they encountered (in certain regions, nineteen out of twenty Indigenous people who came into contact with the British succumbed to disease), the British initiated a number of attacks against Indigenous villages, attacks which often escalated into full-scale wars. British slavers scoured the Atlantic coast for Indigenous people who were sold in slave markets all over the world. Indeed, they began raiding Mi'kmaq territory for slaves in the mid-1600s.[26]

As the British encroached north from New England to Nova Scotia, the Mi'kmaq responded with open resistance. From the mid-1650s until the peace treaty of 1752 (which was reaffirmed in the treaty of 1761), they waged continuous warfare against the British, fighting land battles and capturing almost one hundred British ships. As the long war proceeded, and the Mi'kmaq were gradually weakened, the ascendant British developed policies to exterminate the Mi'kmaq. They used a variety of methods, including distributing poisoned food, trading blankets infected with diseases, and waging ongoing military assaults on civilian populations.[27] These acts of genocide were in addition to the diseases that the European soldiers introduced. In 1746, a typhus and smallpox epidemic spread through Nova Scotia, killing one-third of the Mi'kmaq population. (As late as the 1920s, Mi'kmaw people were still telling stories about the mounds where those who perished were buried.) It was into this decimated population that the British introduced scalping policy as another method of extermination. For two decades, the British paid bounty for Mi'kmaq scalps and even imported a group of bounty hunters known as Goreham's Rangers from Massachusetts to depopulate the surviving Mi'kmaq nation.[28]

Those who survived this genocide were destitute, left with no food and without the necessary clothing to keep warm in a cold climate. Many were reduced to begging. Thousands died of starvation and exposure until limited poor relief was implemented on a local basis. Others eked out a bare existence selling handicrafts, cutting wood for whites, or working as prostitutes (which resulted in outbreaks of venereal disease). Those who struggled to acquire individual land plots were denied title; as a result, it was not uncommon for Mi'kmaw families to engage in the backbreaking labour of clearing and planting a patch of land, only to find that when they returned from fishing, hunting, or gathering excursions that white squatters had taken the land.[29] When the British opened up the region for white settlement, they refused to set aside land for the Native peoples. In British legal thinking of the day, non-Christians who had been defeated by and were subject to the British had no rights to land under the "Norman Yoke," an aspect of the Doctrine of Discovery that the British inserted for their own benefit.[30]

By the early 1800s, the Mi'kmaq population had fallen from an estimated two hundred thousand to less than fifteen hundred people. Most whites were predicting that the Mi'kmaq would soon become extinct. During this period, Mi'kmaw leaders continuously petitioned London, finally managing to obtain a handful of small reserves. Throughout the nineteenth century, however, the Mi'kmaq endured policies that tried to centralize and liquidate the few reserves that had been created, divide their bands, and dissolve their traditional governance. These policies aimed in every way to erase their existence.

Since the signing of the 1752 treaty, which brought an end to warfare, the Mi'kmaq have sought to resolve the ongoing land and resource theft, with little success. In 1973, the *Calder* case decision forced the Canadian government to recognize that it had some obligation to deal with land claims. Although comprehensive claims were held to be worthy of consideration in Western Canada, the Mi'kmaq claims were held to be "of a different nature" and Mi'kmaq participation in this process was denied. In 1977, the Mi'kmaq Grand Council made a formal application for land and compensation under the 1973 policy. The federal government, however, insisted that Mi'kmaq rights had somehow been "superceded by law."[31]

In exploring Mi'kmaq resistance efforts—negotiating a Concordat with the Holy See, waging the longest anti-colonial war in North America, surviving policies designed to exterminate them—we see a picture of Native peoples as resourceful and capable of engaging a powerful enemy in armed conflict for a significant period of time. Perhaps even more important, we see Mi'kmaq people as actors on an international stage, engaging the European powers not only through warfare but through diplomacy, signing international treaties as a nation among nations. Mi'kmaq perspectives of their own history, then, reinstate Native peoples as global citizens and challenge the colonial perspective of Native peoples as powerless victims.

It is impossible to understand contemporary struggles for self-determination without this view of Native peoples as nations among other nations. Today, the spirit that enabled the Mi'kmaq to resist genocide is being manifested in the continuous struggles over the right to fish and in their challenge to their rights under the Concordat with the Holy See. Although the Concordat came to an end in the late seventeenth century, the memory of the alliance has come into play in recent years. When Pope John Paul II committed the Catholic Church to supporting the liberation struggles of Aboriginal peoples in Canada in the late 1990s, the Mawiomi launched its campaign to clarify the settlement terms of the Treaty of Westphalia. It is believed that Canada usurped lands accorded to the Mi'kmaq under the Concordat's international law. By re-establishing communication with the Holy See, the Mawiomi wish to recreate its partnership in ways that enhance the autonomy and spiritual uniqueness of the Mi'kmaq.[32]

☐ Geopolitical Struggles between the Colonizers and Indigenous Resistance in the Great Lakes Region

The British entered the territory now known as Canada from two fronts: the East Coast region (primarily for settlement purposes) and Hudson's Bay (under the charter of the Hudson's Bay Company for the purpose of the fur trade). As British traders spread south into the Great Lakes region, expanding their fur trade, competition with the French escalated. From 1745 onwards, the British adopted policies that regulated trade, protected "Indian" lands from encroachment, and secured military allies among Native peoples through the distribution of gifts. In 1755, the Indian Department was officially established under imperial military authority.[33]

The struggle between Britain and France over the Great Lakes region had profound effects on the Iroquois and Ojibway peoples who lived there. The trade struggle between Europeans forced first one party and then the other to lower the prices of trade goods relative to the furs that were traded for them. Ultimately, when warfare broke out, the effect was devastating, as colonial battles fought in Native homelands destroyed these regions and drew Native peoples into battles, primarily to ensure that a "balance of power" resulted (which would ensure that both European powers remained deadlocked and that one power would not emerge victorious over another).[34]

In 1763, the warfare between France and Britain ended when France surrendered its territorial claims in North America. The trading territory from Hudson's Bay west to the Rockies was claimed by the Hudson's Bay Company and was considered by the British to be its property. Meanwhile, Britain laid claim to most of the territory of eastern North America formerly held by the French, although it lacked any real ability to wrest the land from the Native nations who occupied it. Nor could it control how the nations of these regions would choose to act. Because it was important for Britain to reassert its formal adherence to the Doctrine of Discovery and to ensure that its claims to eastern North America would be respected by other European regimes, the British government consolidated its imperial position by structuring formal, constitutional relations with the Native nations in these territories. The Royal Proclamation of 1763 recognized Aboriginal title to all unceded lands and acknowledged a nation-to-nation relationship with Indigenous peoples which the Indian Department was in charge of conducting. Department agents could not command; they could only use the diplomatic tools of cajolery, coercion (where possible), and bribery.[35] The nation-to-nation relationship was maintained until the end of the War of 1812 when the post-war relationships between Britain and the American government became more amicable and made military alliances with Native nations unnecessary.

In the meantime, Britain's ascendancy in the Great Lakes region marked a disastrous turn for Native peoples. Most of the nations were devastated by years of French and British warfare that they had been drawn into. Once the British had control of the fur trade, they began to drive prices down and violate many of the long-standing trade practices that had been maintained while the French were active competitors. It was also obvious to Indigenous people that one unchallenged European power was far more dangerous to deal with than a group of competing Europeans. During this desperate state of affairs, a number of Indigenous nations attempted to form broad-ranging alliances across many nations in an effort to eliminate the British presence from their territories, culminating in the Pontiac uprising of 1763.

Pontiac, an Odawa war chief, was inspired by the Delaware prophet Neolin. He wanted to build a broad-based multinational movement whose principles involved a return to the ways of the ancestors and a complete avoidance of Europeans and their trade goods. At least nineteen of the Indigenous nations most affected by the Europeans shared this vision. Their combined forces laid siege to Fort Detroit for five months, captured nine other British forts, and killed or captured two thousand British. Within a few months, they had taken back most of the territory in the Great Lakes region from European control.

Between 1764 and 1766, peace negotiations took place between the British and the alliance. The British had no choice in the matter; the Pontiac uprising was the most serious Native resistance they had faced in the eighteenth century.[36] As a consequence, the British were forced to adopt a far more respectful approach to Native peoples within the fur trade and to maintain far more beneficial trade terms. However, the dependency of many of the Indigenous nations on British trade goods and their different strategies in dealing with this dependency weakened the alliance and it could not be maintained over the long term.[37] This unfortunately coincided with the British plan to devise ways of removing the military threat that Native peoples clearly represented without the cost of open warfare. The primary means they chose were disease and alcohol.

There is now evidence to suggest that the smallpox pandemic—which ravaged the Ojibway and a number of the Eastern nations including the Mingo, Delaware, Shawnee, and other Ohio River nations, and which killed at least one hundred thousand people—was deliberately started by the British.[38] The earliest evidence of this deliberate policy is the written request of Sir Jeffrey Amherst to Colonel Henry Bouqet at Fort Pitt. In June 1763, Amherst instructed Bouqet to distribute blankets infected with smallpox as gifts to the Indians. On June 24, Captain Ecuyer of the Royal Americans noted in his journal, "We gave them two blankets and a handkerchief out of the smallpox hospital. I hope it will have the desired effect."[39]

Peter Schmalz suggests, however, that germ warfare was not as widespread against the Ojibway who held the territory north of the Great Lakes as it was against the Native peoples of the Ohio valley and plains. The "chemical warfare" of alcohol, however, was waged against the Ojibway in a highly deliberate manner. Major Gladwin articulated this policy clearly: "The free sale of rum will destroy them more effectively than fire and sword." The effects of widespread alcohol distribution were immediate.

Factionalism increased and the Ojibway could no longer unite for an adequate length of time to solve a common threat to their well-being. By 1780, a split developed between the Ojibway of southwestern Ontario (who had to struggle against devastating social disintegration under the effects of alcohol and their resulting dependency on the British) and the Ojibway situated closer to Lake Huron, Georgian Bay, and Lake Superior (who maintained a stronger cultural cohesion and independence from Europeans).[40]

In the Great Lakes region, chemical and germ warfare were used by the British as the primary means to acquire land and impose control. Despite this, the Pontiac uprising demonstrated the power of Indigenous nations organized in armed resistance to colonization. At the same time, we can see the divisive effect that dependency on British trade goods brought to the nations involved in the fur trade. From these perspectives, these changes to Indigenous ways of life had long-term and highly significant effects on the possibilities of maintaining sovereignty and resistance to European expansion. The centuries-long fur trade changed the course of Indigenous history in Eastern Canada, as the considerable military power of the Indigenous nations was subverted by their need for trade goods to support their changing way of life.

☐ Ojibway Experiences of Colonization

Immigration, Deception, and Loss of Land

As the fur trade spread further west, the British government consolidated its hold over the Great Lakes area by implementing settlement policies. At the end of the American Revolution, Loyalists poured into the territory that had become known as Upper Canada, bringing new epidemics of smallpox that decimated the Ojibway around Lake Ontario. Immigration from the United Kingdom was openly encouraged as a means of cementing the British hold on the territory. In the thirty-seven-year interval from 1814 until the census of 1851, the white population of Upper Canada multiplied by a factor of ten—from 95,000 to 952,000. The Native population, formerly one-tenth of the population, declined into demographic insignificance in the same interval.[41] At the same time local government encouraged the migration of as many American Indians into the colony as possible. This achieved a two-fold goal: securing the potential services of these Native nations against the Americans in times of war, and overwhelming local Ojibway communities with thousands of incoming Ojibway and

Pottawatomi from south of the border. Walpole Island, for example, with a population of three hundred, took in over eight hundred new people between 1837 and 1842.[42] This influx of refugees, while welcomed by their relations to the north, threw many Ojibway communities into disarray at the precise moment when their lands were being taken from them.

Between 1781 and 1830, the Ojibway gradually ceded to the British most of the land north of what is now southern Ontario. The British knew that the Ojibway were aware of the warfare being committed against Native peoples in the United States, where uncontrolled, violent settlement and policies of removal were being implemented. Using this knowledge to their advantage, the British presented land treaties as statements of loyalty to the Crown and as guarantees that the lands would be protected from white settlement. Through the use of gifts and outright lies, to say nothing of improperly negotiated and conflicting boundaries, most of the land of southern Ontario was surrendered over a fifty-year period. The British used the following procedures to negotiate land treaties:

> 1. By the Proclamation of 1763, the rights of Indigenous peoples to the land were acknowledged.
> 2. The Indigenous peoples of each area were called to consider a surrender of lands, negotiated by traders or administrators that they already knew and trusted.
> 3. Only the chiefs or male representatives were asked to sign.[43]
> 4. The surrender was considered a test of loyalty.
> 5. The area ceded was deliberately kept vague.
> 6. Some compensation, in the form of gifts, was given.
> 7. In many cases, the land was left unsettled for a few years, until disease and alcohol had weakened potential resistance. When the settlers began to come in and the Native people complained, they were shown the documents they had signed and told there was no recourse.[44]

The British knew that deceit could drive a better bargain—but as the Ojibway learned to drive harder bargains themselves, the price of land went up. For example, one hundred townships obtained in earlier surrenders might cost the same price as ten townships obtained once the Ojibway understood how negotiations worked. The Ojibway were not, as is commonly believed, fooled by the British. By the late eighteenth century, they were fully aware that Europeans treated land differently than they did. They were familiar with the highly populated centres of British, French, and American settlement and had extensive communication with Native peoples who had already been dispossessed. Earlier land cessions were easier for the British because of the trust that many Ojibway had in the traders and diplomats who had demonstrated a degree of honesty and goodwill in the past. This was combined with the Ojibways' need for trade goods, a certain degree of loyalty, and, especially in the face of the wars of extermination being waged in the U.S., a lack of alternatives. Furthermore, prior to 1825, the Ojibway did not read or write in English and the treaties were ambiguous, incomplete, and often badly worded.[45]

For example, on October 9, 1783, Captain W. R. Crawford negotiated the infamous "gunshot treaty" or "walking treaty"—this was a "blank treaty" which did not specify any boundaries to the land the treaty claimed. Colonial officials were forced to investigate the complaints of the Mississaugas whose lands were taken by this treaty. Crawford argued that they had surrendered all the land "from Toniato or Onagara to the River in the Bay of Quinte within eight leagues of the bottom of the said Bay, including all the islands, extending from the lake back as far as a man can travel in a day."[46] Although later treaties clarified the boundaries (in the interests of Europeans), clear definitions of boundaries were intentionally omitted from the text of treaties and those who signed them were encouraged to include within the ceded lands the territory of other bands.

These practices should not be seen as part of the distant past. As late as 1923, despite attempts to clarify boundaries of the "walking treaty" negotiated by Crawford, the federal government realized that almost half of the City of Toronto, as well as the towns of Whitby, Oshawa, Port Hope, Cobourg, and Trenton were on land that had not yet been ceded. At that point, the government gave $375 to the Ojibway of Alnwick, Rice Lake, Mud Lake, and Scugog for the land.[47] The government showed no more scruples in 1923 than it had in 1783—the land not yet legally ceded was illegally bought for a pittance, two centuries after the fact.

Settler Violence and Loss of Land

When the first two waves of land cessions were over in what is now southern Ontario, two million acres remained in the hands of Native peoples. Over the next fifty years, the British exerted continuous pressure on the Saugeen Ojibway, whose territories of the Bruce Peninsula and its watershed were still unceded. Eager to acquire their land, the British developed a new way of obeying the letter of the law while violating its spirit—they began to use the threat of settler violence to force land surrenders. The constant encroachment of armed, land-hungry settlers forced the Saugeen Ojibway to continuously retreat, negotiating small land surrenders a piece at a time. Often the treaties were negotiated with individuals who had no authority within their communities to negotiate treaties; these treaties, therefore, were illegal. At one point, the Saugeen Ojibway bypassed their angry and unco-operative Indian Agent and petitioned Lord Durham in England to protect their remaining lands. Durham refused, noting that the 1837 rebellion confirmed that the will of the white colonists, especially for cheap land, took precedence over the will of the Indigenous peoples. However, the Saugeen Ojibway continued to petition and, in 1846, obtained a Royal Deed of Declaration, which stated that they and their descendants were to possess and enjoy the Saugeen (Bruce) Peninsula in perpetuity, in addition to receiving regular monies for other surrenders.[48]

By this point, the Bruce Peninsula had assumed major importance in the eyes of the colonial government. A large influx of settlers, primarily refugees from the Irish potato famine and from English industrial slums, put pressure on the colony for even greater tracts of land. Once again, armed squatters were allowed to invade and seize lands. The government, in response to the protests of the Saugeen Ojibway, claimed that the scale of immigration made it impossible for them to control the new settlers. The non-stop violent encroachment forced the Saugeen Ojibway to surrender the Bruce Peninsula in 1854, leaving for themselves five large reserves, many of which were thriving farm communities, and all of the islands along the Bruce Peninsula, which had been their traditional fishing grounds. Three years later, white settlers used extensive force to move in on the farming communities. Within the next twenty years, almost all of the islands were sold by the federal government and all but two of the reserves that still exist today were surrendered. After the British relinquished control of the Indian Department to Canada in 1860, hundreds of acres continued to be carved off the Ojibway reserves in southern Ontario to create farmland for settlers, for the building of roads, and for the expansion of towns and cities.[49]

The above discussion demonstrates how the British fur trade interests in Upper Canada were gradually supplanted by settlement policies, which allowed the Crown to use whatever means were at hand to consolidate its hold over former "Indian" territories. These policies resulted in the endless misery of relocation and land loss for the Ojibway people of what is now southern and central Ontario and left many unresolved claims for restitution of stolen lands. These claims include the efforts of the Caldwell Ojibway to obtain a reserve[50] after being forced off their land near Lake Erie during the first wave of land grabs in the early 1800s, and the monumental struggles around fishing rights waged by contemporary Saugeen Ojibway communities.[51]

☐ Moving North: Resource Plunder of Ojibway and Cree Territories

The consolidation of the land and resource base of what is now northern Ontario became crucial to Canada's westward expansion. This phase of colonization, which took place within the twentieth century, is still being pursued. In many respects, colonial acquisition of the land is still disputed, and as a result, Indigenous histories of this region have yet to be written.

Once the land base in southern Ontario was secure, business interests in the colony looked to the rich resources in the north. Within a few years, the vast timber forests were being cut, and the growing presence of mineral prospectors and mining operations in northern Ontario caused a number of Ojibway leaders to travel to Toronto to register complaints and demand payment from the revenues of mining leases. When there was no response to these or other entreaties, the Ojibway took matters into their own hands and forcibly closed two mining operations in the Michipicoten area. Soon troops, which were not called in to protect the Saugeen Ojibway from violent white settlers, were on the scene to quell the "rebellion," and government investigators began to respond to the issues that leaders were bringing to them.[52] The Ojibway wanted treaties, but they demanded a new concession—that reserve territories be specified before the treaties were signed. After considerable discussion and many demands from the Ojibway leaders, the Robinson-Huron and Robinson-Superior Treaties were signed in 1850. These treaties ceded a land area twice the size of that which had already been given up in southern Ontario, set aside reserves (although much smaller than the Ojibway had hoped for), and provided the bands with a lump-sum payment plus annual annuities of $4 per year per person. Most important, hunting and fishing rights to the entire treaty area were to be maintained.

With these treaties, the colony gained access to all the land around Lake Huron and Lake Superior, south of the northern watershed. All land north of this was considered Rupert's Land, the "property" of the Hudson's Bay Company, and so, by 1867, one of the first acts of the newly created Canadian government was to pay a sum to the Hudson's Bay Company in order to acquire "the rights" to this land. Inherent in the concept of "Canada," then, was the notion of continuous expansion, a Canadian version of "manifest destiny," no less genocidal that the United States in its ultimate goals of supplanting Indigenous peoples and claiming their territory.

Under section 91(4) of the *Constitution Act, 1867,* the Canadian federal government was given constitutional responsibility for "Indians and Lands reserved for the Indians," while section 109 gave the provinces control over lands and resources within provincial boundaries, subject to an interest "other than that of the Province in the same."[53] Through these unclear constitutional provisions, the newly created province of Ontario struggled for the right to open lands far north of its boundaries for settlement and development without a valid surrender of land from the Ojibway and Cree people living there. In 1871, Ontario expanded its borders to seize control of a huge northern territory rich in natural resources. "Empire Ontario," as then premier Oliver Mowat termed it, stretched as far north as Hudson's Bay (although it took a series of legal battles with the federal government to accomplish it), and spurred a rivalry with the neighbouring province of Quebec when it expanded north along the east side of Hudson's Bay.

In the late 1890s, the Liberal regime of Oliver Mowat, dominated by timber "barons" whose immense profits had been made through logging central Ontario and the Temagami region, was succeeded by the Conservative regime of James Whitney. Proponents of modern liberal capitalism, the Conservatives pushed aggressively ahead with northern development, focusing on railways, mining, and the pulp and paper industry.[54] Three northern railways were constructed to access timber, develop mineral resources, and access potential hydroelectric sites to power the resource industries. The railways opened up the territory to predators at an unprecedented rate. As a rule, if the presence of Cree or Ojibway people hindered development, the newly created Department of Indian Affairs relocated them away from the area.

It is important to understand the scale of the mineral wealth taken from the lands of the Ojibway and Cree in the past century, at great disruption to their lives and without any compensation. Since the early 1900s, the Cobalt silver mines brought in more than $184 million; Kirkland Lake gold mines produced $463 million; and Larder Lake produced $390 million.[55] Meanwhile, the Porcupine region, one of the greatest gold camps in the world, produced over $1 billion worth of gold and had the largest silver, lead, and zinc mines in the world.[56]

Across northeastern Ontario, hydroelectric development was sought primarily for the new mining industry. In 1911, however, timber concessions for the pulp and paper industry were granted, mainly to friends of government ministers, on condition that hydroelectric dams be built to power them out of the industry's money. In many cases, pulp cutting and dam construction proceeded well before permits were granted to do so.[57]

☐ Reasserting a Silenced History

This chapter has introduced only a few examples of Indigenous writers, or non-Native historians working with Elders, who have recorded Indigenous nations' stories of their past. These stories introduce new perspectives to what is considered "Canadian" history. For example, a detailed exploration of colonization in Mi'kmaki is frequently left out of most "Canadian" history texts. In part this is because of the Wabanaki Confederacy's links that tied the Mi'kmaq to wars with the Thirteen Colonies and the British Crown, events normally considered outside the purview of "Canadian" history. As Indigenous nations write their histories, we can expect to see more work that disregards the border, insists on the integrity of the Anishinabek nation or the Blackfoot Confederacy or Haudenosaunee territories that span both sides of the international border, and that disregards "Canadian" history.

Writing from the perspectives of the Indigenous nations enables specific communities to give a full and honest account of their struggles with colonizers intent on their removal and elimination as peoples, and to name the racism, land theft, and policies of genocide that characterize so much of Canada's relationships with the Indigenous nations. Even more important, Indigenous peoples are not cast as faceless, unreal "stick figures" lost in a ferment of European interests, but as the living subjects of their own histories.

While accounts of colonization from these nations are important, much remains missing from their perspectives. The Mi'kmaq people, for example, speak of the Jenu, the interval of the Ice Age when the Mi'kmaq retreated to what is now Central America until their lands became liveable again.[58] For Indigenous nations, colonization is only one part of a much older story. The ancient histories and cosmologies of our nations need to be removed from their current mythologized and depoliticized locations inside childrens' anthologies and from the mystical and colourful "origin myths" that inevitably precede television documentaries of "Canadian" history, and written back in as the organizing concepts of the histories of this land. The work of individuals such as Basil Johnston are a valuable beginning. Johnston links Anishinabek stories to the languages, cultures, and contemporary realities of the region that is now considered Quebec, Ontario, Manitoba, and parts of the United States, an area which has been and continues to be occupied by the Anishinabek people.[59] A detailed exploration of the traditional symbols used by many Indigenous nations and how these symbols have shaped the worldviews of the people is another history of the land that needs to be included.

It perhaps goes without saying that the histories of Indigenous nations will decentre the histories of New France and Upper Canada as organizing themes to the histories of this land. Canadian historians who are currently considered the experts could work in conjunction with Indigenous peoples wanting to tell their stories of the land. But the works of the experts alone, which provide powerful and detailed histories of the Canadian settler state, do not represent the full picture. It is the voices of Indigenous peoples, long silenced but now creating a new discourse, which will tell a fuller history.

CHAPTER 2

In Between and Out of Place

Mixed-Race Identity, Liquor, and the Law in British Columbia, 1850–1913

Renisa Mawani

Indians Canoeing Near Nanaimo, c.1860
[BRITISH COLUMBIA ARCHIVES, PHOTO E-06692]

Racial categories and classifications were

central to the "racial order of things" in colonial contexts around the world.[1] In British Columbia, the most westerly of Canada's provinces, the assertion of racial distinctions was particularly salient from the late-nineteenth to the early-twentieth century, a formative period during which federal, provincial, local, and religious authorities endeavoured to construct a strong white Canada and a "*British* British Columbia."[2] While determining who was "Indian" and "white" was important to the making of colonial identities, these constructions also had a material dimension: they specified who had access to land, citizenship, and nation. Racial categories and hierarchies, however, did not simply appear in settler societies like British Columbia. Rather, the European desire for distinct racial classifications meant that whites needed to constantly (re)create their own identities and superiority against the bodies of racialized Others. Yet the permeability of racial boundaries demanded that the policing of the sexual and domestic lives of colonizer and colonized and the legal and extra-legal regulation of mixed-race people remained pervasive strategies in the assertion of European dominance: processes that I argue were all about space.[3]

In this chapter, I explore the colonial anxieties surrounding interracial heterosexual relations between white men and Native women and the resulting imperial gaze that authorities fixed upon the mixed-race progeny of these sexual liaisons in British Columbia.[4] Federal, provincial, and local correspondence, missionary documents, legal statutes, and various court records detailing provincial and federal liquor infractions reveal the social, legal, and political debates over mixed-race people and their "proper place" in the province. Specifically, the following questions are considered: How did government administrators and missionaries (re)assert racial hierarchies when spatial and racial boundaries became blurred through interracial heterosexuality? Why was the "in-between-ness" of mixed-race people so threatening to white elites at this historical moment? In what ways were mixed-race people legally and spatially regulated and displaced? Although I focus on how mixed-race people were disciplined by federal, provincial, local, and religious authorities in the late-nineteenth and early-twentieth century, I also refer to the pre-Confederation era. A brief discussion of the fur trade is necessary to illustrate changing European perceptions of inter-racial sex between white men and Native women. In addition, a review of early statutes maps out the different ways in which government officials defined "Indian-ness" and traces how their definitions became more specific over time.

Canadian historians have put forth a variety of reasons to explain *why* government elites were so frightened by people of mixed-race ancestry on Canada's West Coast and elsewhere across the country. While some scholars have argued that governmental distrust and fears of mixed-race insurgence intensified after the Red River Rebellion, others, drawing from the work of Ann Laura Stoler, have argued that mixed-race people confused racial hierarchies and thus straddled the divide between colonizer and colonized.[5] Mixed-race progeny ambiguously and dangerously bridged the imperial divide by blurring the differences between Native people and whites. However, these fears were not merely symbolic or metaphorical, but deeply embedded in material concerns about land. Many whites feared that the growing class of "half-breeds" in the province would not only destabilize racial hierarchies—as mixed-race people were not always easily catalogued by race—but would also undermine European supremacy by posing *real* geographical implications.

Edward Said has reminded us of the materiality of empire, pointing out that imperialism is at "some very basic level" about "settling on, [and] controlling land that you do not possess, that is distant, that is lived on and owned by others."[6] Although the crossing of racial and sexual boundaries often posed the threat of disrupting racial hierarchies, race-mixing in British Columbia potentially jeopardized European efforts to appropriate Indigenous land. Since European power was contingent upon determining who was "Indian" and who was "white," race had everything to do with who could be included within the nation, and with who had legitimate access to land and how much. Many feared that mixed-race people, if assimilated into the white population, would claim land as easily as white settlers could. If counted as Indians, however, this expanding population would financially burden the provincial and federal governments by placing additional claims on reserve lands.[7] Even worse, the racial ambiguity of mixed-race people raised the possibility that they could duplicitously claim the privileges of whites and Indians alike.

Although authorities relied on a variety of spatial and legal techniques to govern mixed-race people, liquor prohibitions at both the federal and provincial levels were integral to maintaining racial and spatial boundaries and to keeping mixed-race people in their place, or, in other words, *out of place*. Because they were not "Indians" by law, and thus did not fall under federal jurisdiction, provincial and local administrators lamented that this "unruly population" could easily transgress race and space. Many argued that mixed-race people undermined the federal and provincial initiatives to control land, civilize Natives, and build a respectable white settler society in British Columbia. Mixed-race people, then, became the targets of governmental regulatory strategies, particularly the enforcement of liquor prohibitions.

Unlike other vice laws, alcohol provisions—under the *Indian Act*[8] and at the provincial level—were vigorously enforced by local authorities. While governmental interests were partly economic, the enforcement of intoxicant laws was about much more than generating large revenues.[9] Among other things, the regulation of liquor was about space—who could drink, where, and with whom. Thus, the enforcement of federal and provincial liquor prohibitions provided authorities with somewhat precarious means to limit the movements of mixed-race people, restricting them from easily assimilating into white *and* Native spaces. Whereas postcolonial scholars have insightfully documented the multiple ways colonial elites protected their own identities and claims to power,[10] I suggest that colonial authorities in British Columbia were not only concerned with containing whiteness but were also anxious to maintain distinct boundaries around Indian-ness. By cordoning off Indian-ness from the "false claims" of mixed-race people, authorities attempted to restrict and invalidate their claims to Indigenous lands. This allowed both government officials and white settlers to reassert their claims to European superiority and to British Columbia's vast and rugged geography.

☐ Inter-Racial Heterosexuality

The desire for distinct racialized categories and spaces in British Columbia emerged within specific historical and geographical circumstances: when settlement and land became the primary interests of European colonizers.

During the fur-trade era, colonial elites paid little attention to the creation of racial distinctions, as neither the British government nor the Hudson's Bay Company envisioned permanent settlement in Western Canada. It was not until the mid-nineteenth century, when white immigration to and settlement in British Columbia increased and when the "making of Canada" began,[11] that colonial elites expressed a need for distinct racial and spatial boundaries between white settlers, Natives, and other racialized populations. Colonial administrators and missionaries soon realized, however, that the parameters of racial superiority and inferiority were not natural, pre-existing, or easy to establish. Racialized borders in imperial cities and their colonies were incredibly porous to begin with.[12] The land-based fur trade in British Columbia and in various parts of Canada saw the proliferation of mixed-race unions between Native women and white men, which meant that boundary-making in these jurisdictions was even more perilous.

From first European contact on Canada's West Coast, heterosexual relations between Native women and white men—in all their forms—were an important aspect of the social and cultural climate in the "contact zone."[13] These relations were pervasive in British Columbia, where specific social and demographic factors ensured that inter-racial sex flourished from the fur trade throughout the nineteenth century, tapering off in the early part of the twentieth century. British Columbia's racial and gender demography, which was composed largely of Native men and women and white men, undoubtedly influenced these sexual practices, as did the absence of white women. In addition, the Fraser River Gold Rush attracted thousands of unmarried Black, Chinese, and European men to the province, further skewing these proportions, as did the growth of industry and the building of the Canadian Pacific Railway. Although inter-racial heterosexuality was widespread, the Hudson's Bay Company and missionaries did little to prevent it. Inter-marriage and inter-mixture were commonplace, and by the 1858 Gold Rush, estimates reveal that one Native woman out of ten had lived with a non-Native man at some point in her lifetime.[14]

While the Hudson's Bay Company allowed and even encouraged mixed-race heterosexual relations, by the mid-nineteenth century, colonial officials and religious authorities began to fear the consequences of this widespread "race-mixing." As European interests shifted from exploiting natural resources to the acquisition and (re)distribution of Native lands among white settlers, authorities came to see these mixed-race conjugal relations as "illicit," and the mixed-race progeny as undermining the settler society they were aiming to build. Colonial officials and missionaries expressed concerns that the crossing of racial and sexual boundaries would confuse the racial hierarchies they were constructing. In particular, they feared that miscegenation would produce a class of "undesirables" who would thwart their illusory goals of a homogeneous and respectable white settler society.

A strong Euro-Canadian identity and a firm hold on power were the cornerstones of this project. Defining racial boundaries and maintaining them through the management of heterosexuality became important strategies. Ann Laura Stoler observes similar shifts in how European elites perceived inter-racial liaisons between white men and Indigenous women in other colonial contexts. "Local women who had been considered protectors of men's well-being," she writes, "were now seen as the bearers of ill health and sinister influences; adaptation to local food, language, and dress, once prescribed as healthy signs of acclimatization, were now sources of contagion and loss of (white) self."[15]

When British Columbia joined Confederation in the late nineteenth century, European immigration increased significantly and a white settlement began to take shape. The imposition of racial distinctions and the policing of sexual and spatial boundaries became vital to this project. Aboriginal peoples and other racialized communities were socially segregated and geographically (dis)placed. Native peoples were forced into reserves and racialized Others into socially and legally partitioned space, although neither group was entirely removed from white society.[16] Federal, provincial, and local officials invested enormous amounts of time implementing these segregationist strategies to protect the discursive and material privileges of whiteness. Since inclusion and exclusion from the nation and access to land and resources were contingent upon defining who was "white" and who was "Indian," it is hardly surprising that the prevalence of mixed-race relations and peoples elicited such anxiety among government officials.

Differentiating between Indian-ness, whiteness, and everything in-between was necessary for protecting the identity, privilege, and property of whites. Because of their inherent "superiority," white middle-class men in British Columbia were entitled to property (they could pre-empt 160 acres of land and then purchase 480 more),[17] the franchise, and all the other privileges that accompanied full citizenship. If mixed-race people could *pass* as white, officials feared they would gain illegitimate access to these rights and disrupt Euro-Canadian dominance. Protecting the boundaries between "Indians" and mixed-race people was essential to asserting white superiority.

In what was to become British Columbia, Governor James Douglas signed only fourteen treaties with various First Nations residing on Vancouver Island. While Native title was not officially recognized beyond these few treaties, the absence of treaties also meant that Indigenous land claims were not formally extinguished as they were in other parts of the country. Thus arbitrary distinctions between "pure bloods" and "mixed-bloods" became important in British Columbia, as authorities had even more reason to restrict the number of "qualified" Indians who could legitimately make claims to land.[18] The federal government's concerns about "fraudulent Indians" was made clear through their efforts to narrowly legislate the category "Indian" and in later attempts to construct the "half-breed" as a separate racial type.

☐ Legislating Race

The state, argues David Goldberg, often responds to racial transgressions or pollution of its social borders in a twofold way: "first by conceptualizing order anew, and then by reproducing spatial confinement and separation in the renewed terms."[19] In British Columbia, the colonial government responded to the race-mixing through the enactment of various laws that governed both access to land as well as the everyday lives of Native peoples. From the mid-nineteenth century onward, authorities made disparate and contradictory efforts to codify racial differences through the legal construction of Aboriginality. Although whiteness was an "empty category,"[20] and was never explicitly defined in law, white settlers came to know themselves through what they were not, a process to which Indian-ness was central. Just as an invented Africanist presence was crucial to the formation of an American identity, as Toni Morrison has argued, Indian-ness underpinned the discursive and material borders of whiteness in Western Canada.[21] However, federal initiatives not only marked degeneracy onto the bodies of Native people, they also inscribed racial inferiority onto British Columbia's landscape. Reserves were created and Indians were thought to *naturally* belong on them, while white settlers assumed themselves to be the *real owners* and administrators of the "empty 'space.'"[22]

Although racial taxonomies of Indians—as "heathen," "savage," and "immoral"—were frequently articulated and institutionalized by government officials, missionaries, and white settlers, federal attempts to construct a *legal* definition were far more difficult than authorities anticipated. Legislating Indian-ness and then applying this legal construct posed numerous problems well into the twentieth century. Since limiting Indigenous land claims was a primary motive for constituting the "Indian" in law, it is hardly surprising that there was little consensus among state officials and religious authorities about who should be included in this category. In efforts to (re)clarify these questions, lawmakers made repeated attempts to codify Indian-ness. Unclear on how racial identity was to be legally ordered, the federal government vacillated between the importance of "blood" and "culture."[23] The 1850 *Act for the Better Protection of the Lands and Property of Indians in Lower Canada* was the colonial government's first effort to legislate Indian-ness. Under the guise of "protecting" the land of Native people in Lower Canada from the encroachment of non-Indians and trespassers, the Act entrenched the land-ownership rights of the colonial government by limiting Indians to the restricted spaces of reserves. For the first time, the law defined who was an "Indian." Its sweeping definition was based on blood, intermarriage, residence on Indian lands, and adoption. Dissatisfied with such a broad categorization, however, the colonial and later the federal government revised the definition of Indian-ness almost every year between 1850 and 1869.[24]

The *Lands and Enfranchisement Act* of 1869 was another attempt to legislate Indian-ness. Unlike the 1850 Act and its revised versions, the federal government's definition of "Indian" under the 1869 Act was narrower and relied more heavily on blood quantum: an "Indian" was "no person of less than one-fourth Indian blood." The law specified that only an "Indian" who met the blood requirements "shall be deemed entitled to share in any annuity, interest or rents, after a certificate to that effect is given by the Chiefs or Chief of the band or tribal council, and sanctioned by the Superintendent of Indian Affairs."[25] The legislation gave the Superintendent final say as to who qualified as an Indian by law. The Superintendent's veto power and the blood-quantum rule reveal that the federal government was increasingly preoccupied with protecting its own stakes in land by legally constructing "Indian" more rigidly. Defining "Indian-ness" through "pure blood" excluded land claims made by all people of Native descent who had "less than one-fourth" Indian blood.

In 1876, the federal government tackled the definition of "Indian-ness" once again. Under the *Indian Act*, all federal Indian laws and treaties were merged into one statute. Blood quantum remained central to the definition of Indian-ness, but was revised from the earlier wording of the *Lands and Enfranchisement Act*. Tellingly, the new legislation linked blood with *real* property and citizenship. Legislators did not believe that *any old blood* was sufficient for determining Indian-ness, as an "Indian" was no longer defined through definitive gradations of blood. Rather, a "Eurocentric patrilineal principle of descent" replaced the one-fourth rule and became the new doctrine for determining "race" in Canada.[26] The definition of "Indian" was decided largely through a person's relationship with a Native man. Thus, the *Indian Act* defined an "Indian" as "[a]ny male person of Indian blood reputed to belong to a particular band. . . . Any child of such person . . . and . . . any woman who is married to such person." Although the Canadian census continued to delineate Indian status through matrilineal descent, *male* blood became necessary for one to be an "Indian" in law.[27]

The provisions setting out who was *not* an "Indian" clearly reveal the emphasis placed on male blood and the state's impetus for rigidly legislating Indian-ness. Under the 1876 Act, the list of non-Indians included illegitimate children, Natives who continuously lived outside Canada for five years or more, Indian women who married "any other than an Indian or a non-treaty Indian," Indian women who married non-treaty Indians, and "half-breeds." The inclusion of non-Native women and the exclusion of Native women point to the connections between racism and patriarchy, which underpinned the state's racial distinctions.[28] Furthermore, the exclusion of Native people who resided outside Canada for five years, as well as "half-breeds" (who had Indian blood from their mother), suggests that the federal government was driven by economic concerns. In their efforts to control and limit access to property, officials used the *Indian Act* to decide racial identity in a fixed and patriarchal way.

These increasingly narrow federal initiatives, were precipitated by efforts to restrict the "fraudulent" Indigenous land claims put forth by mixed-race people. As Bonita Lawrence argues, the definition of "Indian" under the *Indian Act* placed many Native people outside reserve spaces and land allotments, thus making Euro-Canadian acquisition of land easier. She also points out that the law created deep divisions between and among Indigenous communities,[29] a "divide and conquer" strategy which, in its differential manifestations, has been integral to colonial rule around the world. Federal officials further reinforced these divisions among Indigenous communities by creating a separate racial and legal category for mixed-race people. In some European colonies, mixed-race children who could *pass* as white were often absorbed into the European population. In French Indo-China, for instance, racially mixed children who were given French names, lived in a European environment, and those whose facial features and skin tone made them white enough were either assimilated into the European population or sent to European communities in other colonial regimes.[30] In British Columbia, this was not the case.

Despite their disagreements about racial origins and their inability to define whiteness, local, provincial, and federal authorities agreed that "whites" were racially pure, and since mixed-race children were tainted by "Indian" blood, they could not be absorbed into the ranks of Euro-Canadians. They also agreed that mixed-race people were not "Indians" and were not entitled to the same benefits as Native people. To protect whiteness and Indian-ness from mixed-race people, authorities created the racialized category of "half-breed," which first appeared in the 1876 *Indian Act* under the list of non-"Indians." While officials forcefully debated the meaning of Indian-ness, they spent little time contemplating the definition of "half-breed" and did not specify who constituted a "half-breed" or what the legal status of this category was to be. Rather, federal legislators simply determined a "half-breed" was anyone of European and Indian heritage who was not an "Indian" by law. The ascendancy of a new racial type at this precise historical moment suggests that lawmakers in Canada were deeply preoccupied with racial (im)purity and the ideological and material consequences of miscegenation. By creating a separate category—rather than classifying mixed-race populations as "white" or "Indian"—state officials were once again protecting their own property interests.

By excluding racially mixed people from the legal category "Indian," the federal government created a number of problems for itself and for local and provincial governments. First, and perhaps most important, since mixed-race people fell outside of federal jurisdiction, they could not be legally regulated in the same ways as Indians. Local and religious authorities repeatedly lamented the "notoriously bad character" of mixed-race people and their sinister influences upon the province's well-being.[31] Although many appeared white in skin colour and facial features, local officials and missionaries emphasized that they were racially inferior, not only to whites but also to "pure blooded" Natives. In his 1871 report, the Earl of Kimberley cautioned British and Canadian authorities that the proliferating "race of half-castes" on British Columbia's mainland would eventually "prove a curse to the country in the next generation."[32] Local administrators echoed similar concerns, admitting that mixed-bloods "combine[d] the worst qualities" of both races who grew up to be immoral, lawbreakers, and habitual drunkards.[33] Yet the legal creation of the "half-breed" placed mixed-race people beyond the jurisdiction of the federal government. Provincial and local administrators insisted that they had few legal strategies for disciplining this "immoral" class. They feared that the a-legal status of "half-breeds" would prevent the state from protecting white settlers and the Indians from the criminality of these "degenerate" populations.

Provincial and local authorities were also concerned that "half-breeds" could easily pass for white. To make matters worse, there was nothing in the law that would prevent "half-breeds" from settling in white spaces. On the contrary, the *Indian Act* stipulated that "[n]o person, or Indian other than an Indian of the band, shall settle, reside or hunt upon, occupy any [reserve] land or marsh." If mixed-race people could not legally settle on reserves, authorities feared that they would leave their communities in droves and overrun white settlements. Others feared that "half-breeds" would blur the spatial and racial distinctions between white and Indian by travelling freely between white towns and Native spaces. While obscuring racial and spatial boundaries was a concern in and of itself, the materiality of these transgressions also created fears among government officials. Authorities urged that if proper safeguards were not taken, "half-breeds" could easily gain access to the material privileges of whiteness *and* Indian-ness, illicitly benefiting from both.

The regulation of mixed-race people did indeed pose challenges to local authorities, but their concerns that half-breeds would settle in white spaces were unfounded. Although people of mixed-race ancestry were not legally barred from white spaces, the social and racial climate in the province kept them on the reserves. Several years before the *Indian Act* was passed, "destitute half-breeds" were already believed to be a pressing problem in British Columbia. In 1874, on the advice of Chief Justice Mathew Begbie, the provincial government drafted a bill to provide "for Indian concubines and destitute half-breed children of persons dying intestate and leaving property in the province." Begbie explained that when "concubines" and their children were deserted by white men, they were "thrown to the charity of their neighbors for support, the [Indian] community [was] put to undue expense and the children [were] exposed to physical and moral deterioration to the further misery of the community."[34]

The wording of this bill suggests that Begbie and others wanted to hold white men accountable for their sexual transgressions while removing the financial burden from the federal and provincial governments. If white men were financially disciplined for producing mixed-race progeny, authorities anticipated that these inter-racial liaisons would stop, and more importantly, that the burden of "half-breeds" living illegally on reserves would be lifted off the state. The government of British Columbia never passed this bill, however. Many Native women and children who were deserted by white men and unwelcome in white spaces were thus forced back onto reserves. A "Half-Breed Census," commissioned by Vowell, the Superintendent of Indian Affairs in British Columbia, reveals that large numbers of mixed-race people did indeed reside on reserves well into the twentieth century.[35]

Provincial and federal officials deeply resented the fact that so many mixed-race people were "living as Indians" on reserves. Even though they acknowledged that "half-breeds" lived legally as Indians on reserves in "other provinces and in the Northwest Territories," in the British Columbia context, federal administrators urged that they should be sent off reserves immediately.[36] The close physical proximity between legally defined "Indians" and mixed-bloods exacerbated deep-seated anxieties about racial (im)purity and decline. While authorities feared that immoral "half-breeds" would take advantage of white society, others argued that they would corrupt vulnerable "Indians" by supplying them with liquor. Moreover, their ability to transgress race and space meant that mixed-race people could potentially undermine state initiatives to control land, civilize Natives, and build a respectable white settler society in British Columbia.

☐ Regulating Liquor and Governing Mixed-Race People

In British Columbia, the mid-nineteenth century marked a distinct shift in Euro-Canadian rule as the building of a white settlement was increasingly articulated through the domination of space. The making of a white province was predicated on the construction of multiple racial containments, which began with the legal creation of reserves, followed by the construction of other racialized districts, such as Chinatowns.[37] The social and legal construction of these places and the policing of their boundaries was undoubtedly motivated by the government's desire to secure racial hierarchies and to construct white bodies and spaces as "pure." Even in industrial settlements, where capitalist demands brought the different races into close physical contact, local authorities and employers imposed racially segregated housing, to keep the "inferior races" away from white settlers and from each other.[38]

Regardless of the various provincial and federal efforts to carve up British Columbia's landscape into racially marked pockets, inter-racial social and heterosexual contact remained widespread and pervasive. While mixed-race people embodied the permeability of racial boundaries and the ineffectiveness of spatial segregation, liquor, and drunkenness, especially among Native communities, were also indicative of race-mixing. Alcohol was a crucial aspect of what Adele Perry aptly describes as British Columbia's "homosocial racially plural world of the backwoods."[39] To provincial, local, and religious authorities, however, the sale and consumption of liquor was believed to be an obstacle to civilizing the province's rough male culture and large Native population. Not surprisingly, alcohol became an enormous social reform issue. Fearing that drunkenness would thwart their efforts to build a respectable white society, provincial authorities passed a litany of laws aimed at governing the production, distribution, and consumption of liquor in the province.[40] Since drunkenness among the province's Native peoples was believed to be especially problematic, many of these laws contained explicit provisions making it an offence to supply Indians with intoxicants.

Despite federal and provincial efforts to prohibit drinking among Native peoples, liquor flowed freely on and off reserves.[41] For many, the pervasiveness of liquor consumption symbolized the tragedies of intermingling across racial boundaries. Several authorities argued that working-class whites, "half-breeds," and foreigners blatantly disregarded the spatial restrictions explicitly or implicitly imposed upon them and on the Native population. Ignoring the importance of place, these "undesirables" allegedly supplied Native men and women with liquor and, in many cases, drank and got drunk with them. While local constables and missionaries feared that inter-racial drinking would result in the transmission of vice across place and race, they dreaded that drunkenness would ultimately lead to racial decline. By fostering a fertile climate for immorality and "illicit" sexual relations, many authorities suspected that inter-racial sociability would ultimately result in miscegenation.[42]

Liquor had long been viewed as a devastating influence on Native communities, a racialized notion which underpinned various state efforts to prohibit alcohol consumption. Missionaries and local authorities argued that drunkenness and debauchery among reserves was a clear sign that Aboriginal peoples lacked the European mores of Christianity, self-improvement, and discipline, and as such were especially susceptible to the bad examples set by white traders.[43] While their assumed predisposition to intoxication was used by government officials and missionaries to reinforce Native inferiority, it also rationalized and buttressed the need for spatial segregation. In a 1912 article entitled "The Nanaimo Indian," William Knott, a local missionary, luridly described the conditions that caused inter-racial drinking and the results that ensued:

> In places where the reserve is close to the city limits, as it is in Nanaimo, the [temperance] work requires a much closer watch than would be necessary with more favorable surroundings. . . . For drinking whiskey, some of the Nanaimo's are about as bad as can be, and if some low white man or woman, or Hindu, or Chinaman, or negro cannot be found on the reserve, they go to town and try and find one. In this, they are usually successful and often successful in also finding themselves in the lock up and in the court house, where they usually pay out their hard earned cash or go to jail.[44]

For Knott, "more favorable circumstances" were ones in which Indian reserves were located far away from white settlements and other racialized spaces. While Knott was describing the conditions in urban areas, others argued that inter-racial drinking was equally pervasive in non-urban areas. "In the villages where there is considerable contact with white men and Asiatics," explained another missionary, "the intemperance of the Indian can generally be traced to them."[45] For these missionaries and other authorities, the only way to curb drunkenness on reserves was to actively enforce racial segregation.

Throughout the mid-nineteenth and early-twentieth century, in attempts to limit inter-racial contact, authorities attempted to enforce liquor laws. Many believed that by vigorously policing liquor, they could also eliminate inter-racial mingling and eventually achieve their desired goals of racial segregation and purity. Although British Colombia's sparsely populated and rugged landscape made liquor enforcement difficult, local constables often travelled long distances to apprehend non-Native suspects who allegedly supplied intoxicants to "Indians."[46] Not surprisingly, many white, Chinese, Japanese, and mixed-race women and men were convicted and fined—mainly under provincial prohibitions—for supplying liquor to Indians.[47] Liquor laws, it seems, were used to police racial boundaries and to assert racial and spatial purity. Whereas white men were often arrested for possessing liquor on reserves, Native women and men were prohibited from entering into drinking establishments well into the twentieth century. Notwithstanding these efforts to enforce racial segregation through liquor control, intoxication among Native communities remained a pervasive problem.

Although white men and other racialized groups were implicated in perpetuating drunkenness among Natives, many officials insisted that it was mixed-race people themselves who were ultimately responsible for this condition. Since "half-breeds" were not "Indians" by law, they had no specific legal status and thus could not be legally regulated in the same ways as Natives. By law, then, it was completely legal for a mixed-race person to purchase alcohol, a situation which created deep discomfort for government elites and religious authorities alike. Assumptions about the racial inferiority and inherently "bad character" of "half-breeds" fuelled this panic even further. Superintendent Vowell of the Department of Indian Affairs summarized the perilous combination of "half-breeds" and liquor as follows: The "selling or supplying of intoxicants to such creatures is a source of much evil and is often times dangerous to life, property, and the public peace, by affording opportunities of obtaining liquor for the Indians."[48]

Like Vowell, several Indian Agents and missionaries traced the liquor problem to the large numbers of "half-breeds" living illegally on reserves or within short distances of Native spaces. McKay, an Indian Agent of the Kamloops-Okanagan Agency, explained the situation in his jurisdiction as follows: a "young man," he complained,

> has kept up a steady traffic in spiritous liquors. For the past five years he has been driven from one reserve to another. Lately he ostensibly pre-empted a plot of land on the Similkameen, where he and his brother . . . go through the form of cultivating a small patch of ground; at every convenient opportunity he makes his appearance at

some Indian encampment, where there may happen to be no constable handy and in a very short time supplies intoxicants enough to create a riot.[49]

The Indian Agent's report confirmed all of the provincial and federal government's worst fears about mixed-race people. As the Agent's account
suggests, this mixed-blood man *passed* as an Indian, living on different
reserves for a number of years. His ability to live as a non-Indian and Indian
simultaneously meant that he could access liquor freely and could easily
supply intoxicants to the other residents of the Kamloops-Okanagan
Agency. When compelled to leave the reserve, he simply assumed the identity of a "fabricated" European, *passed* as white, and claimed land to which
he was perhaps legally but not morally entitled. In the eyes of government
and religious officials, his racial ambiguity and that of other mixed-race
people was a sure obstacle to securing white superiority in British Columbia. Moreover, his ability to *pass* as both colonizer and colonized under-
scored the need for authorities to vigilantly protect the real and discursive
parameters of whiteness and Indian-ness from "half-breeds."

In 1895, the Methodist Missionaries sent a petition to the Attorney
General with respect to the "worsening" problem of mixed-race people selling liquor to Indians. They lamented that "there are large numbers of white
men and Indian women who are living in unlawful concubinage throughout the province. As a result of this unlawful union there are large numbers
of illegitimate children who are a standing menace to the laws of our land
and the well being of our communities." The missionaries explained that
when "it suits the convenience of White men they leave both women and
children, who naturally return to the Indian camp—the women to become
the wives of Indians, the children to act as the part of go between in carrying liquor from the Whites to the Indians."[50]

Like others, the Methodists feared that "unruly" mixed-race children
could straddle the boundaries between whiteness and Indian-ness. The
provincial and federal government's inability to govern them also meant
that "half-breeds" could easily subvert white superiority by endangering
the church's civilizing missions. It was bad enough that these depraved
individuals could access liquor for their own use, but, as the missionaries
pointed out, they aggravated the "liquor problem" among Indians by supplying them with intoxicants as well. The Methodist missionaries insisted

that "half-breeds" were solely responsible for this state of affairs and their petition demanded that something be done to suppress, or at least curtail, this ongoing predicament.

The legal and racial ambivalence of racial hybridity posed problems for Indian Agents and missionaries. At various historical moments, authorities suggested different strategies to deal with the growing liquor problem. The first approach entailed the suppression of inter-racial heterosexuality. The Methodist missionaries, for instance, suggested that the state enact some sort of legislation "prohibiting white men from cohabiting with Indian women."[51] Since racial purity was often thought to depend on the vigilant policing of women's sexuality, some officials urged the enforcement of a quasi-pass system to regulate the movements of Native women, keeping them on their reserves and away from white men.[52] Others preferred a less punitive approach, embracing the idea of importing "respectable" white women from Britain to British Columbia.

Each of these "solutions" was intensely debated through extensive letter writing between the Department of Indian Affairs, local Indian Agents, and religious authorities. And while government officials and missionaries deemed anti-miscegenation laws and a pass system unenforceable, they sanctioned the importation of white women, but with much disappointment.[53] For many, including the mayor of New Westminster, the only acceptable solution to this issue was to expand the legal definition of "Indian" to include racially mixed people. Although this proposal received widespread attention from the various levels of government, to include "half-breeds" in the legal category "Indian" would require the federal government to acknowledge their land claims as "legitimate." Authorities quickly put this idea to rest.

Legal distinctions between "Indians" and "half-breeds" remained blurry, causing confusion for Indian Agents and other authorities. McKay, the Indian Agent from Kamloops, sought further clarification from the provincial government on this issue and wrote an angry letter to the Superintendent of Indian Affairs. He requested some guidance as to whether (or not) "half-breeds" were "Indians" and whether they could be treated as such, writing that "considerable diversity of opinion is shown by the local magistrates of my agency, respecting the application of the Indian Act to the illegitimate progeny of Indian women, the results of illicit intercourse with white men." McKay claimed that while he had "always treated them as Indians" in the past and felt justified in doing so, he was becoming increasingly confused about the legality of his decisions. He explained that a "short time ago a Justice of the Peace at Yale is said to have addressed from the bench one of these unfortunate said half-breeds; to the effect that the half-breed has as much right to buy intoxicants at the licensed marts as the worshiped magistrate himself." He urged that if they are "the illegitimate offspring of Indian women but not Indians in the legal sense of the word . . . so long as they keep up their connection with the Indians it is my opinion that they should be treated as Indians in every respect."[54]

The Attorney General's lawyers responded immediately to McKay's queries, pointing out that defining "Indian-ness" in law was "a question of blood" and not morality. As one lawyer explained, "Indians" were to be legally determined as follows: "The word 'Indian' must I think mean a person whose father and mother were Aboriginals. It cannot I think be interpreted as including Half-breeds—the expression is defined in Webster's Dictionary as 'One of the Aboriginal inhabitants of America'—I think the question rests on a question of 'blood' not a 'moral distinction.'" Interestingly, the Attorney General's legal consultant relied on the American Webster's Dictionary's definition of "Indian" to determine the boundaries of racial identity. He added that although "a person with the slightest trace of Indian blood or even without it but of degraded habits might be considered to be an Indian," the uncertainty of determining racial identity would make this difficult to legislate. The lawyer elaborated disappointedly that "the expression Indian in the Indian Liquor Ordinance 1867 does not include an individual who is a half-breed by percentage."[55]

A broader definition of Indian-ness would have enabled authorities to discipline and punish mixed-race people for their racial and spatial transgressions. However, the federal and provincial governments had much to lose by doing so. (Re)constituting mixed-race persons as "Indians" meant that the provincial government could be forced into assigning additional reserve lands to British Columbia's Native population. Since Euro-Canadian rule and the creation of a strong settler society in the province was contingent upon the acquisition and control of land, redefining "half-breeds" as "Indians" was an enormous social and political risk, one which governmental elites were not willing to take. Instead, state officials used their fears of liquor and drunkenness to govern mixed-race people, pushing them off reserves into the periphery of white society, and thus, out of place.

☐ Out of Place: (Dis)Placing Mixed-Race People

Questions of what to do with British Columbia's mixed-race population invoked a series of responses from Indian Affairs officials, missionaries, and local authorities. Despite the fact that "half-breeds" were to be dealt with as a separate racial and legal category, administrators still had much difficulty determining who was mixed-race and where they belonged geographically. In 1892, the Superintendent of Indian Affairs in British Columbia requested Indian Agents to count the number of "half-breeds" in their jurisdictions. In addition, he asked them to record the following details: "what side the Indian descent is [on] in each case, the circumstances of the Half-breed, and why he or she should not be required to be removed from the reserve." More important, Superintendent Vowell emphasized that officials should report "what his or her personal character for morality is, and especially with reference to influences in intoxicants" and "giving them to the Indians."[56] Indian Agents across the province responded with sensationalist stories of large numbers of "half-breeds" with "drunken habits" who "are supplying intoxicants to the Indians."[57] In reply, Vowell sternly advised them that "unless there is a marked change for the better in their conduct," these undesirables should "be ejected from the Reserves," and that local authorities should "keep a sharp oversight as to the future conduct of these parties."[58]

Assumptions of "half-breeds" as debauched, sinister, and as "go-betweens" carrying intoxicants from whites to Indians, were pervasive and resilient. Authorities used these rationalizations in their attempts to force mixed-race people out of Native spaces. As one Indian Agent reported, "[T]here are no half breeds living on any of the reserves belonging to this Agency. I took upon myself the responsibility of dealing with the only case of the kind that has recurred here and I declined to allow a half breed to remain on the Shuswap Reserve: the reserves being in my opinion for the Indians and for the Indians alone."[59] Anxieties about liquor and the spread of vice among "vulnerable" Native communities provided government officials with yet another justification for compelling mixed-race people to leave reserves. Many were convicted under both provincial liquor provisions and the intoxicant sections of the *Indian Act*, and fined for supplying alcohol to Indians. In some cases, individuals were also taken to local jails and incarcerated either for fine default or for breaking the intoxicant provisions. For instance, a "Negro Half-breed" found drunk and disorderly in "the domicile of an Indian" was convicted under vagrancy laws in addition to "supplying liquor to an Indian." He was fined $50 and, in default, was sent to the local jail for three months of hard labour.[60]

Despite state efforts to push racially mixed people away from reserves, many continued to reside there illegally. Several Indian Agents pointed out that removing "half-breeds" from reserves would be futile, "as they have been in the band since infancy—and all their relations and friends are Indians of the reserve" making it "impossible to keep them away."[61] This does not mean that mixed-race people escaped the government's disciplinary techniques. In response to various complaints of this sort, the Department of Indian Affairs created an unofficial three-tiered system of band membership. Individuals deemed to be "Indians" by law were given full membership in band affairs as were "half-breeds" who "have been occupying and cultivating the land on the reserve for a large number of years"; some mixed-race people who lived on reserves for a large portion of their lives were entitled to stay, but with few or no rights to decide band affairs; and, finally, "half-breeds" who were not raised in Native communities from infancy and were not "cultivating land on the reserve" were not permitted to vote in band affairs, nor were they entitled to reside there.[62] While these policies were undoubtedly difficult to enforce, mixed-race people were also disciplined and excluded from Native and white society in a number of other ways.

Many children of mixed-race parentage were denied access to government education. In 1912, the Inspector of Indian Agencies wrote to the Department of Indian Affairs in Ottawa, claiming that two children belonging to a "member of the Chiet Band of Indians [were] placed in the Alberni School." However, he was informed by the Indian Agent that the man "is a half-breed and that his children are not eligible as grant earners in the school."[63] The Departmental secretary responded by saying that the "child of an Indian mother by a white man, or by a half-breed not accounted as an Indian, has no legal right to membership in the band," unless that person was "brought up on the band's reserve since infancy and 'reputed' to belong to the band." He added that "a letter on file" from an Indian Agent in British Columbia stated that half-breeds were always seen "as being on the same footing as those who do not reside upon reserves, and they are allowed to purchase liquor openly as well as the latter. They are also allowed to vote." The Secretary of Indian Affairs stated emphatically that "half-breeds who claim and exercise these privileges [purchasing liquor and voting] have no just right to be accounted as Indians or to live on an Indian reserve," nor are they entitled to schooling.[64]

In the case of light-skinned children, some were forcefully taken away from Native communities. In one instance, an "illegitimate" girl of an Indian woman and white man was placed in the custody of the Children's Aid Society. The girl was apprehended after she had been found with an "immoral" Indian woman who was selling liquor and prostituting herself to white men. Although the girl's mother applied to the court for custody, her request was denied, as the girl was believed to be *too white* to live among the Indians. "This little girl in her ways, traits, living, and aspirations is entirely white" described the Superintendent of the Children's Aid Society. She takes "after her father and grandfather both in manners and appearance, so much so that she passes as a Scotch child," he added. A little girl who looked so white and yet who lived among the Indians was bound to raise questions and anxieties. As an "eighth or a sixteenth breed," the Superintendent observed, she is "entirely out of place among the Indians, and being a white child should not be returned to their care or custody." Since the girl was a non-treaty Indian, the judge acquiesced to the Superintendent's requests, refusing to send her back to what he termed to be a life of "moral destruction."[65] Taken from her family and community, the girl became a ward of the Children's Aid Society and was placed in a Vancouver orphanage.

Racial classifications were fundamental to the ways in which government authorities constituted a provincial identity and affirmed Euro-Canadian rule in British Columbia. Specifically, establishing who was "white," "Indian," and mixed-race was crucial for determining who belonged where, and who had rights to land and to citizenship. While the federal government attempted to legislate these distinctions into the *Indian Act*, a large mixed-race population in the province made codifying and regulating these racial boundaries a challenge for local authorities. Whereas in other contexts, colonial elites insulated whiteness from the potential demands of mixed-race people in various ways,[66] authorities were equally concerned with protecting Indian-ness from the "fraudulent" claims of "half-breeds." Since the parameters of Indian-ness and whiteness were materially about who had access to land and how much, government officials exercised vigilance in safeguarding these categories, albeit often unsuccessfully.

In their efforts to protect whiteness and Indian-ness and to assert a racial order in the province, state officials forced mixed-race people in what Ann Laura Stoler has called the "gray zones along colonial divides."[67] In other (post)colonial contexts, people of mixed-race parentage who fell between the categories white and Native were sometimes successful in slipping through or subverting dominant power relations. Under apartheid in South Africa, mixed-race people had an unstable social position and fewer rights than whites, but for the most part experienced better living conditions than Black South Africans.[68]

In the British Columbia context, the "grey zones" meant that those of mixed-race ancestry enjoyed fewer rights than both whites and Native peoples. The federal government's decision to legislate the "half-breed" as a separate legal and racial category translated into an erasure of identity, rights, and territorial claims. The in-between status of many mixed-race people enabled government officials to deprive them of their rights to land and community, while displacing them to the margins of the emerging white settler society. Robert Young remarks that "the repressive legacy of the desiring machine of colonial history is marked in the aftermath of today's racial categories that speak of hybrid people, yoked together."[69] In British Columbia and elsewhere in Canada, this legacy is also materially evident in the struggles by mixed-race people to reclaim their Native ancestry and their real and symbolic space in the nation.[70]

CHAPTER 3

Cartographies of Violence

Women, Memory, and the Subject(s) of the "Internment"

Mona Oikawa

Tashme, British Columbia Internment Camp, c. 1943

[JAPANESE CANADIAN NATIONAL MUSEUM, PHOTO 94/60.015a-c]

It really made me angry that she lives in [northern Ontario]. And I was seeing that. I was making the connection to that being part of the internment process. I'm all pissed off that I have to [travel by plane and then take a bus for three hours]. And then I thought my grandmother lives there and has lived there for over fifty years.

—Naomi[1]

During the 1940s, twenty-two thousand

Japanese Canadians were forced to leave their homes on the Canadian West Coast and were imprisoned, dispossessed, detained, pressed into low-waged labour, and displaced. Forcibly moving twenty-two thousand people across provincial, municipal, and national boundaries was a profoundly spatialized and deliberate orchestration. The extant literature on the Internment describes some of the spaces of incarceration and displacement—the internment camps in the B.C. interior, the sugar-beet farms, the prisoner-of-war (POW) camps, "self-support" sites, and the work camps.[2] As is also illustrated through the literature, Canadian law played a pivotal role in the production of these incarceration sites. The *War Measures Act*[3] and various Orders-in-Council established who went where.

Yet, while scholars have described these laws and sites of incarceration, they have devoted relatively little attention to the long-term effects upon those who were subjected to these laws and forcibly displaced through their enactments. Similarly, very little attention has been paid to the role that the multiple spaces and the forced movement of twenty-two thousand people has played in the reproduction of a racial social order and a white nation-state. In this chapter, I critically examine the production of the "carceral"[4] spaces of the Internment, asking, as have many critical geographers of historical violence, what the spaces enabled both in the past and present.

Tracing the specific geographies of the Internment uncovers both the scale of the violence perpetrated on Japanese Canadians and the microprocesses of power required to accomplish it. It also reveals the enduring effects of the incarcerations and displacements. As the opening quote from the daughter of a survivor so powerfully reminds us, there is a critical connection between space and memory, a connection that refashions itself from one generation to the next. While Naomi experiences anew the violence of her grandmother's expulsion from her original community, survivors' memories of the Internment are themselves affected by the spatial details of the Internment. For each generation of Japanese Canadians, then, the spaces that emerged out of a series of laws enacted during the 1940s, produced and sustained racially subordinate subjects who continue to experience their exclusions from the nation. These spaces also produced and sustained dominant subjects. It is the production of Japanese-Canadian subjects in space and time that is explored here.

The women's testimonies I draw upon in the text are taken from my larger study that investigates the cross-generational transmission of memories of the Internment—I interviewed eleven women who were incarcerated and ten of their daughters. I examined how the sites of incarceration were remembered and described, and how memories of these spaces and what they produced were conveyed to daughters of survivors. What was clearly articulated in these twenty-one interviews were the long-term effects of the Internment upon survivors and subsequent generations, effects that underlined the systematic exclusions of white racial domination over time and space. In this chapter, I analyze the testimonies of six women who were expelled from their homes in British Columbia. The women were between the ages of twelve and twenty-two at the time of their expulsion in 1942. I do not suggest that these testimonies are representative of the experiences of all Japanese Canadians. Rather, I am insisting we see the effects of the Internment as heterogeneous experiences of violence. To make the full measure of the violence visible, I show how individuals experienced the Internment in multiple ways and at multiple sites.

I use the notion of cartography to convey the mapping of the physical and the social: the spaces of the incarceration and displacement, the social relations producing these spaces and produced through them, and the subjects who were displaced to these spaces and affected by the violence of these displacements. More important, the notion of cartography of violence illuminates that the mapping of Canada—the making of the nation and the subjects within it—is based upon systematic racial exclusions and other social divisions. Re-mapping the spaces of the Internment, therefore, reveals the ideological framework through which Canada was made and the forgetting of violence that is essential to this project of nation-building and the making of citizens.

The counter-mapping of Canada illuminates the cartographies of violence lived by the subjects of the Internment. In contesting the fixed and immutable atlas version of Canada, the women interviewed verbally re-map the nation where their identities as racial Others were imposed and reinforced through spatial exclusions. Their cartographies make visible the violence that is made invisible through sanitized landscapes and hegemonic ideologies of forgetting. Their memories of racism and their lived geographies of racial exclusion, including the very production of the separate geographical spaces in which they currently live, enable us to see how racial social order was historically and geographically produced in Canada, and hence how it produced Canada.

My task, however, is not to detail the particularities of each incarceration site but to illustrate how carceral spaces were constructed relationally, producing relational subjects who remember the Internment differently. Nor do I furnish the life histories of the women whose oral testimonies are used here. Rather, their testimonies provide a verbal mapping of the spaces of incarceration and illustrate some of the ways in which the very heterogeneity of these spaces affects what is remembered and named. In this way, survivors' testimonies provide a counter-map to a sanitized landscape of national forgetting. At the same time it must be emphasized that the enormity of national violence[5] can never be exhaustively remembered or "known."

I am profoundly aware of the fissures in the cartographies attempted here. As Robert Shields states, "Place-images, and our views of them, are produced historically, and are actively contested. There is no whole picture that can be 'filled in' since the perception and filling of a gap lead to the awareness of other gaps."[6] Detailing some of the embodiments of this violence will never convey its full extent or effect. I welcome an interrogation of the means through which we remember the Internment, in ongoing efforts to contest the forgetting of the violence actively produced within Canada. It is this difficult process of remembering our own social locations, forged through domination and subordination in the Canadian nation-state, that I offer as a challenge to all readers as we witness these fragments of testimonies.

☐ **Spatializing the Narrative of Internment**

The temporal limitations imposed by the historical narrative relegate the violence of the Internment to the past. If we view history as a linear march of progress through time, we may fail to see the long-term effects of national violence and the multiple ways in which violence is continually being perpetrated against subordinated communities. In this way, the temporal focus of historical narrative may serve to obscure our understanding of this multiply constituted violence and hinder our abilities to see its processes and effects.

In contrast, spatializing the historical narrative, so that we conceptualize history as not solely about time but also about space, enables us to develop a picture of violence. What this spatial analysis makes visible is how social relations are produced through geographical constructions and at the same time produce these constructions. Edward Soja calls spatial analysis an "interpretive geography," a way of recognizing "spatiality as simultaneously . . . a social product (or outcome) and a shaping force (or medium) in social life." Soja's work reminds us that space is not "fixed, dead, undialectical," but has a critical relationship to the people who inhabit a space and to the spaces and people seemingly exterior to that space.[7]

This analysis is particularly useful in understanding the complex spatial construction of the Internment in relation to the now sanitized and overgrown sites of the former spaces of incarceration. Keeping in mind that twenty-two thousand people were removed from their homes on the West Coast and incarcerated in different and separate geographical locations, we can begin to understand how spaces organize different forms of surveillance and how "discipline proceeds from the distribution of individuals in space."[8] What my work seeks to emphasize, therefore, are the ways in which the physical spaces of incarceration, the social processes produced through these spaces, and the ways in which these spaces impinge upon the memory and representation of these spaces are all interconnected. As I trace the spatialization of the Internment, I will discuss how these "three spaces (physical, mental, social) . . . interrelate and overlap."[9]

An examination of spatial arrangements is critical to an interrogation of the making of Canada as a white nation. The white supremacy of British Columbia and of the nation necessitated the continual creation of pathologized populations of Aboriginal people and people of colour who could be spatially segregated. David Goldberg has described cordoned off, pathologized areas as "periphractic spaces." The boundaries of these spaces can be physical or imagined and they imply the processes of "dislocation, displacement, and division." Goldberg suggests that periphractic spaces have become "the primary mode by which the space of racial marginality has been articulated and reproduced."[10] Degenerate spaces, therefore, are established in relation to white bourgeois spaces to produce differing entitlements to power.

The Second World War presented an opportunity to ascribe the mark of "enemy alien" upon Japanese nationals and "disloyalty" upon Canadian citizens of Japanese origin. These ascriptions were the pretext given for their spatial removal from the coastal area, away from the "respectable" space of the white bourgeois metropolis. Dispossession and discounting the citizenship of even those who were born in Canada, normalized their erasure from the B.C. coastal area; hence, their imposed statelessness became attributed to an invented monolithic allegiance to the nation of the "enemy." The expulsion, incarceration, and servitude integral to the Internment had to be spatially imagined and rationalized, and by expelling Japanese Canadians from the one-hundred-mile restricted coastal area they were re-cast outside the imagined white collective space of the Canadian nation.

☐ **Creating a Nationless People**

Canada's declaration of war on Japan gave the pretext for greater and greater spatial restrictions placed on all people of Japanese origin living in the country. Audrey Kobayashi has documented how "spatial discrimination" was imposed upon Japanese Canadians between the years 1942 and 1949. Her work emphasizes that the spatial exclusions transpiring during this period were but a "logical extension" of a fifty-year history where geographical rights were denied through a "social context of racism."[11]

The Canadian government used the *War Measures Act* to authorize the wholesale expulsion, detention, incarceration, dispossession, and deportation of Japanese Canadians.[12] Orders-in-Council issued by the federal government clearly specified where and when they could travel. For example, on December 8, 1941, all fishing boats were impounded, thus claiming the waters out-of-bounds. Order-in-Council P.C. 365 issued on January 16, 1942, designated a one-hundred-mile "protected area" from the Pacific Ocean to the Cascade Mountains and from the Yukon to the United States border. Order-in-Council P.C. 1486 issued by the federal cabinet on February 24, 1942, allowed the Minister of Justice to control the movements of all people of Japanese origin in "protected areas."[13]

Delineating the allowable times for Japanese Canadians to be outside of their homes was a step towards spatially separating them in internment camps and far-flung regions of the nation. A "dusk to dawn" curfew imposed on all people of Japanese origin on February 28, 1942, limited their access to public places and to each other, thus curtailing their abilities to gather in numbers and to work outside daylight hours.[14]

Community infrastructures supporting communication and intracommunal relations were hastily dismantled and rendered illegal by the federal government. Japanese-language schools and the three vernacular newspapers published in Vancouver were closed.[15] Public community gatherings were forbidden and churches were not permitted to hold services except in the case of funerals.[16] Prohibitions placed upon communal gatherings were the first steps towards the separation of friends and family members.

Part of the process of creating a placeless and hence nationless people was to dispossess them. Being without place ensured an uncontestable disentitlement to the rights of citizenship. While Japanese Canadians were already excluded from many of the rights of citizenship prior to the Internment, the processes of dispossession and displacement served to strip them of any legal recourse, solidifying the continued abrogation of their claim to legal rights well into the future. Thus dispossession and displacement go hand in hand with the legislation aimed at controlling Japanese Canadians.

Order-in-Council P.C. 288 established a three-man committee responsible for the disposal of fishers' boats.[17] On December 8, 1941, twelve hundred fishing boats were impounded and placed under the control of the Japanese Fishing Vessel Disposal Committee.[18] All of the men whose boats were confiscated were Canadian citizens. Motor vehicles, radios, and cameras were confiscated by the government. When people were ordered to move from their homes to various incarceration sites, all property left behind was held by the Custodian of Alien Property. Order-in-Council P.C. 1665 of March 4, 1942, stated that the property was under the "control and management" of the Custodian.[19] Since the displaced people were allowed to take only 150 pounds of baggage per adult and 75 pounds per child over twelve with a maximum allowance of 1,000 pounds per family, the possessions left behind were often looted or destroyed. Thus dispossession began well before the issuance of Order-in-Council P.C. 469 on January 19, 1943, allowing the Custodian to liquidate all property under its control.

☐ Cartographies of the Carceral

When the Internment is admitted into sites of popular culture, for example representations in journalistic texts, it is sometimes depicted spatially as camps somewhere in British Columbia.[20] The geographical and social distinctions among the Internment camps are effaced through the unitary word "camps." This singularizing of space in the collective memory is part of the production of its forgetting. Spatially conflating the incarceration and displacement of twenty-two thousand people to the (sometimes) admitted sites of amorphous internment camps denies the spatial scope of the incarcerations and displacements. Like the rendition of the Internment as a temporal moment, a "sad chapter" or "page" of Canadian history, the singularity of space conceals the extent and materiality of the violence involved in destroying communal and familial relations. What is also obscured through such monolithic representations is the way in which multiple spatializations produced heterogeneous gendered subjects.

"Camps" were in reality numerous heterogeneous carceral sites scattered across the country. While I cannot undertake an extensive examination of all of these sites and the social relations constituting them, I will map out some of their interconnections.[21] To counter-map the mythologized terrain of Canada, we must understand how social relations are used to create, legitimize, perpetuate, and forget spatial segregations. Each site of incarceration and displacement was characterized by particular physical qualities and social relations. Each site presented different spatial arrangements and different encounters with white people. Who inhabited each site and its spatially specific social processes influenced the production of memories of that site. Spaces of incarceration and displacement were differentially and relationally constructed. This construction was both material and discursive and entailed the mobilization of interlocking systems of domination—male domination, white supremacy, economic domination, heteronormativity, and ableism—to accomplish it.

This process was also one in which white subjects were formed in relation to Japanese Canadians: white bourgeois respectability depended upon the pathologizing of Japanese Canadians.[22] Racializing, gendering, and classing processes were spatialized through these carceral sites. Japanese-Canadian masculinities were produced in relation to white masculinities. Japanese-Canadian women were constructed in relation to white women. Japanese-Canadian men and women were constructed in relation to each other. Dominant and subordinate discourses positioned white bodies and white spaces in relation to Japanese-Canadian bodies and carceral spaces, and were relationally constitutive. Carceral sites, therefore, depend upon and produce relations of power. When these spaces become visible as heterogeneous and related sites, the matrices of power producing these spaces also become more discernible.

Work Camps and Prisoner-of-War Camps

In the expulsion of Japanese Canadians, fifteen hundred non-citizen males were the first to be moved, separated from their families and sent to forced labour or "road camps" in British Columbia.[23] Seven hundred and fifty citizen and non-citizen males were incarcerated in prisoner-of-war (POW) camps in Ontario; six hundred and fifty single males who were Canadian citizens were also sent to the forced labour sites in B.C.

The government mobilized a particular notion of racialized masculinity to produce the site of the work camps through Order-in-Council P.C 1271 issued on February 13, 1942. Men who were not Canadian citizens were the first to be removed from the one-hundred-mile restricted coastal area. This expulsion and the imprisonment of male citizens and non-citizens in the POW camps in Ontario operated by the Department of National Defence, depended upon the heightened image of a demonized and racialized masculinity, that of the "enemy alien," constructed to legitimate their incarceration. While more analysis of the representation of Japanese-Canadian masculinity is needed, it is evident that racializing discourses depicted Japanese-Canadian men as Other in relation to a normative white bourgeois masculinity. The government accused those detained in the Petawawa and Angler, Ontario, POW camps—what they called

"Internment camps"—as "those Japanese known to be dangerous, or to have the slightest subversive tendencies and, therefore, considered to be a potential menace."[24] As has been documented by Ann Sunahara and others, many of the men forced into POW camps were in fact those who protested the separation of their families.[25]

The demonization of Japanese-Canadian men and their spatial separation from women were critical to the government's legitimization of the Internment and promoted its notion that Japanese men were essentially "different" from white men and inherently dangerous. Language was used to further social distinctions, not only between white Canadian citizens and Japanese Canadians, but also among those removed from the coast. As Ann Sunahara has demonstrated, the government was careful to describe those born in Canada as "not interned," even those who were in POW camps, since only non-citizens could be legally interned according to the Geneva Convention.[26] Yet government officials used the term "internees" to describe men incarcerated in POW camps. The space of the POW camp was then used to construct those forcibly moved to other sites as "evacuees."

Through Order-in-Council P.C. 1271, fifteen hundred male nationals were moved to road-camp sites—two-thirds were married and had an average of two or three children. In addition, Canadian-born, unmarried, able-bodied men were sent to road camps in Ontario and British Columbia. In total, 2,150 men were sent to road camps in British Columbia and Ontario; numbers of men who lived in the interior-B.C. prison camps were forced to work full-time outside the camps and were sometimes allowed to return on the weekends.[27] Over three thousand men were removed from their families in 1942. Over seven thousand women, fifteen years of age and older, were moved to various incarceration sites. Over eight thousand children under the age of fifteen (approximately thirty-five hundred girls and forty-six hundred boys) had to be cared for in these carceral sites.[28]

Spatialized segregations produced notions of racialized men as non-citizens while disguising the Canadian citizenship status of those who were incarcerated. A tension between the denotation of "Japanese" and "Japanese Canadian" exists in the discursive production of the displaced subject. The spaces of incarceration were used to produce these relational categories through multiple segregations. When bodies were moved to particular spaces, they took on particular meanings. These shifting signifiers, all constructed relationally to notions of white bourgeois citizenship, justified the deportation of the "Japanese" and the forced relocations of "Japanese Canadians." Allowed to stay in Canada, displaced Japanese Canadians could then provide labour for white citizens who, in turn, were entitled to discipline and monitor them.

Hastings Park Prison

The first site of incarceration for eight thousand people,[29] particularly those who did not live in Vancouver at the time of the expulsion, was Hastings Park Manning Pool in Vancouver. Sunahara describes it as "a holding pen for human beings . . . converted from animal to human shelter in only seven days . . . the ever-present stink of animals and the maggots and the dirt . . . encrusted the buildings in Hastings Park."[30] Her description contrasts sharply with a government report describing Hastings Park as "[a]t all times . . . kept scrupulously clean." The report also states: "Many valuable lessons in food values were learned by the Japanese during their stay in Hastings Park and while they were there every effort was made to educate them to the correct standard of proper diet. Sanitary and laundry conveniences and all the more simple accoutrements of *modern civilization* were installed."[31]

The construction of Japanese Canadians as uncivilized hinged upon the Orientalist notions of their Otherness, and this difference had to be repeated to justify the violent actions committed against them. Meyda Yeğenoğlu has delineated how temporality is used to legitimate the violence of colonialism by rendering the colonial project as one which seeks to modernize and raise to the "advanced" moment of the colonist the "backward" and "primitive" Other.[32] I would extend her analysis to include spatial as well as temporal processes through which dominant subjects legitimize their use of power.

During the Internment, separation from family and destruction of community were continually legitimized by the state and citizenry in the goal of assimilation (read civilization). Confining Japanese Canadians to pathologized and dehumanized spaces enhanced the illusion of respectability of white citizens outside these spaces and of those who inhabited them not by force but by choice. In seeking to obscure the violence of incarceration and displacement, the white bourgeois subject secured for itself the notion of being "civilized," and the continual repetition of the assimilation discourse was essential to erasing the violence inherent in incarceration and forced displacement. To paraphrase Yeğenoğlu, "the dissimulation of the violence" was promoted under the guise of "dissemination of the benefits of modernity to uncivilized cultures."[33]

Kazuko was seventeen when she was moved to Hastings Park from her home in Haney. Her comments shed light upon what was deemed as "modern civilization" by the government. They also reveal what "valuable lessons in food values" were imparted:

> The first place where we went was Hastings Park, with lots of other people. You know, you just sleep on the floor and . . . the sugar was rationed, so even when you got porridge, the sugar was not even a teaspoon full. And milk didn't even cover the porridge. Porridge was like a paste. You know because it was so many people to cook for. And then also we had to help with the dishes afterwards, which is natural. But the meals were, oh gosh, I'm telling you, were like, you wouldn't even feed it to a dog. It was just terrible. So we were very happy to get out of there.

Haru, who was forced to move from her home in Vancouver at the age of nineteen, described her memories of Hastings Park in this way:

> The men were taken first to Hastings Park. My father and my mother, then even in Hastings Park we couldn't stay together. The men were all in one building and the women and children were in another building. That was an experience. And then once you're there, it's like a prison. There was a gate, you couldn't go out. You had to get a special permit to go into Vancouver if you wanted to go and do some business . . . you slept in a horse building or manufacturer's building where they had bunks. And they gave you blankets that you could put a rope on to make a partition. And it was very hard because there were hundreds of people there and you didn't know who they were. They came from all over Vancouver and Vancouver Island. They were total strangers. Regardless of how hot, how rainy, we had to go to another building to stand in line for hours to get our food, for breakfast, lunch and supper. And we all got a tin plate. I can remember that it was so hot one day. By the time you got there, you just thought you were going to pass out, just to get your supper.

Haru describes the horror of Hastings Park and how the men, including her father, were "taken" and separated from the women. Married men were prohibited from entering the building that housed their wives and young children.[34] While white men were entitled to family, Japanese-Canadian men were not, a distinction that helped to convey their lack of status as men. Put another way, men denied access to their families were emasculated, unable to exercise that most basic of patriarchal functions as head of the family.

On September 30, 1942, the Hastings Park prison site was closed.[35] The eight thousand men, women, and children incarcerated there were dispersed to other carceral sites.

Interior-B.C. Prison Camps

Over twelve thousand Japanese Canadians were moved to the internment camps in the interior of British Columbia located in Greenwood, Slocan City, Bay Farm, Lemon Creek, Popoff, Rosebery, Tashme, New Denver, Kaslo, and Sandon. Most of those sent to these camps were women and their children, along with elderly and physically ill men, and men who were unable to undertake the physical labour required in the work camps.

Although some of the Internment literature alludes to the patriarchal practices of "Japanese," Japanese-Canadian, or Japanese-American men, there has been little analysis of how male domination and gender-specific roles were promulgated through practices enacted by the white politicians, public servants, administrators, and other participants in this violence. With males over the age of thirteen separated from women and children in Hastings Park, it was assumed by government officials that women would care for all of the children. The gendered presumption that women must care for children was used by white politicians and administrators, and were actualized through the removal of men from the sites where these activities took place.

A gendering discourse also produced the female subject in the internment camps where many women were separated from their male partners, unmarried adult sons, and brothers. Women in these sites, therefore, became primarily responsible for the care of children, elderly men and women, and women and men with disabilities. While the government may have at times rendered women invisible, as in the case of a 1942 government report where women and children were listed as one category of the "Canadian-born,"[36] gender was always a critical discourse during the Internment.

It is also important to underline that a category of physical ability was iterated through the Internment—some of the men and women sent to the interior prison camps were defined as "not able-bodied." Gendered divisions of work and social space, enforced through spatial separations, marked bodies with hegemonic notions of ability and created a hierarchy of able-bodiedness within the sites.[37] Separating men who could not labour in the work camps for reasons of disability was a way to mark them as "dependents" and emasculate them within this hierarchy. Further to this gendering discourse of dependency, which was regulated through spatial separations, women who did not work at paid labour in the interior internment camps, yet who were responsible for the care of the elderly, people with disabilities, and children, were also described by administrators as "dependent" upon the government.[38]

Just as the removal of men constructed Japanese Canadians in relation to a white hegemonic able-bodied masculinity, so too the removal of Japanese-Canadian women produced a white hegemonic femininity. The separation of women from their partners, lovers, children, parents, siblings, extended family, friends, and neighbours privileged white spaces where particular arrangements of family and community were ensured of their continuity. While the removal of many men from families with children ensured that women assumed the childcaring function prescribed in hegemonic male-dominated family structures, the subject position of Japanese-Canadian women was not unitarily similar to that of white women. White women's "respectability" was discursively produced in relation to the women and men living in degenerate spaces. They clearly benefited materially from the exclusions that the violence of the Internment produced, for example, in their use of the labour of Japanese-Canadian women as domestic workers and farm workers.[39]

"Self-Support" Carceral Sites

The government understood that some Japanese Canadians were in a financial position to lease sites for their own use. These "self-support" carceral sites were established in Lillooet, Bridge River, Minto City, McGillivray Falls, Grand Falls, and Christina Lake and were accessible to Japanese Canadians who had the funds to lease them. Twelve hundred Japanese Canadians leased and moved to these sites, and during their incarceration, they were not eligible to receive any government financial support. The description of people in internment camps as "not self-supporting" was dependent upon the construction of the notion of "self-support." Class distinctions, however, obscure the racializing and gendering processes of these sites. While the government maintained that families were kept together in the "self-support" sites, some men were removed. People also worked at paid labour, including women and girls who were hired to do domestic work.[40] Just like those imprisoned elsewhere, the people in the "self-support" sites paid for their own incarceration, depleting their savings and any proceeds from the confiscation and sale of their property in order to do so. Despite the hierarchical arrangements of class in the delineation of the carceral sites, people in all of them were policed and their movements restricted. Extended family members and friends were separated through these arrangements. One woman I interviewed described how she and her parents were moved to Lillooet but her grandparents were moved to a internment camp.

Sugar-Beet Sites, Domestic Work, and Exile

Driven by a policy of administering the incarcerations through minimal cost, the government's construction of carceral sites hinged upon using the labour of Japanese Canadians.[41] In this way, labour shortages caused by the absence of men fighting in the war could be alleviated and Japanese Canadians could further contribute towards funding their own incarcerations through the purchase of necessities for their families or sending money to relatives.[42]

The displacement of men, women, and children to sugar-beet farms in Alberta, Manitoba, and southwestern Ontario intensified hierarchical divisions. The very name given to these sites by the government—sugar-beet projects—masked their function as carceral sites.[43] Thirty-six hundred Japanese Canadians were moved to Alberta and Manitoba, many of whom lived in poorly insulated shacks through prairie winters. Harvesting and processing beets required strenuous labour, so farmers running the farms preferred Japanese-Canadian families with adult male members. Ontario farmers requested single males only for sugar-beet work, and, in 1942, four hundred men were moved to these farms. Women and children also laboured on the farms in Alberta and Manitoba. Nevertheless, a masculinized discourse maintained men as heads of households in relation to the "non-self-supporting" men in the prison camps. Racialized masculinities were always being shaped through the dominant discourses of white masculinity, in this case through contact with farmer employers and employees of the government.

Women and girls were employed as domestic workers by camp administrators and townspeople in various carceral sites. Whereas single men were sent to work sites in British Columbia and Ontario, single women were moved from their families to undertake domestic work outside of British Columbia.[44] One hundred women were sent to Ontario in 1942 to work in private homes and institutions. That fall, women were moved to Winnipeg and placed by the Young Women's Christian Association in domestic service positions for employers who were "influential Winnipegers." In 1945, a "repatriation survey" was conducted by the federal government.[45] The survey required Japanese Canadians to commit to moving "east of the Rockies" or to Japan. Single women who agreed to move east had few options but to separate from their families to take domestic service positions in private homes. Although some men and boys were also employed as domestic workers, domestic servitude was clearly a feminized process.

The women I interviewed were moved from site to site, sometimes from internment camp to internment camp, and were separated from different family members and friends in this continual displacement. All of this occurred after the initial traumatic removal from their homes. Although historians of the Internment have struggled to name the processes of forced movement after the initial coastal expulsion, the term "second uprooting"[46] used to describe what is sometimes referred to as the "dispersal" from the interior internment camps does not quite capture the multiple displacements that occurred after 1941. Each departure, including the one from "home," to unknown spaces of confinement and restriction, from familiar geography to changing landscapes and climates, was a leaving of cherished people and all the people who had surrounded them, a weeding through again of ever-diminishing possessions, and was replete with the accumulation of loss.

The most geographically distant site of expulsion was Japan: many Canadian citizens of Japanese origin visiting Japan in 1941 were not allowed to return to Canada for the duration of the war. Despite a protest launched against the deportation of Japanese Canadians after the coerced signings of the "repatriation survey," close to four thousand were expatriated to Japan. As Sunahara has demonstrated, most of those who went to Japan felt they had no other choice.[47] Those who had partners or children in Japan had to leave Canada to reunite with them. Dispossessed and impoverished, people knew they would face economic hardship in Canada and Japan; they also knew they would have to continue to contend with racism if they remained in Canada. As one man answered when asked why he was going to Japan, "The white people hate us and we have no other place to go."[48]

☐ Counter-Cartographies of Nation: Remembering the Subject(s)

The spatial fragmentation and separation of carceral sites masks the violence of the Internment; by placing people in isolated geographical areas, distance was created between those incarcerated and the politicians who gave the orders. Making the violence less visible protected the legislators from witnessing the actions they had legislated.[49] The use of euphemistic language distanced the government and its administrators from the effects of their actions and left a semantic legacy with which we continue to struggle.

Legislators, administrators, and a participating citizenry used words such as *interior housing centres, self-support communities, road camps, sugar-beet projects, domestic-service placements* to describe the different spaces to which Japanese Canadians were forced to move after their expulsions from the British Columbia coastal areas. These terms conjure up images of hierarchical work and living arrangements but not the notion of incarceration. To see the spaces as carceral might necessitate *seeing* the people who were incarcerated. Similarly, the social processes of expulsion, incarceration, forced displacement, and deportation were euphemistically named *evacuation, relocation, resettlement,* and *repatriation.* These descriptors connote a sense of voluntary movement on the part of Japanese Canadians or benevolence on the part of the government and mask the violence and the force producing these processes and the force produced through them. Although I am unable in this chapter to trace the ways in which politicians, administrators, and citizens produced the forgetting of the violence simultaneous to the production of the violence, I would suggest that this discursive and material production of forgetting affects Japanese Canadians' abilities to remember and name the violence they experienced.

This euphemistic language delimits Japanese-Canadian women's capacities to name their own experiences of violence. The ability to remember the violence is also affected by the material: how could one person acquire and retain the multiple complexities of the innumerable spaces of loss and separation? Forgetting on the part of Japanese Canadians is evidence of the violence—as remembering the Internment invokes an engagement with trauma, the effect of violence. Yet despite the historically produced forgetting by those who perpetrated the violence, what is remembered in the testimonies are the multiple and geographically diverse spaces that served to separate women, men, and children. What is remembered is the violence of separation and loss.

The testimonies of five women—Aya, S., May, Ann, and Kazuko—guide us through some of the complex spatial arrangements of the Internment. These women were incarcerated in the Greenwood, Tashme, New Denver, Slocan City, and Rosebery camps. They were interviewed in the cities where they now live between the years 1992 and 1996.

While focusing on these testimonies may risk reproducing the image of the "camps" as emblematic of the Internment, I hope to illustrate how people incarcerated in the prison camps remember their own incarcerations as constructed in relation to their spatialized separations of family and community. Juxtaposed with the government's description of these sites of confinement are women's descriptions of what these relational sites produced in their own lives. The geographical and social specificities of each site and the women's connections to other sites shape how they remember their own experiences of incarceration. Yet despite the limitations of remembering through trauma and semantic and spatial confusion, the violence of loss is unmistakeable, mnemonically traceable, corporeally inscribed.

Greenwood—Aya

In a government report, Greenwood was described as a "once prosperous mining town," "nine miles north of the international boundary in central British Columbia."[50] In 1942, 1,777 Japanese Canadians were forced to move there. The "white population" in the area numbered one hundred and fifty at that time. Aya was twenty-three when she was forced to leave her home in Steveston; she and her four children were moved four times between 1942 and 1946. Aya was born in Steveston, a predominantly Japanese- Canadian community, and had lived there all of her life until the expulsion. Up to that time, all of her friends were Japanese Canadian. She was pregnant when she and her children were forced to move to Greenwood:

I had my two eldest daughters and my son was still a baby when we had to evacuate from Steveston. . . . But the men couldn't go because they all, you know, went to road camps. And so I left my husband who went to Hastings Park and then with my kids and with the neighbours we all went to Greenwood . . . I hadn't heard from my husband for quite a long time, over two months after I went to Greenwood. And I was wondering what happened to him. . . . And then I finally got a letter from him, from the internment camp. Angler. I wasn't too sure why he was sent there. And after the war, when we got together, he told me. . . . So we were separated four years. So we both had a hard time.

The censorship of the mail prevented Aya from knowing that her husband had been arrested while trying to return to her. She did not find this out until reuniting with him four years later. He had wanted to be with her when she gave birth to their fourth child, but was arrested en route to Greenwood and sent to Angler, the POW camp in northern Ontario. Aya's memory of Greenwood's geography is haunted by the memory of her missing husband. Her narrative of displacement inevitably includes her spatializing of absences as well as the gendered embodiments of her own birth-giving, childcaring, and living with the constant fear of the unknown.

The Greenwood internment camp was unique in that there was a substantial population of people who had been moved from one community—Steveston—to this prison site. Some of Aya's neighbours and friends were also imprisoned here. Yet, after two years, Aya was forced to leave them and move again. She explains the reason she was given for this move: "And then after two years the Security Commission, they called it. . . . Well they informed us that they wouldn't have internees' families—they called us internees' families because our husbands were interned—in Greenwood. So they sent us to Tashme. And I was there until the war ended."

Even within the internment camps, notions of "difference" were imposed, creating different categories of inmates. At Tashme, hierarchical arrangements included a feminized space associated with the wives of men incarcerated in the POW camps, thus marking their association with government-instituted gradations of "foreign."

Tashme—S. and May

A government report emphasizes how Tashme was named by using the "first two letters of the surnames of each of the three commissioners of the

British Columbia Security Commission," the governmental body responsible for administering the processes of explusion and incarceration.[51] The report describes the prison camp as "situated on a ranch . . . leased for the duration of the war," "14 miles south-east of the village of Hope . . . situated on the scenic Cariboo highway, a beautiful three-hours drive from the city of Vancouver." The road from Hope to Tashme was but a "rough, narrow mountain trail," and became a work site for Japanese-Canadian men who were forced to upgrade in preparation for its becoming "part of the Hope-Princeton Highway."

Despite the government's travelogue description, Tashme was a carceral site. The report was ominously clear in its purpose: "the valley in which Tashme nestles is about one mile wide and about 15-miles long, surrounded by precipitous mountain slopes closing in at each end into very narrow and easily guarded entrances. A better place could hardly have been found to house a large number of Japanese evacuees." The efforts of the Royal Canadian Mounted Police (RCMP) in maintaining the "security" of Tashme and other prison camps noted that "[t]he settlements are situated in mountainous valleys from which the only outlets are by a few roads. On these roads the Royal Canadian Mounted Police established road blocks at which special guards check all passersby."[52]

In 1942, 2,636 Japanese Canadians were forced to move to the Tashme prison camp. The fact that the government report does not even list white residents in the area is an indication that there were few people living in the Tashme environs: Tashme and its buildings were constructed solely for the purpose of incarcerating Japanese Canadians. As at all the incarceration sites, white workers were required to police and administer the camp.

S. was approximately twelve years old when she was moved to Tashme; she refers to it as one of the places that "wasn't a ghost town." After four years there, she was moved to New Denver, and, in 1948, three years after the end of the war with Japan, she was moved to Toronto. S. remembers that some of her white friends from Vancouver visited her family while they were in Tashme. Upon their second visit, they were stopped at the entrance by the RCMP and forbidden entry. She explains, "anybody coming in or going out would have to stop there at the Mounties' office." She also indicates how white officials monitored and delineated the boundary between Tashme and the "outside world" and that this authoritative whiteness was a dominant presence in the prison site: "You couldn't come into Tashme unless you went past the Mounties' office. So you would see them all the time." S. describes this failed visit by her friends as a "reminder that we were, what do you call it, not in prison, but there was a control factor there."

S.'s struggle to name the spatial confinement of Tashme reflects the semantic legacy of the Internment. It was "not a prison" in the sense of what she knew and it is this spatial differentiation that the government used to define it as "not internment." What is also clear in S.'s description of Tashme is how the memories of the Internment are constructed relationally by comparing one's own situation to that of others who experienced violence. S. added how she was not in a "ghost town" as were other Japanese Canadians who were sent to abandoned mining towns. What is apparent here are the limits to language when describing spaces whose meanings were discursively blurred and whose existence has been, for the most part, officially erased in the collective national memory. S., however, also demonstrates the care that is taken in making semantic differentiations, acknowledging the specificity of the sites of exclusions.

Such complicated struggles to contextually name experiences as "not" conforming to a common-sense notion of a particular space or experience (for example, "prison") are sometimes problematically interpreted by researchers as acceptance of incarceration. Memory and forgetting are interwoven in these testimonies, yet these memory texts are contingently produced in relation to the memories and forgettings of dominant subjects. What gets remembered and forgotten is therefore embedded within relations of power, forged across time and space. While an inordinate amount of attention has been paid to "silent" Japanese Canadians who were incarcerated, little has been given to the "silence" of the white beneficiaries of the violence. How did the white "visitors"—friends, clergy, teachers, police officers, businesspeople, politicians, administrators, farmers, employers—and those who lived in their environs remember them, and why are their silences rarely noted in the Internment literature?

S. was moved to New Denver in 1946 because her family had signed to move east in response to the "repatriation survey." She describes how they had to leave Tashme "because people [who] came from the other ghost towns . . . who were going to go back to Japan were gathered together in Tashme." May, who had been moved to Slocan when she was fourteen, described how her mother and sister had to leave Tashme for New Denver after they had signed to go east. Although May was moved to Toronto to undertake domestic work in 1944, she recalled her family's further displacement and the process of reconfiguring the spaces of incarceration as "pool[ing] them together . . . the one kind of people in one place and one kind of people in another place." Hence bodies took on meanings through these spatial hierarchies. Just as some of the wives of men who were incarcerated in POW camps were forced to move to Tashme, moving those who signed to go to Japan to Tashme marked the location both discursively and materially as the carceral site for those the government imagined to be most associated with the "enemy." Legitimizing the physical removal of people from the nation requires the continual imagining and materializing of people who occupy only the margins within it. Hence Tashme became, for some, the last spatial move before their physical ejection from Canada.

When S. described her move to New Denver in 1946, she noted that members of her family had already been separated—her sister and brother had been moved to Ontario and her other brother was living near Kamloops, B.C. It is important to note that the displacement of S. took place after the end of the war with Japan and the incarceration in the prison camps continued years beyond armistice. It was not until 1948 that S. was moved to Ontario to take a domestic service position where her brother worked as a "schoolboy," doing domestic service for a white family while attending school. Displacement was and continued to be a far-reaching process across time and geographical space.

Slocan City—Ann

The area known by the government as the Slocan Extension included the internment camps of Slocan City, Lemon Creek, Bay Farm, and Popoff. In 1942 there were 4,814 Japanese Canadians in the Slocan Extension sites. A government report described Slocan City as an "abandoned mining town," "situated in the West Kootenays at the foot of Slocan Lake."[53] The report also described how Slocan was used as a transfer point for the New Denver, Rosebery, and Sandon internment camps. There were three hundred and fifty white people in the Slocan and adjacent areas.

Ann lived in a tent with her two small children when she first arrived in the winter of 1942. Her husband had been moved to Tashme, and she did not see him for six months. Ann remembered living in the tent for three or four months, enduring the freezing temperatures at night. In Slocan City, the temperatures dipped as low as twenty degrees below zero in the winter. When her children contracted measles, Ann was moved to a quarantine area of Slocan. The body and its gendering through various spaces are vividly remembered through Ann's testimony: her pregnancy and living in a tent, her children's illness and being moved to a separate area of Slocan, her understanding of how difficult it was for women to raise children in such hardship and confinement.

Ann described how hierarchical divisions were created in the camps by administrators. She was eventually moved from a tent to a shack, which she did not have to share with another family. She explained how some people with four or more children lived in the pre-existing "ghost town" shacks without sharing this space with other families. Ann pointed out frequently in her interview that she felt other people suffered greater hardship. When I asked her if there were predominantly women and children in Slocan, she replied: "Yes. And the men that were there were veterans of World War One." Ann's father was a veteran and died before the incarceration. She described her mother as being "with the older group there. She had a sort of special [arrangement] . . . because she was a veteran's widow. . . . She had one room. They were lucky to have a room to themselves. And so were we to have a house to ourselves. Rather than shared kitchens. I think that's the worse thing . . . and especially if you have children."

The one room becomes loaded with the weight of privilege in Ann's remembering of the many who shared one-room spaces and her acknowledgment of the hardship of those who had children in them. The implications of Ann's mother's incarceration and all of the male veterans in Slocan, loyal soldiers and their families whose incarceration Ann remembers, are also witnessed in her words even as she attempts to minimize their traumatic effect. The privilege of the one room masks the inferiorized positioning of the veteran whose military service was rewarded with incarceration.

Ann's comments were sometimes filled with a sense of irony and conveyed her knowledge of relations of domination and how these were spatially articulated. When I asked her whether there was a store in Slocan, she responded by associating ownership of the Slocan store to a Doukhobor family who owned property in the area. She mentioned a woman from that family whom she saw again "years later in Vancouver." Ann discovered that the woman then lived in Shaughnessy Heights, on "the better part of Dunbar."[54] In this way, Ann emphasized that people profited from the incarceration of Japanese Canadians and this profit went beyond a spatial and temporal notion of the Second World War to produce future spatial and economic entitlements.

Rosebery—Kazuko

Rosebery was an incarceration site, which was part of the "New Denver Evacuation Area," sixteen miles north of New Denver City. It was inhabited by 219 adults and 137 children by June 3, 1943.[55] Kazuko was among those living at the camp.

Kazuko described growing up in Haney and living in a community where most of her friends were Japanese Canadian and "everybody was very close to each other and friendly." She was eighteen when she was removed from her home in Haney and moved to Hastings Park. She was later moved to Rosebery without her friends from Haney—"we were all scattered" is how she describes it. Her description of Rosebery is constructed in relation to the internment camp in New Denver. She reported there were few organized activities in Rosebery as compared to what she knew of the activities held in New Denver. She remembered Rosebery as being on the outskirts of New Denver and "there was nothing" there.

More than once in her interview, however, Kazuko indicates how her family was "lucky," as compared with those whose families were separated. Despite the financial difficulties her family experienced during the Internment, she realized that men who contributed to the family income were usually removed from the family in order to earn the income. She states, "actually the men had to separate from the family. But fortunately we were very lucky. Somehow we were all together, most of the time, the evacuation time." However, she is also clear that the Internment profoundly affected their lives: "But it wasn't really a life at all, all those years."

Kazuko's memory of the Internment was also constructed relationally when she was asked to describe meeting her husband after she was moved to Toronto. She immediately responded by describing where he had been incarcerated:

> He was in an internment camp and he was treated terribly. They were whipped around, all over—he said he worked for seven cents an hour. And oh, they really, they were just watching you and the minute you just light a cigarette or anything—they got a whipping. He had a terrible time. I think he had a worse time than I did.

The knowledge of her husband's experience in a POW camp influences how Kazuko remembers her experience of Rosebery, as does the knowledge that others were separated through this period. Her own pain and trauma are displaced in remembering her husband's incarceration in another site. Their displacement displaces memories; the piecing together of fragmented geographies is always incomplete; the fissures of the "missing" and geographical spaces haunted and haunting. These "past" ruptures of relationships and communities continue to leak into the present. Our memories suffer from the weight of incompletion, reminded as we are in the momentary "image" flashing "up at the instant"[56] of meeting one of the missing or someone who notes we or our loved ones are missed.

In the totality of the Internment, Kazuko situates herself relationally to others who suffered and lost differently than she. Later in my interview with her, I asked her about the "repatriation survey," which triggered the memory of her eldest brother, with whom she had lost contact when they were separated. Remembering the spatial configurations of their separation and her brother's decision to go to Japan invokes this memory of her loss:

> Oh, I forgot to tell you . . . I had a big brother, too, that was born in Japan. But he didn't come with us. He went on his own. Yes. . . . And then he went to Tashme but he got married in New Denver. And then when we had a choice of going to Japan or coming here, well, he chose to go to Japan. So ever since that we haven't got in touch with him. . . . We don't know whether he's dead or alive or. . . . We tried everything.

How to keep the threads together, how to remember everyone who was lost, how to forget/not forget one's own losses or remember that others' losses are one's losses too?

In reconstructing the spatial differences, sites of exile spread across a nation, Kazuko remembers her brother's exile from nation, from family, from her. She remembers she hasn't seen him since her family was allowed to attend his wedding in New Denver and in her urgent telling of nearly forgetting, I feel she is reminding me that I must remember him. Efforts to find him across the geographical borders dividing "enemy" nation from Canadian nation, across the boundaries that imprisoned and simultaneously excluded Japanese Canadians within a nation through legislative restrictions, censorship of mail, continued displacement, and economic hardship proved futile. She describes the pain of this interminable separation: "We don't know how he is, what he's doing or if he's not living. . . . It's a terrible feeling, you know. . . . We really feel bad about that. . . . But it's too late now. We think that he is gone anyway."

The spatial configurations of the Internment, its violence and relations of power, were legitimized through Canadian law. The women's testimonies map out the long-term effects of this violence and how racial, gendered, and classed segregations and incarcerations were used to geographically and socially divide and separate families and communities. They see and articulate the interconnections between the carceral spaces through their relatedness to each site and the people known and unknown incarcerated in them. They struggle to name the interconnections among the different sites because their lives were touched by all of them in varying ways. This awareness of other sites' conditions and the partners, lovers, parents, children, friends, acquaintances, and families who inhabited them inform their memories of that experience. They are aware of the multiple elisions—who is missing and missed—in dominant narratives of the Internment.

The testimonies generated from memoryscapes forge a social space integrally linked to the physical sites of their incarcerations simultaneously remembered in relation to the sites where family and community members were incarcerated. These complicated cartographies of inclusion re-map the physical, mental, and social terrain of loss and effect, offering a remembrance of violence iterated by politicians and citizens in multiple sites. Women's reconceptualization of the violence of expulsion, forced separation, dispossession, homelessness, and loss of community reconstructs their sense of selves relationally to different physical carceral sites and the social relations producing materialized divisions.

The heterogeneity of the carceral sites produces particular memories of landscape and social relations simultaneous to the memory of sites unseen, yet always remembered. For example, Haru reported that she knew life in the "self-support" carceral sites was difficult because one of her relatives had been moved there. Another woman was thankful that her father was able to stay with her family while they worked on a sugar-beet farm because she knew that many children in the interior internment camps were separated from their fathers. It is this very awareness of the hardships inherent in each site and how people were differently located within them (according to age, class background, gender, physical ability, parenting responsibilities, religious affiliation, immigrant/citizen status, language spoken) that affects a woman's ability to name her own experience as uniquely difficult. This memory of entire communities destroyed and how one constructs oneself in relationship to remembering them, therefore, profoundly affects how women describe their own experiences of violence.

More complex readings of Japanese-Canadians' testimonies are usually replaced by an Orientalist scrutinizing of the testifier in a search for flaws of social/cultural difference. It is better to focus on *their* silences than on the unutterable, than on the loud incongruencies their/our embodiedness in different spaces signify, than on their confrontations with national spaces and citizens whose memories are devoid of the Internment and other histories of violence. The normalized erasure of communities and their histories differently affects the ability of us *all* to admit the extent of the violence and to name it. The gestures to remember the loss of others and others' losses, sometimes problematically interpreted by researchers and writers as demonstrating passivity or an attitude of *shikata ga nai*, are in fact revelatory of the extent of the violence.[57]

These articulations of the interrelatedness of the physical, mental, and social spaces of the Internment and the memory of the losses produced through displacement and spatial separation in many ways continue to contest the erasure of communities. The ability of these women to locate their losses spatially and relationally instructs us to think further about our implication in the enforced scattering of Japanese Canadians and in the "scattered hegemonies"[58] of nation-building and citizen constitution.

CHAPTER 4

Keeping the Ivory Tower White

Discourses of Racial Domination

Carol Schick

University of Saskatchewan, 2001

[DAN COGGINS]

As a marker of difference and an indicator of

respectability, space cannot be underestimated as a sign of personhood and legitimacy. This chapter examines a university space that remains dominated by those who identify as white. It examines how discourses in this university space function in ways that privilege whiteness, so that whiteness persists as what is worth knowing and as an identification worth performing. Ironically, the efforts to maintain the university space as white-dominated were instigated by the presence and acknowledgement of diverse populations in the university as well as a potential shift in power relations within the academy which was brought on by alternative political thought.

At the education faculty in the Canadian university in which this study is set, racial privilege was used to reconfirm the space as white in the midst of and, in part, because of the introduction of a compulsory cross-cultural course in a pre-service teacher-training program. I conducted semi-structured interviews with twenty-one white pre-service teachers who had attended this course. By applying a discourse analysis[1] to the interviews, I examined processes by which white identification is affirmed and supported by educated white participants who claim liberal values of equity and tolerance. My research indicates that racial identification processes, to which these participants have access, establish them as "rightful occupants" of university space. In many examples drawn from their discourses, participants perform themselves as belonging "in here," a place characterized by abstraction, objectivity, and rationality; quite unlike "out there," where others belong and which participants describe as political, embodied, and not necessarily rational. In their association with the university as a site of white domination, participants reinforce their identities, a process that further supports their performance of whiteness in other teaching arenas.

My understanding of how space produces subject identifications is drawn from the work of Sherene Razack,[2] whose analysis argues that space produces identities of both privilege and degeneracy. As a production of difference, the designation of space constructs and contains identities that are said to belong in a particular site. Social relations that converge in specific sites mark out places of privilege and elite formation against contamination by an outside Other. Since spaces produce identities, continuous surveillance is necessary to prevent the loss of privilege and respectability. My research findings illustrate that the surveillance and disciplinary practices that support the production of dominant identifications also produce intellectual identities in this site. Participants from this education faculty struggle to establish themselves as legitimate occupants of this white space in which their own claims to whiteness are insecure. In describing the multicultural course, they use the intellectual discourses of the university so that the influence *of* the Other is turned into discourse *about* the Other. These participants come to know themselves as knowledgeable, innocent, and in control; and their access to privilege is measured by how they use this compulsory multicultural course to confirm their rightful place in the university.

☐ Spatial Arrangements

In 1988, the College of Education at the University of Saskatchewan accepted the proposal of the Subcommittee on Multicultural Teacher Education, which acknowledged that newly graduated teachers could expect to meet a diverse ethnic, racial, and minority student body within the province. The proposal constituted the framework for the motion passed at Academic Affairs (University Council), which required a compulsory course in multicultural education for all pre-service teachers with a specific focus on Aboriginal culture. The proposal's rationale reflected "the changing nature of the responsibilities of teachers and teacher educators in a country in which multiculturalism and human rights have become the cornerstones of Canadian citizenship."[3]

Multicultural education, framed as an issue that was "not going to disappear," was described as "consonant with the changing balance among ethnocultural groups in this country." The rationale and philosophical ethic of the proposed course were "concerned with equality of educational opportunity and outcome," and the "creation of multiculturally literate citizens who respect and promote linguistic and cultural diversity, social equality, racial harmony, and national cohesiveness as cornerstones of Canadian society." Finally, the compulsory course would ensure that graduates would "be able to function effectively in situations requiring cross-cultural perspectives, understandings and competencies."[4] After many course proposals and incarnations of the committee, a course was finally piloted in 1993–94.

In the multicultural course under discussion, over 90 per cent of students were white. Although Saskatchewan is a province made up of widely diverse ethnocultural groups, it is Aboriginal peoples whose critical mass most sharply challenges the discourses of hegemonic whiteness at all intersections of personal and institutional contact. Though the overarching view was to produce teachers who can teach "students from majority and minority backgrounds,"[5] and despite the variety of populations at this particular Canadian university, a significant purpose of this course was to produce white teachers who would "know something about" Aboriginal culture.

Since 1988, the course has become a requirement without which pre-service education students cannot graduate. Each year, several sections of the course are taught by both Aboriginal and white teachers. What, then, is produced by this compulsory multicultural course in a setting where students already perform dominant subjectivities? How is the setting contained and strengthened as an elite white space through the development of a compulsory curriculum that requires multicultural, cross-cultural learning of all its students?

☐ **Desiring Whiteness**

The research participants were interviewed following their completion of the course. It is hardly surprising that the participants' greatest desire is to be accepted as legitimate entrants into a professional college of education and as successful teacher candidates. Many of the students are of non-Anglo European ancestry and from working-class origins; many have direct contact with older relatives for whom English is not a first language. Gaining access to norms and values formed in the privileged space of the university allows these participants to claim a "toehold on respectability."[6] The security of their white identities is dependent upon their construction of themselves as not-Other. As white ethnic minority participants, they claim entitlement by moving closer to the centre of white norms and values by means of "dominance through difference." They need the credentials the university will give them and the ideological training to "become a teacher."

I am not assessing participants' interviews for particular racist or non-racist claims, nor suggesting that they express some essential white identity. I am examining their discursive practices for the processes they use to perform their subject identities in spite of, and perhaps because of, compulsory multicultural education. This includes tactics by which participants justify their university attendance as normal and appropriate. These discursive practices are not necessarily peculiar to a particular geographic location or a particular individual, but rather they are peculiar to a community of speakers in which the discourses are easily understood. I explore some of the discursive practices participants use to access the elite space of the university: specifically, their knowledge of how domination is organized and produced in this site.

For example, participants use discursive practices to justify their own positionings as respectable, innocent, and "well-intended." Kim pointed out that "when you see someone else getting stepped on . . . your heart goes out to them because you know, hey, I've had it happen to me."[7] At other times, however, his identity as defender of the oppressed conflicts with his delight in experiencing the privileges of his educated white male status. He can hardly conceal his pleasure, for example, when describing how surprised he was, on a trip to the Philippines, to be called "Sir" by elders. Even though he suggests that others are elitist, this same position has become available to him as a university-educated white male.

Because participants' own dominant identities are not yet fixed, they require the university to uphold the racial configurations of a white teaching profession. By aligning themselves with this elite space, they secure their own legitimacy and respectability. Before I address the substantive issue of how participants produce themselves as white subjects in this elite space, it is necessary to discuss the contexts in which their claims to legitimacy are considered the norm.

☐ Threatening Ideas

Cross-cultural, multicultural initiatives—also called anti-racist or oppositional—frequently meet with resistance. Difficulty in implementing and teaching such courses suggests that they pose some kind of threat in the spaces where they are introduced. Equity initiatives appear to be inevitably disruptive, no matter how carefully worded or ideologically mild the agenda. What is being endangered by a cross-cultural course in this white-dominated university of the Canadian Prairies? What are anti-oppressive courses up against? How might multicultural, cross-cultural stories implicitly undermine claims of white entitlement? What common-sense assumptions do they disturb?

From the very beginning, the compulsory nature of the cross-cultural course was considered an affront, even though it was by no means the only mandatory course in the participants' program. Margaret Wetherell and Jonathan Potter indicate that "[t]o define something as compulsory is, in terms of the liberal discourse of freedom and human rights, to define it negatively. Compulsion is automatically rhetorically bad."[8] Many view cross-cultural matters as a private affair and therefore resent the suggestion that they require preparation in a public space before they can encounter their racialized Other in the classroom.

The compulsory nature is also at odds with a popular Canadian persona: the laissez-faire individual who has no particular ideology except to allow others to live with their differences. The participants treat the course as an objectifying, intellectual exercise akin to mathematics and language instruction. However, their negative responses in describing the effects of the course indicate that they actually have had very little success at maintaining objective distance, suggesting instead the extent to which the experience of the course was more of a moral and ethical issue for many participants. They attempt to distance themselves by saying: "I really felt alienated in that class," "I was taking it to be almost a form of forced reverse discrimination," and "Why is this being shoved in our face all the time?"[9] By describing the course in such negative terms, participants can dismiss any effects the course may have had on them.

Multicultural education also threatens Canadian stories of immigration in which Europeans produce a national narrative that establishes them as the "original inhabitants." Heroic tales of successful occupation by white settlers are narratives that legitimize European, especially Anglo, claims of entitlement. Another part of the national narrative, however, one which is more conveniently "forgotten," is the colonizing process that threatens Aboriginal people with geographic, cultural, and economic erasure. The notion of historic Anglo entitlement shapes Canada as a white space in which Aboriginal land claims need not be taken seriously; this spatial configuration—which is a *dis/placement*—establishes European immigration as instrumental in the founding of Canada. The claims of Aboriginal people are ignored in the celebratory heroism attached to immigration mythology, and the construction of dominant white-identified people is established through the production of Aboriginal peoples as Other. The control of space, on which domination depends, also requires a relationship with another whom it is necessary to designate as abject and Other. Lenore Keeshig-Tobias describes the necessity of the Other for the production of dominant Canadian identities in her poem "O Canada":

> We have always walked on the edge/of your dreams, stalked/you as you made wild your way/through this great land/generation after generation/And, O Canada, you have always been/Afraid of us, scared, because you know/you can never live without us.[10]

In Western Canada, both degeneracy and privilege are produced as effects of spatialization. White entitlement is produced and rationalized as survey lines, deeds, boundaries, purchase prices, and mortgages—signs of ownership and belonging.[11] White entitlement is also produced relationally against the Otherness of original habitants. Production of the space as white, therefore, is never complete, and the identities that depend on the legitimacy of domination are forever insecure.

What else is challenged by a compulsory course on multicultural education? The proposal from the University of Saskatchewan refers to the recommendations of "definitive Canadian and international texts which implicitly critique the historical context of discrimination and racism"[12] in Canada. Canadian institutions are subject to the Canadian Charter of Rights and Freedoms, the Constitution, and the Universal Declaration of Human Rights, in which the rights of minorities are defended. Responding to diverse populations is not simply an act of conscience or a desire to "do the right thing." Mandating a multicultural course "reflects the changing nature of the responsibilities of teachers and teacher educators."[13] In an increasingly pluralist society, elite institutions can no longer maintain race, class, and gender barriers, that is, they cannot keep out the Other. Diverse populations and legal documents that protect minority interests may motivate multicultural studies, yet diverse bodies of knowledge on university campuses threaten the knowledge and space of the elite. David Sibley describes how alternate knowledge threatens established hierarchies and power structures in academia:

> There are certain parallels between the exclusion of minorities, the "imperfect people" who disturb the homogenized and purified topographies of mainstream social space, and the exclusion of ideas which are seen to constitute a challenge to established hierarchies of knowledge and, thus, to power structures in academia. In both cases, there is a distaste for mixing expressed in the virtues of pure spaces and pure knowledge. In both cases, it is power—over geographical space or over the territory marked out by groups within an academic discipline—which is under threat.[14]

How is this threat to "power structures in academia" averted or at least contained? One way is to offer a multicultural course. This course may forestall demands the Other might make on white space, contain challenges of racism and discrimination brought against the white spaces, and limit accusations that the academic space is exclusionary. Being supportive of diverse bodies of knowledge is consistent with inquiry and open-mindedness, the cornerstones of white liberalism. Ironically, while the multicultural course may be threatening, it strengthens the space as liberal and as one in which whites welcome the Other. The multicultural course threatens participants because it presents symbolic reminders of the Others' demands. Participants' whiteness and "toehold on respectability" are always insecure and they rely on their exclusive access to elite spaces to produce themselves as dominant. They also rely on the university space as a site for the reaffirmation of their bourgeois, racialized identity as the not-Other.

Space as a major metaphor in participant discourses is indicated by the often-repeated expressions "fit in" and "out there." The desire to fit in is protected against the unconstrained, illogical space where unpredictable, potentially harmful, outdated, and contrary knowledge resides. Participants are very much aware that "that kind of knowledge is *out there*"; even the "real" world of teaching is contaminated space. Participants take great care to keep their knowledge and identities safe so that they themselves are not "outed." They want to "fit into" an elitist knowledge centre with its access to a "regime of truth," which is characterized by middle-class status, whiteness, ability, normative sexuality, post-secondary education, up-to-date training, possession of cross-cultural knowledge (politically correct attitudes), assumptions of moral superiority, idealism, and innocence.

In the next section, I show how participants' discourses indicate that educational institutions work to their advantage in the formation of their entitlement. In these central places of education and learning, participants attempt to distinguish themselves from "other" ways of life found "out there." What is already in place to make these discourses understandable? To which discourses do white pre-service teachers already have access in the construction of white privilege?

☐ Securing White Entitlement

Rationality Rules

There are two techniques that participants use to secure white entitlement. The first is the identification with ideological space of rationality and objectivity. As a source of white bourgeois legitimacy, the university, like no other place, represents the establishment and practice of that most distinguishing trait of white male legitimacy: rationality.[15]

Participants use a variety of rhetorical strategies to claim this ideological space, including reporting the reactions of classmates, objectifying self- and others' reactions, making disclaimers, claiming credentials as a feminist sympathizer, offering evidence of supportive actions, and offering extensive qualification of negative remarks.[16] These strategies produce participants as utterly reasonable people, ones who understand the necessity of civility, rationality, and self-control. Participants have an interest in claiming these identities because logic and reasoning are not only highly prized in the teaching profession, they are also markers of civility and the right to govern. Their claims create a distinction between "us" and "them" around the ownership and distribution of emotions and intellect. In possession of intellectual control, participants offer their own rationality and moderation as the basis for dismissing other remarks with which they disagree; their demonstration of what is considered rational and reasonable maintains their identities as non-prejudiced supporters of tolerance.

Participants express negative remarks about the course in a variety of ways—not as biased opinions, but as statements of reasoned fact. For example, the course content is questionable because it implicates white participants in a racist history. This revised history undermines the participants' positions as neutral players; it calls into question issues of knowledge—who holds it? how is it constituted? what knowledge can be considered legitimate? Their conclusions lead them to believe that the "facts" of the course, which do not necessarily present a flattering image of racially dominant people, are merely a point of view or a particular slant; they are unfounded notions that need not be taken seriously. Participants also report that issues were forced on them, either by means of materials or by the professor's methods. Some hold that it was mildly coercive and others that it was outright manipulative: "I didn't like what the class was doing to me because it was changing how I felt and it wasn't changing it in a really positive manner." "This class was very much directed at trying to get you to believe, focus on cultural ideas and make you think those ideas."[17]

The expression "make you think those ideas" may be intellectually impossible, but does suggest that some kind of coercion is at work. Participants defend themselves against the implications of the course by describing it as something forced on them, further evidence of its emotional, irrational, and unreasonable premises. Both presentation and course material are suspect: "The Native focus was a little too Native."[18] The phrase "too Native" implies abandonment of all that is rational and civil while retaining the potential to *go Native*, a prospect that must be guarded against.

Even though the course is seen as unfairly emotional and irrational, the participants see their hostile reactions as completely justified and reasonable because they have been provoked. As Chris points out: "I really thought that [the course] was a travesty in many ways because I thought there was some really . . . uncalled for situations that we were placed into."[19] Justification of their emotional responses signals participants' assertion of dominance. Even though their emotional response is a deviation from reasonableness, the contradiction goes unacknowledged. Instead, their manipulation of "rationality" indicates their insider knowledge about conditions under which deviations may occur. By rejecting the course, participants declare authority or superiority over it; similarly, their performance of a credible, dominant identification includes the authority to pronounce that their own extreme actions are reasonable. Citing that other classmates were similarly affected is further evidence of credibility.

These discourses rely on the university as the home of official white rationality and knowledge—the markers by which a taxonomy of difference may be established and where "different from" means "unequal to." Here is the mythological, safe, and pure place of abstraction and objectivity; the world of knowledge and theory; a place for the "disembodied" mind. There is no awareness of the university as a site where power relations exist. The assumption is that knowledge and intellectual teachings are objective and neutral and need not be challenged. Chris expresses her dissatisfaction when issues in the classroom became political and were no longer objective:

> I know there's problems that go beyond the university class. Like there's *problems with politics and things like that and I think that those are being brought into the classroom* rather than being sort of left at the door, and we were all people, looking for a better, some sort of a solution. *But those problems weren't left at the door, they were brought in.*[20]

The real-world politics of gender, culture, and classroom management are strongly resisted. When this intrusion happens—when an issue becomes too personal for comfort—participants use their indignation to re-establish their dominant identities and central positions. The space must be maintained; the identities—those who are in control and those who are not—cannot be confused. If participants' reactions are described as unreasonable, their authority and their ability to discern what is reasonable are undermined.

Taking Place

The second technique participants use to secure white entitlement is to identify themselves with the physical space and with the normative designation of who is likely to be found there. It is hardly surprising that participants desire identification with the university. The attendance of people who do not fit any of those categories does not belie the claim that the university is a white, elite, male-dominated place. Indeed, the point of interest is how these hegemonic European values are maintained in spite of the presence of others who are neither male nor European. Criticism of university elitism is typically managed by suggesting that such arguments are one sign of the university's legacy of liberalism and rationalism as evidenced in its capacity for tolerance and open debate. Pat describes one of the attractions of the university in comparison to his workplace:

If I took this class and I went back to [my trucking job], I wouldn't be able to go in and say, "You know, you can't really call the, you know, the Hispanic janitor, you know, a spic. You can't do that. That's bad." That part wouldn't go over very well in the coffee room full of, you know, huge stereotypical truck drivers. *At university you can discuss these things and talk about them.* . . . [21]

Participants are very interested in associating themselves with the university; they look to it for the legitimating function it offers to those who do not necessarily come from the ranks of the social elite. In exchange, the speed with which participants are able to comply with the normative values and requirements determines how well they are prepared to "fit in" with university life and performance. For Pat, university is a place of privilege where learning takes place with intellectual types who are his equals: "You get spoiled at university, I find, because you're with a certain type of people all the time." The university is a rational place where differences on issues of race and gender can be discussed as intellectual topics. The social, economic, and intellectual gulf between the truckers' coffee room and the university is well marked; it is unreasonable to expect that the coffee room can accommodate what participants consider the same high standards of behaviour found in the pure space of the university. Pat, however, considers himself a liberal thinker and agrees that the ideas in the cross-cultural course should be taught to all university students, no matter what their course of study:

Actually I'm saying that every course should be happening across the disciplines but this course in particular because we're talking about it; because when you step *out in the street in Canada* you can't get away from issues of culture or gender. They're all around you so to not integrate them I think is an *injustice to the very ideas.*[22]

Pat has indicated that he is a moderate in all things, therefore he is willing to discuss "culture and gender," which he assumes are part of what he will meet "out in the street in Canada." He identifies this street venue as separate from where he now resides. This meeting on the street will not be voluntary, but forced; and in a place that lacks order and control such as the street, one will have to expect such irrationalities as "culture and gender." In the pure white space of the university, these issues can be discussed as intellectual topics so as not to do "injustice to the very ideas." In his position as a privileged insider, he can assume that these are disembodied "ideas" that do not touch him personally and are separate from the life he now lives.

This participant offers himself as innocent and naive; he is shocked to learn that his levels of self-determination and rationality are not experienced by all people. Although he is perhaps even more naive in his ignorance than he would care to claim, he is proud of his arrival at liberal thought and the level of control and autonomy he describes. He finds himself in a dilemma; he says that his liberal, autonomous outlook—characterized by such qualities as "saying whatever I like"; "having common sense, being rational"; "being a strong, independent thinker"; "being in charge of one's own destiny"—is not unique but neither is it a widely held belief. Furthermore, he assumes these qualities are his personal possession, his property, and warrant him taking up his position of privilege. These are the possessions that mark his dominance and of which he is proud. His expression of surprise that these qualities are not widely circulated or in general use does not completely cover his pride that his possession of them affords him a unique and powerful status.

The dilemma he faces is in trying to appear both humble about his access to elite space and, at the same time, maintaining that his privileges are available to everyone. He resolves his dilemma by claiming innocence and naïveté as well as by referring to his associations with other people from other cultures to refute any notion that his own access is culturally enhanced. Aída Hurtado suggests that "most [whites] can detect when whiteness is being questioned and its potential privilege dismantled."[23] The response is to de-emphasize its function as a group while at the same time universalizing its privilege by saying, like Pat, that "anybody" can achieve merit,[24] pretending that the value attached to being white does not exist. The contradictions in participants' discourses are most interesting for the use participants make of them and the tension participants produce by holding these conflicts.

Pat struggles continually, through many rhetorical devices, to keep himself in a good light, which is defined by objectivity, rationality, the life of the mind, and an uninvolved stance separate from gender and culture. He is the "anti-imperialist" "seeing-man"[25] who claims to be supportive of the cross-cultural course because it fits his liberal philosophy. He has figured out the "correct way" to think about Otherness; he knows what an anti-racist stance should sound like. Maintaining this particular identity as a sympathetic white male enhances his credibility in and entitlement to this dis/embodied white space. The university site recuperates whiteness and accomplishes the very successful performance of this participant identity in a way that cannot easily be questioned.

☐ Beings in Outer Spaces

Yet there are those in the university whose identities—such as the representative Aboriginal professor—who are perceived as being "out of place." Her embodied presence poses a dilemma for many of the participants; some of their greatest hostility is reserved for her. For, if she can be a legitimate authority in this site, and if participants' own legitimacy is dependent on their whiteness, the presence of the Aboriginal female professor undermines their entitlement. The Aboriginal professor triggers conflicting desires such as authority/subordination in the professor–student relationship. Some participants find it confusing and some reassuring that even though at a distance they reject the professor's authority, they find her agreeable one-on-one. Chris displays a distinct lack of control, however, in that she both desires the professor for her difference and is repelled by her attraction:

> Before the class . . . *I had respect for the Native culture* and I understood the issues. . . . But *after the class I felt resentful in some way*. It wasn't . . . a growing experience. To me, it was a diminishing experience because I felt I became more narrow-minded. And since I've taken that class I've tried to put the class out of my mind because it wasn't a good experience. *And I think a lot of it had to do with the professor.*[26]

Chris rejects and anticipates the presence of the Aboriginal body as it is positioned to provide her with an experience of Western culture that is not otherwise available to her. For Bev, however, the smooth objectification of cultural knowledge is continually interrupted by personal relations:

> The professor at the university was not liked by our class as a whole. *We didn't like her because we felt she didn't like us*. . . . It wasn't enjoyable to go to class because of the instructor. We challenged what she had to say. *We didn't accept everything she said word for word. We spoke our minds* and I don't think she liked that much. . . .[27]

Participants consider their rejection of the professor as reasonable because it is in response to the professor's unreasonableness. That participants don't accept "everything she said word for word" indicates that they are discerning and rational, not slavish believers of what anybody tells them.

Jan, who reacts to contested spaces, has portrayed herself as credible and sympathetic by means of her personal interest in cross-cultural issues as well as her voluntary enrolment in a number of Native Studies courses. She frequently refers to her "place" in her interview, speaking of "out there" and "coming back," wondering where she and others "fit in."

Jan is caught in a dilemma of her own making. She is a supporter of Aboriginal issues and of what she calls "differences." But now that Aboriginal people are claiming the sites of their children's education for themselves—by organizing more band-controlled schools and hiring more Aboriginal teachers—Jan suggests that differences don't really matter that much. At the same time that she doesn't want her whiteness to be held against her or to exclude her from a job, she continues to rely on her white privilege for access to jobs in an Aboriginal school—a space that has never belonged to her and that has only recently been denied to her. She is very confused about her "place" and finds that her question of where she fits in is her greatest concern:

> Even after the information, I'm seeking it out, there's people out there that are saying well *you don't fit in*. I've had profs where I've asked that question in Native Studies or otherwise and got told well we don't want your help. . . . And as far as I'm concerned *I have to try to fit in,* and I mean maybe one day I'll be the minority. You know, *I want to fit in. I don't want to have no rights like you [Natives] had no rights.* Like, if one day I'm to come to Saskatchewan and you [Native] people make up the majority of the population, which could very well be, I'd like to know that *I'm going to fit in* somewhere. *I don't want to be treated the way you've been treated,* you know.[28]

The circle of benefits leads back to white control, even when the sense of place is not clear. The question "Where do I fit in?" must be answered so that white identity, as a condition of its privilege, will be secure. There is a strong sense of place in describing the "pure" and the "impure," but she questions how white dominant people are to "take their place" "out there" in areas where white privilege may be less secure than in the white space of the university. Even at times when sense of place may be uncertain, white participants assume that they will maintain their place as identity keepers and definers in their own lives and those of Aboriginal peoples.

An assumption that presupposes the contradictions and dilemmas of these participants is that cultures and identities are "settled," separate, and real. They rely on a realist approach when it supports their entitlement to attend the clean, well-lighted space of the university, or when they wish to secure the teaching job of their choice, or when they are granted privilege in hiring practices. In contrast, when participants explain their need for further entitlement to space to which they may not have ready access—such as teaching in Aboriginal-run schools—they eschew the notion of separate and divided identities. They assume that their privilege need not be a barrier to access because, with privilege, comes the ability to change at will the significance of their embodied status. Participants assume that they can transform their identities as required by performing themselves, in chameleon-like fashion, as "not really white." When coming up against the walls of contested space, white participants imagine they can pass through the walls by leaving their bodies behind.

These participants, as do many others, position themselves at the centre of a place-knowledge-privilege repertoire of self-definition. This repertoire occurs most often in the distinctions participants make between "here," where the participants are, and "out there." "Here" typically refers to a university environment, which is mainly white, middle-class, elite, straight, privileged, and often liberal in rhetoric if not in action. "Here" is a protected, enlightened, and enlightening place in the middle of raging storms of prejudice, unrealistic claims, and misinformation. By definition of quantity, "here" may be considered a minority position; but in these circumstances, adopting a minority position marks the exclusive rather than the excluded. This exclusive access supports participants in the performance of their roles as reliable witnesses in which they claim that various life circumstances have provided them with unique and unclouded perspectives. These unique positions are contrasted with participants' illustrations of how others have failed to be rational, moderate, knowledgeable, and fair.

When this self-referential place-knowledge-privilege cycle is interrupted by experiences such as found in the cross-cultural course, the participants struggle to re-establish their central positions. It is the disruption of the cycle that makes visible the norms that support it. Pat describes how the contested site of white privilege is neither exclusive nor secure: the "in here" place of the university is not completely pure, having among its members some aberrant character types:

> The things that happened in the course, I think, are a reflection of character . . . for good or for bad. . . . When you go into the washroom and you see somebody scrawling some racial or gender slur on the wall, I'm actually a little bit surprised about that because you think, geez, I mean, in university and they didn't even spell . . . that word right. What's going on? Oh, they didn't flush the toilet either, that doesn't surprise me. But when you get outside the walls of this institution, you're exposed to it everyday. I think I'm going to see it.[29]

That the university space has been invaded and contaminated by unreliable characters is an indication that white privilege and its power to exclude and define are continuously under siege. The contamination is an exception in this place where the walls typically act as borders between space that is rational and the space "out there" where disorder cannot be contained. Pat suggests that it is not rational to be racist and sexist, that evidence of discrimination and prejudice in the university would seem to be a problem of irrationality and an individual's bad character. Because whiteness signals innocence, it is inconceivable that this contagion could be from someone who "belongs" here.

The notion of secure spaces for the production and control of identities is a myth and an impossibility. Michel Foucault's illustration of the production of sexuality offers a good analogy of the production of racial identity.[30] He claims one is mistaken to assume that identities can be controlled or limited or that contagion is from without. In the case of sexuality, it is false to assume that everything learned about sexuality within the family is normative, proper, and "safe." On the contrary, as Ann Laura Stoler points out, the family is the site where sexuality acquires social meaning, where we begin to identify as sexual beings; as the family is the site where sexuality is learned, it is not a haven from "sexualities of a dangerous outside world, *but the site of their production.*"[31]

I suggest that the same is true regarding the production of whiteness in university spaces. Like the familial context, these white places produce identities in which codes and expectations of proper white behaviour are vigorously enforced by reiterative, normative practices and designations of what is worth knowing. It is inconceivable to Pat that white privilege and racism are what one *learns* at university. He must maintain that elite white space is safe from contamination and innocent of racism because, tautologically, university space is elite and white. It is in these ideologically coded spaces that the performance of whiteness is most thoroughly embodied and reinforced as normative, especially in the midst of a course on multicultural education. Sexuality, class, ability, and ethnicity are learned through whiteness as the embodiment of what the Other is not. Here is the site where the performativity of whiteness coheres—in the "unsettled and unsettling"[32] population of the discursively absent Other.

☐ Self-Preservation

The division of identities into site-specific locations supports a "grid of intelligibility"[33] through which a white bourgeoisie comes to define itself. Participants' access to white-identified spaces does not necessarily follow from racist practices or confrontations or from particular events. Rather, access is gained through using "historical discourse as a strategic weapon of power."[34] For example, class-and-race-specific sites of education—such as universities that are instrumental in the production of white identities— are one tactic for maintaining distinct spaces in Canadian society.

The participants' responses are reactions to a cross-cultural studies course, as I have tried to make clear, do not represent individual racist actions per se. Yet as Stoler explains, there are ways in which current discursive practices are used to "work up" and "assemble" older forms of racism already in place. Following Foucault, Stoler provides this understanding of racism:

> [R]acism is more than an ad hoc response to crisis; it is a manifestation of *preserved possibilities,* the expression of an underlying discourse of permanent social war, nurtured by the biopolitical technologies of *"incessant purification."* Racism does not merely arise in moments of crisis, in sporadic cleansings. It is internal to the biopolitical state woven into the weft of the social body, threaded through its fabric.[35]

The assumption that society must at all times be protected from the biological dangers of its ever-present "sub-race" produces an "internal racism," requiring "incessant purification" as one of the fundamental dimensions of social normalization.[36] Participants desire "incessant purification" as a justification for their claim to innocence.

"Preserved possibilities," which remain available for reproduction of the social order, can be contrasted with the effects of university space on the construction of Aboriginal students' identities. Rick Hesch describes the process of social reproduction in a teacher-education program for Aboriginal students attending a Prairie university. Hesch states that in spite of the affirmative nature of the program, Aboriginal students' experiences are racialized, gendered, and classed in ways that contribute significantly to their overall problem of staying in the university and completing their programs. Describing students' decisions to leave as a "choice" is ironic considering the exclusionary nature of the institution. Hesch continues, however, that even the successful completion of the program—constrained as it is by a university environment—"both enables and limits the possibilities for the development of [A]boriginal teachers."[37] At the same time, the affirmation of white identities in this site continues apace in that any lack of success Aboriginal education students may have in the university system leaves those jobs and the ideological spaces they might have filled still available for prospective white teachers. Through these spatial arrangements and preserved possibilities, the entitlement and belonging of white students is affirmed.

The "preserved possibilities" of the white participants are their rights to reject or access anything they choose such as the knowledge of cross-cultural teachers, positions in Aboriginal-controlled schools, or proprietarial status at a university. These "preserved possibilities" were in place long before they participated in their cross-cultural course, which for some participants was a moment of crisis.

For most of the participants, their interactions with the course placed them in contradictory positions which they struggled to explain: they defend their dominant subjectivities against the implications of the cross-cultural course and the anger and uncertainty it arouses; they affirm their identities as non-prejudiced, liberal individuals. They support their liberal identities by claiming their responses are rational and unemotional, quite unlike the responses of anyone with whom they might disagree. Participants justify their own emotional responses by implying that it is only what reasonable people would do when provoked by the unreasonableness of others. Participants rely heavily on a particular understanding of rationality and emotional control to mark them as self-determining individuals. Regardless of their own conduct or that of others, it is their description of the events that performs participants as insiders and demonstrates their control of the definition of rationality which is, perhaps, the single, most highly prized claim of white bourgeois subjects.

In ideologically white spaces such as university campuses, identities are produced both inside and outside the specific site. The maintenance of domination is actively supported by white students, as the participants in my project demonstrate. Their grasp on bourgeois white identification relies on their allegiance to prestigious white space and their access to privilege and social respectability. They depend on university processes and make full use of a mandatory multicultural course to support white domination so that they may establish and produce their own legitimacy as "good" teaching bodies and "respectable" Canadian citizens.

CHAPTER 5

Gendered Racial Violence and Spatialized Justice

The Murder of Pamela George

Sherene H. Razack

*Painting of "western scene," McCall Field,
Calgary airport, 1960*

[GLENBOW ARCHIVES NA-2399-76]

To unmap literally is to denaturalise geography, hence to undermine
world views that rest upon it.

—Richard Phillips, *Mapping Men and Empire*

On Easter weekend, April 17, 1995,

Pamela George, a woman of the Saulteaux (Ojibway) nation and a mother
of two young children, was brutally murdered in Regina, Saskatchewan.
Beyond the fact that Pamela George came from the Sakimay reserve on
the outskirts of the city, and that she occasionally worked as a prostitute,

something she was doing that weekend, few details of her life or the life of her community are revealed in the court records of the trial of the two white men accused of her murder or in the media coverage of the event. More is known about her two murderers—young middle-class white men. Easter marked the first weekend since the end of their university exams. There was a week or so of freedom before summer jobs began, and nine-teen-year-old university athletes Steven Kummerfield and Alex Ternowet-sky set out to celebrate the end of term. They went out drinking in isolated areas under bridges and behind hockey arenas, and then cruised "the Stroll," the city's streets of prostitution. Eventually, after failing to per-suade one Aboriginal woman working as a prostitute to join the two of them in the car, one man hid in the trunk. Approaching her twice and being refused twice, they finally succeeded in persuading another Aborig-inal woman, Pamela George, to enter the car.

The two men drove George to an isolated area outside the city, a place littered with bullet casings and condoms. Following oral sex, they took turns brutally beating her and left her lying with her face in the mud. They then drove to a fast-food restaurant and later to a cabin on Saskatchewan Beach, which belonged to one of their grandfathers. The next morning, upon returning to town, they heard a radio report describ-ing a body found outside the city. After both first confided their involve-ment in the murder to a number of friends and to one of their parents, one man left town to take up his summer job planting trees in the northern forests of British Columbia. The other man flew to the mountain resort of Banff, Alberta, where he joined other white male university athletes celebrating the end of term. In early May, nearly one month later, after fol-lowing a tip and having exhausted the list of suspects who were mostly Aboriginal or of the "streets" of the Stroll, the Royal Canadian Mounted Police (RCMP) arrested both men for the murder of Pamela George. The arrest of two young middle-class white men for the murder of an Aborigi-nal woman working as a prostitute sent shock waves through the white population of this small prairie city. Pamela George's own family endured the pain of losing a loved one violently.

At the trial two years later, the defence at first tried to argue that Pamela George managed to walk away from the isolated field and was killed by someone else, an Aboriginal man. They also argued that since both men were highly intoxicated, they bore diminished responsibility for the beating. The boys did "pretty darn stupid things," but they did not commit murder. Both the Crown and the defence maintained that the fact that Pamela George was a prostitute was something to be considered in the case.[1] The judge sparked a public furor when he instructed the jury to bear this in mind in their deliberations. The men were convicted of manslaughter and sentenced to six-and-a-half years in prison, having already spent twenty months in prison. The objections of the Native community and some members of the white community stemmed from their belief that the crime was, at the very least, one of second-degree murder and that the judge acted improperly in directing the jury to a finding of manslaughter.[2] Alex Ternowetsky was paroled in 2000 after having served only two-thirds of his sentence. In August 2001, he faced new charges of assault, robbery, mischief, impaired driving, and refusing to take a Breathalyzer test.[3]

Why write about this trial as spatialized justice and this murder as gendered racial or colonial violence? Some readers of early versions of this essay have commented that the prison sentences for manslaughter meted out to the two accused were not highly unusual and therefore not indicative of the court's leniency. Others noted that a finding of murder would have required more evidence than was available. In agreement with this latter view, in 1998, the Saskatchewan Court of Appeal rejected an appeal by the Crown that the trial judge had failed to fairly present the Crown's position that the two men had murdered Pamela George. The Appeal Court concluded that Mr. Justice Malone had made it clear to the jury that a finding of murder, whether first or second degree, would require evidence that the accused intended to commit murder or knew that their actions would result in Pamela George's death. There is some indication, according to the Appeal Court, that the jury did indeed carefully consider whether there was enough evidence to convict on a charge of murder rather than manslaughter. Further, the Appeal Court continued, the trial judge's direction to the jury to consider that Pamela George was working as a prostitute the night of the murder did not degrade her in any way and thus cannot be considered to have led the jury to its conclusion that the men committed manslaughter and not murder.[4]

I propose to show that a number of factors contributed to masking the violence of the two accused and thus diminishing their culpability and legal responsibility for the death of Pamela George. Primarily, I claim that because Pamela George was considered to belong to a space of prostitution and Aboriginality, in which violence routinely occurs, while her killers were presumed to be far removed from this zone, the enormity of what was done to her and her family remained largely unacknowledged. My argument is, in the first instance, an argument about race, space, and the law. I deliberately write against those who would agree that this case is about an injustice but who would de-race the violence and the law's response to it, labelling it as generic patriarchal violence against women, violence that the law routinely minimizes. While it is certainly patriarchy that produces men whose sense of identity is achieved through brutalizing a woman, the men's and the court's capacity to dehumanize Pamela George came from their understanding of her as the (gendered) racial Other whose degradation confirmed their own identities as white—that is, as men entitled to the land and the full benefits of citizenship.

In the same vein, I race the argument made by some feminist scholars that women working as prostitutes are considered in law to have consented to whatever violence is visited upon them.[5] While I wholeheartedly agree, I underline how prostitution itself (through enabling men to mark the boundary between themselves and degenerate[6] Others) and the law's treatment of it as a contract sustain a colonial social order. Finally, I reject the view that the spatialized justice I describe, the values that deem certain bodies and subjects in specific spaces as undeserving of full personhood, has more to do with class than it does with race. In this view, it is her poverty and her location in the inner city that most influenced how Pamela George was treated in life and in law.[7] A white woman in a similar circumstance and place would be treated the same way, or perhaps only slightly better. Again, while I would not disagree (indeed I would argue that a white woman working as a prostitute on the Stroll would be racialized), I emphasize here that race overdetermined what brought Pamela George *and her murderers* to this brutal encounter. Equally, race overdetermined the court's verdict that the men bore diminished culpability for their actions.

The racial or colonial aspects of this encounter are more prominently brought into view by tracing two inextricably linked collective histories: the histories of the murderers, two middle-class white men, and of Pamela George, a Saulteaux woman. Significantly, history is precisely what was absent in the trial. Pamela George stood abstracted from her history and remained for the court only an Aboriginal woman working as a prostitute in a rough part of town. The two men, Alex Ternowetsky and Steven Kummerfield, were also abstracted from their histories. They were simply university athletes out on a spree one Easter weekend. As abstractions, neither side could be seen in the colonial project in which each was embedded. The history of dispossession, and its accompanying violence, that brought both Pamela George and her murderers to the Stroll; white people's historic participation in and benefit from that dispossession and violence; and the law's complicity in settler violence, particularly through an insistence on racelessness and on contract, all remained invisible. At the end of the day, the record showed only that two white "boys" lost control and an Aboriginal woman got a little more than she bargained for. That an Aboriginal woman was brutally murdered sometimes seemed lost during the trial.

The collective histories I trace are also geographies. In examining the transcripts of the case, one can hardly miss the spatiality of the violence and its relationship to identity as well as to justice. The men leave the university and their families' and girlfriends' middle-class homes in the suburbs to spend time with each other, in places that are "outside" civilized society. From drinking under bridges, beside airports, and behind hockey arenas, they proceed to the Stroll, the streets of prostitution occupied by racial Others, and ultimately to the murder scene. In the elite spaces of middle-class life (the university, suburban homes, chalets, and cottages), they learn who they are, and, more important, who they are not. Moving from respectable space to degenerate space and back again is an adventure that confirms that they are indeed white men in control who can survive a dangerous encounter with the racial Other and who have an unquestioned right to go anywhere and do anything.

These journeys of transgression are deeply historical ones. White settlers displaced Pamela George's ancestors, confining her Saulteaux nation and others to reserves. Pamela George's own geographies begin here. Colonization has continued apace. Forced to migrate in search of work and housing, urban Aboriginal peoples in cities like Regina quickly find themselves limited to places like the Stroll. Over-policed and incarcerated at one of the highest rates in the world, their encounters with white settlers have principally remained encounters in prostitution, policing, and the criminal justice system. Given the intensity of this ongoing colonization, white men such as Kummerfield and Ternowetsky had only a very small chance of seeing Pamela George as a human being. When the court itself undertook the same journey from respectable to degenerate space during the trial, as it reviewed the events surrounding the murder, her personhood again remained invisible. White complicity in producing the harsh realities of her life never surfaced, and the men's own activities were subjected to very little critical scrutiny. The "naturalness" of white innocence and of Aboriginal degeneracy remained firmly in place as the conceptual framework through which this incident of gendered racial violence could be understood.

I propose to unmap these journeys. That is to say, I want to denaturalize the spaces and bodies described in the trial in an effort to uncover the hierarchies that are protected and the violence that is hidden when we believe such spatial relations and subjects to be naturally occurring. To unmap means to historicize, a process that begins by asking about the relationship between identity and space.[8] What is being imagined or projected on to specific spaces, and I would add, on to bodies? Further, what is being enacted in those spaces and on those bodies? In the first section of this chapter, I discuss the factors that brought Pamela George to the Stroll and those that brought two white men to it. I suggest that the encounter between the white men and Pamela George was fully colonial—a making of the white, masculine self as dominant through practices of violence directed at a colonized woman. In the second section, I explore how various legal and social constructs naturalized these spatial relations of domination, highlighting in the process white respectability and entitlement and Aboriginal criminality. In the conclusion, I explore how we might contest these practices of domination through a resurrection of historical memory of colonization and its continuing effects. In essence, I suggest that we insist that in law, as in life, we inhabit histories of domination and subordination for which we are accountable.

☐ Space, Gendered Racial Violence, and the Making of White Settler Societies

Why was she prostituting herself when the Queen promised her a prosperous life on the reserve? . . . Why would she prostitute herself if the treaties had been fulfilled? . . . Many times I wonder at nights whether she screamed "Canada, Canada" like that Somalia kid that was killed by the Airborne Regiment.

—Morning Child, commenting on the death of his daughter, Calinda Waterhen[9]

Two white men who buy the services of an Aboriginal woman in prostitution, and who then beat her to death, are enacting a quite specific violence perpetrated on Aboriginal bodies throughout Canada's history, a colonial violence that has not only enabled white settlers to secure the land *but to come to know themselves as entitled to it*. In the men's encounter with Pamela George, these material (theft of the land) and symbolic (who is entitled to it) processes shaped both what brought Pamela George to the Stroll and what white men from middle-class homes thought they were doing in a downtown area of prostitution on the night of the murder. These processes also shaped what sense the court made of their activities.

In *Racist Culture*, David Goldberg writes about the spatial configurations of colonial societies, arguing persuasively that racial categories have been spatialized. Colonizers at first claim the land of the colonized as their own through a process of violent eviction, justified by notions that the land was empty or populated by peoples who had to be saved and civilized. In the colonial era, such overt racist ideologies and their accompanying spatial practices (confinement to reserves, for example) facilitate the nearly absolute geographical separation of the colonizer and the colonized. At the end of the colonial era, and particularly with urbanization in the 1950s and 1960s, the segregation of urban space replaces these earlier spatial practices: slum administration replaces colonial administration. The city belongs to the settlers and the sullying of civilized society through the presence of the racial Other in white space gives rise to a careful management of boundaries within urban space. Planning authorities require larger plots in the suburbs, thereby ensuring that larger homes and wealthier families live there. Projects and Chinatowns are created, cordoning off the racial poor. Such spatial practices, often achieved through law (nuisance laws, zoning laws, and so on), mark off the spaces of the settler and the native both conceptually and materially. The inner city is racialized space, the zone in which all that is not respectable is contained.[10] Canada's colonial geographies exhibit this same pattern of violent expulsions and the spatial containment of Aboriginal peoples to marginalized areas of the city, processes consolidated over three hundred years of colonization. Here, however, both colonial and slum administration persist. Reserves remain lands administered by the *Indian Act*, while city slums are regulated through a variety of municipal laws.

Regina, a city of almost two hundred thousand people in which Aboriginal peoples make up approximately 8 per cent of the population,[11] is estimated to have a higher urban Aboriginal population per capita than all other major Canadian cities. The Aboriginal population is also the youngest one in Canada—43 per cent of Aboriginals are fifteen years old or younger.[12] However, the presence of a significant Aboriginal population in an urban centre is a relatively recent historical development. Canada's colonizing endeavours confined the majority of Aboriginal peoples to reserves by the second half of the nineteenth century, establishing in the process the geographical configuration of Regina today as a primarily white city in the midst of the reserves of the Qu'appelle Valley. This nineteenth-century spatial containment of a subject population was never secure and often required brutal policing and settler violence. In 1885, for example, white settlers of Regina who were fearful of Native rebellions organized a Home Guard and pressed vigorously for the North West Mounted Police (NWMP) to police Natives and to hang Native leaders arrested after the Riel Rebellion.[13]

Sexual violence towards Aboriginal women was an integral part of nineteenth-century settler strategies of domination. In her research on the appearance during this time of captivity narratives (stories about the abduction of white women and children by Aboriginal peoples), Sarah Carter documents the important role that stereotypical representations of Aboriginal women played in maintaining the spatial and symbolic boundaries between settlers and Natives. Prior to 1885 there had been relative co-existence between fur traders and Aboriginal peoples, but the Métis rebellion and general Aboriginal resistance to their spatial confinement, as well as the increasing presence of white women on the Prairies, led to powerful negative images of Aboriginal women that portrayed them as licentious and bloodthirsty. These images helped to justify the increasing legal regulation of Aboriginal women's movements and their confinement to reserves. As Carter demonstrates, "the squalid and immoral 'squaw'" helped to deflect criticism away from the brutal behaviour of government officials and the NWMP, and it enabled government officials to claim that the dissolute character of Aboriginal women and the laziness of the men explained why reserve land was not used to capacity and were pockets of poverty.

After 1885, the pass system was introduced and required Aboriginal peoples to obtain a pass from a government employee before leaving the reserve. One rationale was that the system would limit the numbers of Aboriginal women "of abandoned character" entering the towns. Relying on diaries of policemen, newspapers, and court records, Carter discusses a variety of oppressive practices towards Aboriginal women. For example, government agents sometimes withheld rations to reserve communities unless Aboriginal women were made available to them. The NWMP often turned a blind eye to such practices, engaging in their own coercive relations with Aboriginal women. White men in positions of authority often beat Aboriginal women, sometimes fatally. Oral narratives of late-nineteenth-century Lakota women suggest that the NWMP had easy sexual access to Aboriginal women whose families were starving.[14]

Newspaper records of the nineteenth century indicate that there was a conflation of Aboriginal woman and prostitute and an accompanying belief that when they encountered violence, Aboriginal women simply got what they deserved. Police seldom intervened, even when the victim's cries could be clearly heard.[15] In one case explored by Sarah Carter, which bears an uncanny parallel to the trial of Ternowetsky and Kummerfield for the murder of Pamela George, a Cree woman, referred to in the newspapers as a squaw named Rosalie who was working as a prostitute, was murdered by William Fisk, a white man of a well-established family. Even when Fisk confessed to the murder, the Crown expressed his sympathy for Fisk as a man whose activities in capturing rebellious Natives clearly marked him as a patriot and an upstanding citizen. When a jury declared Fisk innocent, a judge ordered a retrial and, unusual for the period, urged the new jurors to forget the victim's race and consider the evidence at hand. Ultimately convicted of manslaughter, Fisk was initially given a life sentence, but this reduced to fourteen years of hard labour when testimonials of support for him poured in. Rosalie, as one newspaper boasted, had a "respectable burial" even though she was not white, an honour swiftly diluted when the church refused her burial in the mission's graveyard because she had died in "sin" while engaging in prostitution. The lesson of the case, one Calgary newspaper opined, was that it was important to "keep the Indians out of town."[16]

The nineteenth-century spatial containment of Aboriginal peoples to reserves remained in place until the 1950s. As professor Jim Harding of the University of Regina noted in his presentation to the Royal Commission on Aboriginal Peoples (RCAP), a white boy growing up in Regina in the 1950s would know Regina as almost exclusively white and as bordered by the reserves of the Qu'Appelle Valley: "two different worlds."[17] By the 1960s, however, a steady stream of Aboriginal peoples flowed from the reserves to the city. With a high birth rate, Aboriginal peoples left reserves in increasing numbers, impoverished among other things, by a series of federal government cutbacks for housing. In 1971, the census indicated only 2,860 Aboriginal peoples living in Regina, but unofficial estimates placed the number closer to thirty thousand by mid-decade.[18]

This pattern of migration from reserves to cities is well documented for other Canadian cities. For example, Russell Lawrence Barsh studied the high rates of relocation from reserves to Lethbridge, Alberta, a city also bordered by reserves, in the 1990s and concluded that migration was primarily linked to housing rather than to the lure of economic activities in the city. Barsh suggests that housing shortages were created by cutbacks in federal grants to reserves during the 1980s.[19] These patterns are confirmed in the Ontario context by Allison Williams, who has reviewed a number of Canadian studies of migration of Aboriginal peoples to cities.[20] Between 1986 and 1991, the urban Aboriginal population in Canada increased by 55 per cent in contrast to the non-Aboriginal urban population increase of 11 per cent.[21]

Pamela George's homeland, the Sakimay reserve, is typical of the spatial configurations that emerged in Canadian colonialism and produced the migration from reserves to the city. The link between the material privilege of white settlers in the cities and Aboriginal marginalization is a direct one, as the Indian Claims Commission (an independent body set up by the federal government to aid in the settlement of land claims) established with respect to the Sakimay and other reserves in the area. The Commission found that, in the 1940s, the federal government failed to consult the six First Nations involved before passing the *Prairie Farm Rehabilitation Act*, which authorized the construction of dams and the flooding of reserve lands along the Qu'Appelle River. The government also failed to expropriate or obtain surrenders of affected reserve lands. These practices left the Sakimay reserve tremendously impoverished, while white farmers profited from the enhanced irrigation.[22]

The three Prairie cities of Winnipeg, Regina, and Saskatoon have a higher in-migration from reserves than other Canadian cities. Women form the majority of these migrants (58 per cent), relocating to the city for a variety of reasons, including loss of tribal status, violence, and lack of housing and employment. Once in the city, however, the majority of urban Aboriginal peoples are left in a "jurisdictional limbo" between the city and the reserve.[23] As the authors of a case study of the First Nations economy in Regina conclude, the urban Aboriginal population remains more marginal than their reserve counterparts, without access to social services and networks. Aboriginal people also remain outside the city's economy—only 2.8 per cent of the workforce is Native, while Aboriginal people constitute 8 per cent or more of the population. In Winnipeg, Regina, and Saskatoon, according to the 1991 census, 60 per cent of urban Aboriginal households live below the poverty line and, for single-parent households headed by women, the figure is 80 to 90 per cent.[24] In Regina itself, this picture is even worse: 81 per cent of Aboriginal households live in poverty and the high-school drop-out rate for Aboriginal children is 90 per cent—higher than in any other city.[25]

Despite three decades of significant urbanization, the spatial configuration of the nineteenth century and the social hierarchies it both engenders and sustains remain firmly embedded in the white Canadian psyche and in social and economic institutions. The Native Council of Canada put it directly to the Royal Commission on Aboriginal Peoples: "There is a strong, sometimes racist perception that being Aboriginal and being urban are mutually exclusive."[26] In their own testimonies to the Royal Commission and other bodies, Aboriginal peoples report on the considerable racism in their lives in the cities. Robin Bellamy, a front-line worker in inner-city Saskatoon, told commissioners of the fear Aboriginal people had described to him in entering white areas of the city. Bellamy also described in considerable detail the almost complete exclusion of Aboriginal people from Saskatoon's institutions—in banks, for example, Aboriginal people regularly encounter difficulties cashing cheques.[27]

There are perhaps no better indicators of continuing colonization and its accompanying spatial strategies of containment than the policing and incarceration of urban Aboriginal peoples, a direct continuation of the policing relationship of the nineteenth century. Between the late 1960s and the early 1970s, the number of Aboriginal peoples in Regina's jails increased by 10 per cent. In 1971 the city stepped up downtown patrols, and in 1975 created a special task force for the purpose of policing Aboriginal peoples. By 1994, the province of Saskatchewan (of which Regina is the capital) had the highest level of incarceration of Aboriginal peoples in Canada: 72 per cent of the population in the province's jails were Aboriginal.[28] According to a "One-Day Snapshot" survey taken in October of 1996, 76 per cent of Saskatchewan's inmates on register in adult correctional facilities were Aboriginal.[29] In 1999, Patricia Monture-Angus tells us that Aboriginal men made up approximately 80 per cent of the population at Saskatchewan Penitentiary.

The rates of incarceration are even more dramatic for Aboriginal women. Ten years ago it was estimated that in Saskatchewan a treaty Indian woman was 131 times more likely to be incarcerated than a non-Aboriginal woman, while Métis women were twenty-eight times more likely to be incarcerated. According to Jim Harding's 1993 testimony to the Royal Commission, Aboriginal women then made up 80 to 90 per cent of the prison population at Pinegrove, a correctional facility in Regina. Thus, while the number of admissions to correctional centres increased in Saskatchewan by 46 per cent between 1976 and 1992, the rate of increase for Aboriginal women was 111 per cent for the same period.[30] Looking to a national scale, and to more recent statistics, First Nations women (registered or "Status" Indians) made up only 1 to 2 per cent of the Canadian population in 1997, but represented 19 per cent of federally sentenced women.[31] Harding connected Saskatchewan's provincial carceral scene, in particular, to the history of colonization, reminding RCAP commissioners that it was in Saskatchewan that Louis Riel was hanged and eight Indian leaders were executed in 1885. Perhaps, he speculated, the lessons of 1885 remain "deeper in our psyche [and] in our social structure than we would like to realise."[32]

Not surprisingly, the encounter in policing between white people and Aboriginal people maintain all of the characteristics of the nineteenth-century colonial encounter. Commenting on the use of police dogs to terrorize Native youth, Professor Harding recalled witnessing the police unleashing a dog in the house of a Native woman engaging in prostitution. Describing to the commissioners the scene of terror that ensued, Harding underlined the fact that the typical offender is also the typical victim: a young Native woman. Indeed, Native women can seldom count on the police when assaulted. Harding estimated that in the decade preceding the RCAP hearings, at least ten Aboriginal prostitutes had been murdered in Regina. René Dussault, co-chair of the Royal Commission, aptly concluded that Harding's presentation described "the dark side of the city," a zone where Aboriginal women are particularly at risk.[33]

The evidence that Aboriginal peoples live in a state of colonization as direct and coercive as prevailed two centuries ago is nowhere better demonstrated than in the high rate of suicide among Aboriginal peoples in Canada. As a government report concludes, the suicide rate, one of the highest in the world and four times higher than that of the non-Aboriginal population, is an expression of the "collective anguish" of three hundred years of colonial history. Illustrating the sources of this anguish and the depth of despair, one young Aboriginal woman told the report's authors of her own former life on the street, a past which included prostitution. Exemplifying what the report calls "a mixture of sexual and racial exploitation," "Missy" described how men from high-class communities go downtown to look for Native kids to rape and assault, knowing that the Native kids who survived would not talk. She commented on how she was generally perceived by such men: "One thing that really used to bother me was that men looked at me differently [from the other girls]. I always felt really dirty all the time. Men used to look at me and undress me with their eyes just anywhere, or try and pick me up thinking I was just easy. That used to really bother me." As Missy concluded: "So I felt really dirty being an Indian."[34]

Although there is no systematic study of the sexual violence Aboriginal women endure today on the streets at the hands of white men,[35] the cases that do surface suggest that the nineteenth-century perception of the Aboriginal woman as a licentious and dehumanized squaw (a perception described by Missy near the end of the twentieth century) continues to prevail. The Aboriginal Justice Inquiry's discussion of the 1971 murder of Helen Betty Osborne in The Pas, Manitoba, elaborates on its prevalence. Brutally murdered by two white men, Osborne, an Aboriginal student who was walking along a downtown street, was picked up in town and driven to a more secluded spot where she was assaulted and killed. As the Commissioners of the Aboriginal Justice Inquiry concluded, Osborne's attackers "seemed to be operating on the assumption that Aboriginal women were promiscuous and open to enticement through alcohol or violence. It is evident that the men who abducted Osborne believed that young Aboriginal women were objects with no human value beyond [their own] sexual gratification."[36]

Such assumptions often appear to be operating when the police fail to respond to the disappearance of Aboriginal women, citing their involvement in prostitution and their practices of moving from place to place. In the early 1990s, John Crawford, a white man, was convicted of murdering three Aboriginal women—Calinda Waterhen, Shelley Napope, and Eva Taysup. In each case, Crawford and another white friend began by drinking and having sex with the woman in question who was possibly working as a prostitute. The women's disappearance attracted little attention. When their families reported them missing, police appeared to assume that such women were simply transients on the move. As police sergeant Dave

Kovach told a reporter, the police don't look for transient adults because such individuals often go missing and often don't want to be found.[37] Crawford's victims were indeed, as Denise McConney has written, "caught up in the ongoing displacement, relocation, and search for a safe place that is a consistent theme in the lives of most native women."[38] Ironically, it is their very dispossession that is held against them when Aboriginal women encounter violence on the streets.

The Making of White Men: The Two Accused

Alex Ternowetsky and Steven Kummerfield's histories begin in the colonial practices described above. In their everyday life, they would have had almost no chance of encountering an Aboriginal person. Absent from the university, the ordered suburbs of their families, the chalets and cottages, Aboriginal bodies had to be sought out in the marginal spaces of the city. Why would white men seek out these bodies? Why would they leave their own spaces of privilege? How do young white men such as Alex Ternowetsky and Steven Kummerfield come to know themselves as beings for whom the definition of a good time is to travel to the parts of the city inhabited by poor and mostly Aboriginal peoples and there to purchase sexual services from an Aboriginal woman? I argue that the subject who must cross the line between respectability and degeneracy and, significantly, return unscathed, is first and foremost a colonial subject seeking to establish that he is indeed in control and lives in a world where a solid line marks the boundary between himself and racial/gendered Others. For this subject, violence establishes the boundary between who he is and who he is not. It is the surest indicator that he is a subject in control.

I have argued elsewhere[39] that the spatial boundaries and transgressions that enable the middle-class white male to gain mastery and self-possession are generally evident in his use of a woman in prostitution. When they purchase the right of access to the body of a prostitute, men, whether white and middle-class or not, have an opportunity to assert mastery and control, achieving in the process a subjectivity that is intrinsically colonial as well as patriarchal. Naturalized as necessary for men with excess sexual energy, prostitution is seldom considered to be a practice of domination that enables men to experience themselves as colonizers and patriarchs, that is, as men with the unquestioned right to go anywhere and do anything to the bodies of women and subject populations they have conquered (or purchased). Instead, the liberal idea that we are autonomous individuals who contract with each other is used to annul the idea that prostitution is non-reciprocal sex and thus a violation of the personhood of the prostitute. The contract cancels the violence, although we readily recognize the violence of other financial transactions (such as Third World youth who sell their corneas to First World buyers). The space of prostitution, which Malek Alloula describes as "*the very space of orgy*: the one that the soldier and the coloniser obsessively dream of establishing on the territory of the colony,"[40] is the space of license to do as one pleases, regardless of how it affects the personhood of others.

How did the two men enact their colonial histories? Race is not, at first glance, as evident as gender although neither exists independently. The men's behaviour bears some resemblance to the young hockey athletes researched by Laura Robinson in her *book Crossing the Line: Violence and Sexual Assault in Canada's National Sport*. Robinson describes the masculinity that is actively fostered in the world of young athletes as one where violence and sexual aggression, and a hatred of the softness that is female, are positive signs of masculinity. The normalizing of abusive relationships and male-bonding rituals designed to foster team relationships help to produce men for whom relationships with other men become the primary source of intimacy. Drawing on the work of scholars researching sports and masculinity, notably Peggy Reeves Sanday, Robinson suggests that sexual violence collectively enacted enables the men to get as close to each other as they can without endangering their sense of themselves as heterosexuals. To debase and degrade a woman in the presence of other men secures the masculinity that must be aggressive and that must disavow sexual feelings for other men.[41]

Scholars pursuing these themes in the context of university-educated men on sports teams share Robinson's emphasis on the relational features of this masculinity. S.P. Schacht, for instance, concludes of male rugby players that a kind of "order-by-violence" often prevails in which the definition of a real man is someone who sexually harms women. The players resorted to a variety of violent practices to "distance themselves from the feminine," continually reminding one another what masculinity is.[42] Peter Donnelly and Kevin Young also note "the fragility of reputations" in sports subcultures, that is, the need to make and remake masculine identity and the constitutive role that violence plays in this cycle.[43] Laurence Wenner describes the male adolescent for whom excessive public drinking (as well as buying the services of a prostitute) is a rite of passage into manhood, an exposure of oneself to a dangerous situation from which one emerges triumphant. Sport, Wenner suggests, works in a similar way, enabling men to establish their reputations with other men and to mark off the distinction between themselves and women.[44] As I show below, such practices also enable men to mark themselves as different from and superior to racial Others.

Kummerfield and Ternowetsky inhabited a world in which the homosocial bonding, drinking, and aggression were important features. Their counsel presented a unified picture of boys who started drinking at fourteen and who steadily progressed into a regular pattern of weekend and summer drinking. Both of the accused noted that as the youngest members of their university sports teams, they were initiated into more serious drinking by older teammates. Described as an "up and coming basketball star" of the University of Regina, Steven Kummerfield was cautioned about his excessive drinking by his basketball coach and saw an addictions counsellor while in his first year of university.[45] Kummerfield's drinking led on one occasion to his becoming a young offender, when in 1994 he damaged some unoccupied farm buildings.[46]

For his part, Alex Ternowetsky described socializing and drinking with his hockey teammates at the University of Northern British Columbia. Returning to Regina for a visit a few months after beginning his first year, Ternowetsky drank to excess with his friends (Tyler Stuart and Ryan Leier) and ended up at a convenience store in the early morning. While there, he tried to hug a girl emerging from a nearby vehicle and when confronted by her boyfriend proceeded to smash the latter's car with a golf club handed to him by his friends. He received a conditional discharge and his father paid the damages of $3,000. The assault charge was dropped. Shortly after, he sought some addictions counselling, although it is not clear if this was as a consequence of the court case.[47]

On the weekend of the murder, both men indulged in extensive drinking with their friends. Ternowetsky's account of his activities over the Easter weekend prior to the murder provides some idea of his social world. Arriving via Edmonton, he contacted a friend, Rod MacLeod, with whom he went drinking at one of their old haunts behind the Balfour hockey arena. Later, at a bar, his friend Eric Willrich got into a fight with a man he assumed was harassing Ternowetsky. Eric broke his leg during the fight. The following day, Ternowetsky continued drinking with MacLeod on the roof of the Optimist's arena.[48] Nostalgically sharing a bottle of rye in memory of a good time the summer before, the two also went drinking behind

Massey Pool. Finally, when neither Willrich nor MacLeod was available to continue partying, Ternowetsky arranged to meet Kummerfield at Rainbow Bridge and took a cab there, stopping at a bank machine en route to withdraw money for the night's activities.

Of the dozen or so male friends of the accused who testified, all were white male athletes attending university. In this remarkably homogeneous shared world of young, white, athletic, middle-class men (some of whom even had the same first Christian names), drinking and socializing occurred in isolated spaces outside their respectable homes. Parental surveillance and the financial costs of drinking in a bar were undoubtedly factors contributing to this pattern; during the Easter weekend, Ternowetsky was not allowed into the home of a friend and Kummerfield's parents refused to lend him the car to go out drinking. The men relied on their allowances to obtain drinking money. Their places of drinking and socializing were invested with special meaning, a testimony to the importance of their friendships. The accused testified that the places were secluded and a tradition, a place where they shared good times. A strip of gravel beside the airport runways was Alex Ternowetsky's favourite place and his friends named it the "Alport" in his honour. Steven Kummerfield's favourite place to drink was underneath Rainbow Bridge, a cement bridge over the Waskana Creek, which he described to a correctional officer as "a special place" for himself and Alex.[49] It was in this spot that "Allie" and "Stevie," as the accused called each other, began drinking on the night of the murder.

The sense of identity that both accused gained from their activities with other men was premised on a shared whiteness. Their sports activities cement white settler identity in ways I do not explore here,[50] but evidence of their shared whiteness is most apparent in their own and their friends' and families' responses to Pamela George and to the Stroll. The men told several of their friends about the events the night of the murder and received considerable support and advice. Alex Ternowetsky told at least four of his friends. One of these, Rodney McLeod, with whom he had been drinking at Massey Pool and whose fleece jacket he was wearing the night of the murder, reassured him that no one would find out. To another, Tyler Harlton, he confided that he had killed "an Indian hooker." Ryan Leier, with whom Ternowetsky had been in trouble before and to whom he confided the full details of the night while both were in a hot tub at a chalet in Banff, reassured his friend with the advice "you shouldn't assume you killed her." Finally, Ternowetsky told his fried Eric Willrich, whose jeans he was wearing the night of the murder and at whose house he is alleged to have washed the blood stains off.[51]

Steven Kummerfield confided to his best friend Tyler Stuart, with whom he had once gone to the area of prostitution, that "we beat the shit" out of "an Indian hooker." In Tyler Stuart's account, Kummerfield also elaborated that he said to Pamela George, "If you don't give us head, we're going to kill you." Stuart, apparently mostly concerned about the transmission of disease to Kummerfield's white girlfriend, advised his friend to break up with her if he hadn't worn a condom the night of the murder.[52] In none of these conversations was there any indication that the men acknowledged that a woman had been brutally murdered; her death seemed almost incidental and simply inconvenient. The men seemed to possess a collective understanding of Pamela George as a thing, an objectification that their exclusively white worlds would have given them little opportunity to disrupt.

In contrast to these spaces of intense white male bonding, the men's relationships with white women and parents appeared to be less intense although no less supportive of their practices of white masculinity. Kummerfield had dinner with his girlfriend Shannon Johnstone before the murder and then went out drinking with Ternowetsky. Although each said they were in love, he never told her about the murder. Suspecting that he had been with another woman, she apparently interpreted his withdrawn manner in the days following the murder as irritation at her questioning about where he had slept on the night of the murder. Kummerfield did confide in his mother about his involvement in the murder, the morning after. Far from counselling her son to go to the police, she suggested that she could call Crimestoppers and provide the police with a false tip. His mother also washed his jeans and cleaned his shoes. Other parents were equally protective of their sons once they became aware of the gravity of the charges. For example, Tyler Harlton's father mailed newspaper clippings of the trial to his son but took care to return unopened a letter from Alex Ternowetsky.[53] Here, too, there appeared to be little anguish over the fate of Pamela George.

In addition to their own isolated spaces, the men also inhabited those of middle-class respectability—white spaces of the university and sports arenas. The suburban households out of which they came enabled them to wear expensive clothing, including the labels of Club Monaco, Nike, and Timberland; Kummerfield used his father's credit cards to withdraw money for prostitutes, and Ternowetsky used his own account to buy a plane ticket to Banff.[54] There were cabins and chalets, the former owned by a grand-father who was formerly a member of the provincial legislature, the latter rented by hockey-playing friends. These privileged spaces provided the men with another male space for drinking. Alex Ternowetsky, who flew to Banff the day after the murder, was able to book himself into a hotel room in the resort town and to continue partying, activities that required cabs and money for the room, food, and alcohol.

The testimonies of the men staying at the chalet in Banff suggest that, at least in the all-male spaces, sexual aggression was normalized. Ternowetsky's drunken talk at the chalet did not strike his listeners as unusual. (He is reported as saying eight times in a half-hour period that "I want to go find a hooker and beat and rape her," and replying to a question about whether he had ever done this with "Yeah . . . it was fun and it was a rush.") They objected to his loudness but, as Curtis Doell testified, nothing struck him as unusual. The normal pattern was to ski and follow this up by eight hours or more of drinking. It was also typical to bring white women picked up in bars to the chalet.[55] Presumably, this talk about women and "Indians" was entirely normal.

In this all-white masculine world of privilege, the Stroll, the area of prostitution described in the trial as encompassing St. John and Ottawa Streets and involving a specific set of streets and hotels in between, represented the dangerous world of racial Others, a frontier on the edge of civilization. Police described the Stroll as a world of drugs and prostitution, and most of all, as a space of Aboriginality. Steven Kummerfield and his friends visited the Stroll "out of curiosity." Alex Ternowetsky and his friends took their girlfriends on an adventure to the Stroll, "sort of seeing who was there," as his lawyer put it.[56] The young women hid under blankets while the young men negotiated for the services of an Aboriginal prostitute: a thrilling excursion to the slums that would have helped these young white people to know their own place in the world.

On the night of the murder, after leaving Rainbow Bridge, Kummerfield and Ternowetsky drove to a place where they could buy liquor and then headed to the streets of the Stroll. They encountered Charlene Rosebluff, an Aboriginal woman working as a prostitute. In her account, they offered her $60, which neither of them had. Rosebluff refused to get in the car because there were two men and both were drunk. When she refused, the two men yelled at her using a string of racial slurs. At the trial, they acknowledged that this was possible and that they were likely to have used racial epithets.[57] One man then got into the trunk of the car while the other drove around and tried to persuade Rosebluff twice again. (At the trial, it is unclear whether they recognize her to be the same woman.) She again refused. The men switched positions and tried once more. This time, when Pamela George agreed to get into the car, they drove her to a country field two miles outside the city.

When young white men enter racialized urban spaces their skin clearly marks them as out of place. They are immediately read as johns, as rich white men who have come "slumming." This visibility no doubt contributes to white (particularly more affluent) city dwellers' tendency to perceive themselves as likely targets of robbery or violence in racialized urban space.[58] Steven Kummerfield once paid for the services of a prostitute and alleged that she disappeared with the money without providing her service. Such perceptions of white vulnerability frequently exist in a manner disproportionate to actual documented incidence of crimes, violent crimes in particular.[59] It is perhaps the men's perception that they were marked and at risk on the Stroll that prompted them to drive Pamela George outside the city to a borderland between the country and the city, a no-man's-land that offers greater anonymity.[60] In this no-man's-land, violent acts can be committed without meaningful consequence. Although the accused both maintained that they did not know the area, the RCMP and the neighbouring farmers testified that it was isolated and that it was routine for prostitution to occur there.[61]

What normally happened in this space was mostly undisputed during the trial. The Crown referred to activities in the space as "romantic" activities, while a farmer stated that couples and prostitutes often used the area and that there was "necking or petting in vehicles." The defence lawyer Kovach asked an RCMP officer (who testified that he often stopped vehicles in this area) if "we're talking males, females, homosexuals, whatever, we don't know the kind of people—or you don't know the kind of people that frequent that road." The accused had no response when they were asked by the Crown why they would drive George to this area if all they wanted to do was have sex with her, a question the judge later directed the jury to ignore. Presumably, since Pamela George and the men were engaged in a contract of prostitution, something that occurred routinely in this space, the jury was directed to draw no special conclusion from their having taken George there.[62]

It is difficult to avoid both the historical and contemporary racial and spatial parallels between the murders of Helen Betty Osborne and Pamela George. Equally, newspaper reports in 1999 calling attention to cases of Aboriginal men found frozen to death after Saskatoon police apparently dropped them outside the city limits in the dead of winter, outline the tremendous violence of the eviction of Aboriginal peoples from urban space.[63] In each instance, white men forcibly and fatally removed Aboriginal bodies from the city space, a literal cleansing of the white zone. The violence is itself cleansing, enabling white men to triumph over their own internal fears that they may not be men in control. The evictions are to areas where white men are able to evade responsibility for their violent acts, areas where there are few witnesses and where, significantly, the norms of civility are suspended and violence by contract is known to occur.

Although there are several instances which neither of the accused can recall, they generally agreed that once at the country field, Pamela George was frightened and tried to defend herself. They talked to her and gave her false names. She ultimately agreed to perform oral sex and all three remained in the front seat of the car while this was in progress. While George was performing oral sex on Ternowetsky (having finished with Kummerfield), Kummerfield announced that they should leave. Ternowetsky asked that George be allowed to finish but a short time later, Kummerfield dragged her from the car and hit her. Ternowetsky, at first surprised, joined in. Neither recalled the extent of the violence but each remembered her face in the mud and the fact that she tried to defend herself. They later claimed that when they drove off (after having bent the license plate to conceal the numbers), Pamela George was still standing.[64]

During the trial, the murder scene and the Stroll were described as spaces somehow innately given to illicit and sexual activity. The bodies of Charlene Rosebluff, Pamela George, and a number of Aboriginal men were represented variously as bodies that naturally belonged to these spaces of prostitution, crime, sex, and violence. This degenerate space, into which Kummerfield and Ternowetsky ventured temporarily, was juxtaposed to the spaces of respectability. Each space required a different legal response. In racialized space, violence may occur with impunity. Bodies from respectable spaces may also violate with impunity, particularly if the violence takes place in the racialized space of prostitution.

☐ Unmapping Law: Gendered Racial Violence in Anomalous Zones

When I identify Ternowetsky and Kummerfield's transgression into racial space as an identity-making process (the men entered the zone, came into close contact with its degenerate occupants, and survived to tell the tale), it is worth reiterating the important connection between prostitution, race, space, and justice. Prostitution emerged in its modern form as distinct and confined to sharply demarcated areas of the city at the historical moment when liberal nation-states emerged. Bourgeois subjects, the new citizens of the nation-state, knew themselves as respectable and civilized largely through a spatial separation from those deemed to be degenerate and uncivilized. Degenerate spaces (slums, colonies) and the bodies of prostitutes were known as zones of disorder, filth, and immorality. The inhabitants of such zones were invariably racialized,[65] evacuated from the category human, and denied the equality so fundamental to liberal states.

During the trial, Pamela George came to be seen as a rightful target of the gendered violence inflicted by Kummerfield and Ternowetsky. Put another way, her murder was characterized as a natural by-product of the space and thus of the social context in which it occurred, an event that is routine when the bodies in question are Aboriginal. This naturalizing of violence is sustained by the legal idea of contract, an agreement between consenting and autonomous individuals. Because she consented to provide sexual services, the violence became more permissible. The moment of violence is contained within the moment of the contract and there can be no history or context, for example the constraints on her choice and the historical conditions under which the bargain was made. Trapped in the moment in time of the contract, Pamela George remained simply "the prostitute" or the "Indian."

In the absence of details about George's life and critical scrutiny of the details of the lives of the accused, a number of subject positions remained uninterrogated. Thus, not only did George remain the "hooker" but Ternowetsky and Kummerfield remained boys who "did pretty darn stupid things"; their respective spaces, the places of white respectability and the Stroll simply stood in opposition to each other, dehistoricized and decontextualized. If Pamela George was a victim of violence, it was simply because she was of the Stroll/reserve, Aboriginal, and engaging in prostitution. No one could then be really held accountable for her death, at least not to the extent that there would have been accountability had she been of spaces within the domain of justice.

The Stroll and the Street

The perception that the Stroll and Aboriginal bodies are spaces of violence, while the university and white suburbs are spaces of civility, is first demonstrated by the candid responses of the police when questioned as to whom they initially pursued and why. The boundary between the streets and the university and suburbs was so firmly entrenched in the minds of the police that they spent the first three weeks after the murder "rounding up the usual suspects." The testimony of Corporal Torgunrud in reply to the Crown attorney's question as to who is a murder suspect is revealing in this respect:

Q   Who do you usually suspect when you get a murder?

A   Well – . . .

Q   Let me give you a better example. If it's a woman who's killed and there is [sic] boyfriends, husbands, are those people often the suspects?

A   Yes.

Q   And that's simply because of the reality of life because oftentimes there is violence in relationships?

A   That's right.

Q   And do you often suspect associates?

A   Yes.

Q   And if a person happens to live a life on the street, involved in that type of world, you might suspect other associates in that area?

A   That's right.

Q   Did you suspect anybody who was attending the University of Regina when you first got the case?

A   No.

Q   And why not?

A   Nobody had ever come forward or there was never anything to point to anybody there.

Q   And why would you suspect somebody *far removed from Pamela George's life,* I take it?

A Right.

Q And did you get much, make much headway in this case pursuing the leads where the suspects were street people, people involved in sort of a lifestyle different, maybe, than most of us have?[66]

It is, of course, only possible to consider the world of the university as entirely apart from the world of the streets if one discounts that there are two parties in prostitution: the prostitute *and* the client. Pursuing suspects on the street, the RCMP interviewed a number of Aboriginal men, and the white man described as George's common-law husband. The suspects all speculated that George was murdered by a "bad Trick,"[67] but this made little impression on the police and they continued looking for Aboriginal men or men from the "streets." The police had to overcome a number of obstacles in order to keep their focus on suspects from the streets, obstacles that ultimately defeated them. For one thing, the shoe marks at the murder scene indicated that the murderer likely wore Caldera Nike hiking boots, expensive shoes that no suspect from the streets possessed. It was only when they followed up on Charlene Rosebluff's tip that the police considered the men who were most likely to possess such shoes: white middle-class athletes.

The first suspect the police pursued, George's common-law husband, Lenny Hall, was a white man who was consistently described by the defence as "an elusive character" whose "whereabouts are pretty scarce," a man with long greasy hair all the way to his mid-back. The police described Hall as extremely distraught when they told him of Pamela George's death. He later took a polygraph test and was cleared. In spite of being white, Hall was so thoroughly racially marked and identified as "of the street" that when the defence hired a private investigator to find him (on the strength that he was still a suspect), she looked in the downtown hotels, the salvation Army Hostel, the Souls Harbour Mission, the food bank, and the correctional centres. She asked "certain street people . . . that generally sort of keep tabs on each other" but did not think to ask George's family if they knew where Hall was.[68] At the trial, both she and the police concluded that Hall was unlocatable, a conclusion the Crown attorney quickly attempted to qualify with his own spatial assessment:

> . . . you can appreciate to some extent who we're dealing with here,
> this is someone who, from his background, has moved around a fair

bit, he is an Ontario native to begin with. . . . Saskatchewan isn't home, he's not born and raised here . . . for example, Charlene Rose-bluff's evidence, why people don't want to get involved in this, especially street people . . . the last thing Mr. Hall, quite frankly, wants to be doing is getting involved in this thing.[69]

In his awkward naming of Hall as an "Ontario native to begin with," the Crown attorney very nearly made an explicit and subtextual conflation of Hall and "Natives," a predictable slip given the extent to which Hall was invested with racial characteristics and regarded as degenerate and therefore not white enough.[70] One should not read anything sinister, the Crown attorney suggested, in Hall being difficult for the police and the private investigator to find: such people are hard to find and are reluctant to become involved with the police. Again, Hall's elusiveness was naturalized as an innate feature of someone of this background, almost a cultural characteristic (or an acquired racial one), and not in any way an effect of ongoing police violence towards individuals racialized and policed in urban Aboriginal spaces.

In contrast to Hall, the Aboriginal suspect, Lloyd Issac, was easy to find since in the weeks following the murder he was arrested and jailed for robbery. As with other Aboriginal suspects, Issac had no Caldera boots and his own running shoes were free of mud and blood. Nonetheless, the defence maintained throughout the trial that he was possibly the killer. With a history of encounters with the police, Issac was reported to be very agitated when asked if he would take a polygraph test. (He was earlier falsely accused on the basis of one.) Issac had several theories about the murder and had heard from other Aboriginal men in prison, including George's cousin, about some of the details of the investigation. In the retelling of the police's interview with Issac, the court heard details of how prisons, conflated with Aboriginal spaces, operate. They learned of prison networks of information, for example.[71]

The street thus remained, in the space of the courtroom, an aggregate of individuals who form a mass and who function according to their own rules. From this perspective, criminality sticks to the Aboriginal bodies, entrenching a view that such bodies can be associated with little else. In the court transcripts, we do not learn, as newspaper reports revealed, that Issac had been struggling to overcome a drug habit, that he had been subjected to several beatings by police, and had feared being framed for the murder of Pamela George. He had been interrogated by the police four times in relation to the case and was unable to find legal assistance, circumstances that possibly contributed to the taking of his own life in March 1996.[72] Since the over-policing, incarceration, and high suicide rates of Aboriginal peoples were not brought to bear on the details, the stain that is Aboriginality could not be seen as socially constructed.

Aboriginal women did not fare any better than the men in failing to materialize as subjects during the trial. They too remained "of the streets" and therefore of the violence. Charlene Rosebluff, who was originally of the Sakimay reserve, as was Pamela George, and who the men first approached on the night of the murder, remained in the judge's mind as "the prostitute." When she was late for her second court appearance, the Crown attorney explained that she was upset by the way in which "her world" was being described. The judge instructed the jury to read nothing sinister into her failure to show. Kummerfield described her to his friend Tyler Stuart as a hooker and not very good-looking. As an expert on substance abuse revealingly suggested to the court, it was likely that the men were unable to positively identify Rosebluff as the person they approached three times, not because of their state of inebriation, but because they couldn't tell one Indian from another and viewed all Indians as being the same. Later pressed by the defence to explain once again what the men's failure to recognize Charlene Rosebluff might mean, the expert witness, Dr. Aubrey Levin, again suggested that while such behaviour might be explained by memory loss due to the effects of alcohol, the use of insulting language towards Rosebluff would more strongly suggest that the men were unable to recognise her because of "a certain attitude towards that kind of person," a person who is a prostitute.[73] His expertise, and thus his opinion of the source of the men's confusion, was later discredited by the judge in his address to the jury.

Apart from a few moments, such as when Charlene Rosebluff remembered her as a nice person and a mother with two children, and when her mother and sister recalled that she liked doing crafts, could cook anything and was a good mother to her ten- and five-year-old, Pamela George never left the racially bounded space of prostitution and degeneracy during the trial, a space that marked her as a body to be violated. We never learn of the Sakimay reserve and the extensive familial networks of her life there, nor do we learn anything about why she resorted to prostitution a few times a month, and why she left the reserve in the first place. It is only in newspaper articles that we learn that she helped her father through his crisis with alcohol abuse, supporting him in his journey to become an addictions counsellor. When details of her life emerged, such as the fact that Pamela George had a cousin in prison, and her father had himself been falsely accused of a crime,[74] they only confirmed the equation of Aboriginality with violence, a state of affairs that remained unconnected to the violence of the colonizers. In place of details that might have given her personhood, there were a myriad of other details that instead reassured the court of her belonging to spaces of violence. The needle marks on her arm, the tattoos on her body with the words "Ed" and "I love Mom," the stories of her ripping off clients (stories the police report they heard from Lenny Hall), the mention of her sister who was also a prostitute, and the detailed descriptions of how prostitutes conducted their business (but not how clients participate) leave a powerful image of degeneracy. This degeneracy was clearly racial. She was described as a member of the Mongoloid or Mongolian race when a strand of her hair was classified in evidence. Stephen Kummerfield described her as "shuffling" away from him in fear when she saw Alex Ternowetsky jump out of the trunk.[75]

Perhaps most telling of all were the accused's sense of the crime they committed. Ternowetsky told his friend Tyler Harlton that they picked up an Indian hooker, got kind of mad at her, started to hit her and did it too much and so probably killed her. Tyler was asked on the witness stand how Ternowetsky regarded the murder, to which he replied: "He kind of glanced over it, looked at it sexually." When asked to clarify, he explained that his friend did not describe the sexual act but instead made a noise like grunting. Ternowetsky did not apologize to the George family until relatively late in the trial. Questioned by the Crown attorney as to why he felt he had to leave town quickly if all he thought he had done was hit someone a few times, Steven Kummerfield replied:

> I was basically disgusted with what took place that evening, and I really didn't want to be arrested or anything like that just because there are so many opportunities I had, you know, to be successful and stuff and, you know, I just felt so ashamed and things like that.[76]

Lost opportunities weighed more heavily on Kummerfield's mind than the thought that he might have severely injured if not killed a woman. Kummerfield's response to the violence parallels those of hockey players like Jarret Reid, who described in his statements to the court the tragedy of the loss of his hard-won hockey career and his reputation as an adored and respected athlete.[77]

Ultimately, it was Pamela George's status as a prostitute, hence not as a human being, and her belonging to spaces beyond universal justice, that limited the extent to which the violence done to her body could be recognized and the accused made accountable for it. Although it was central to the defence to spatialize accountability in this way, neither the Crown attorney nor the judge contested these relations between space and justice. The defence naturalized the violence by framing it as merely something that happens in prostitution and in those spaces. Describing the murder scene as a "quiet" rather than isolated location in which to have sex,[78] defence attorney Kovach suggested at sentencing: "They were out in the country doing what happens apparently on that road on a regular basis. . . . This is a fairly common area for that type of activity to be taking place. . . . She wasn't stabbed forty times. There wasn't a hammer used."[79] In perhaps the most convoluted but revealing of arguments that prostitution lies beyond the space of universal justice, the defence lawyer for Alex Ternowetsky suggested that if the court was going to ignore that Pamela George was working as a prostitute (and thus consider the beating and murder as one would any other), then the same consideration must be extended to his client:

> But I think the same consideration has to apply when you look at the evidence as it applies to Alex Ternowetsky. Alex admits that he drank excessively, that he picked up a prostitute, that he hit her and he left her out in the country to walk back to the city on her own, and no one can blame you if you look at that and say that's disgusting behaviour. But the issue that you have to consider is whether or not he's guilty of murder. . . .[80]

Although it is difficult to follow his logic, defence lawyer Aaron Fox appeared here to be suggesting that if the court ignored that the violence occurred within the context of prostitution (and is thus a lesser violence), then it must also ignore that his client drove George to a place of prostitution and inflicted the violence that caused her death. The social meaning of places and bodies must all be studiously ignored even as the law depends on these meanings to evaluate the violence. Presumably, his client would then be guilty of disgusting behaviour but not of murder. A parallel was being made between George engaging in prostitution and his client's drinking, both being examples of risky and ill-advised behaviour. Prostitution in particular "may not be pleasant but that's the reality." Further, Pamela's alleged drug addiction can be equated to their client's drunkenness. It was indeed central to the defence's arguments that the accused were simply young men who went out drinking. As Fox sums up: "You come to realize how easy it is for two otherwise rather average young boys with a booze problem to find themselves in a whole pile of extremely serious criminal difficulty, difficulty that could indeed effectively wreck their lives for years to come." For the defence, if there was a problem to be named in this trial, it is "substance abuse,"[81] and not racial or sexual violence that ended in murder.

The defence had to go to considerable lengths to make the argument that their clients were drunk and incapable of formulating an intent to injure or kill. The accused performed a number of deliberate actions (hiding in the trunk, hiding the license plate, having oral sex, and so on). While one expert witness saw such actions as indicating consciousness of what they were doing, the defence's own expert on substance abuse declared the men "alcohol tolerant" to the point that they could perform intricate tasks while very drunk.[82] Drunkenness as a defence for what was being viewed as a temporary loss of control on the part of the men may have made sense to the court not only because of the men's firm belonging to their own social space but also because of the victim's position outside of it. In other words, given her status in the trial as an Aboriginal woman prostitute and thus of the space of violence, was Pamela George seen as having simply gotten what she deserved?[83]

In his summation, after noting that Pamela George worked as a prostitute, the Crown attorney reminded the court that everyone was entitled to the protection of the law.[84] He nevertheless concluded in his summary remarks, after sympathizing with the families of the accused, that "Pamela George obviously lived a lifestyle far removed, probably from yours and mine. . . . The fact that she was a prostitute obviously is a fact, and you have to consider that as part of the case."[85] In his address to the jury, the judge directed the jury as follows:

> Now, if you should find that Pamela George consented to the sexual
> activity of the two accused, notwithstanding Kummerfield's remark

about killing her if she did not give them head, or if you should have a reasonable doubt as to whether the accused consented or not, bearing in mind that the evidence indicates that she indeed was a prostitute, then the Crown has not made out its case with respect to first-degree murder occurring during a sexual assault, and you must find the accused not guilty of first-degree murder but guilty of second-degree murder.[86]

He then clarified that forcible confinement was a separate and distinct issue from confinement for sexual assault. For there to be forcible confinement, Pamela George would have to be shown to have been dragged to the car and held against her wishes; she cannot simply have been forced to have sex. He directed the jury to remember that George consented to perform sexual acts and that the accused were within their rights to hire her. Even Kummerfield's remark that he would kill her if she did not perform the sexual acts had to be considered in light of the fact that he had in fact hired her to perform these acts. While George was to be judged for engaging in prostitution, the men were not to be judged for having purchased her services. Put more plainly, her activity was a crime which carried the risks of violence, while theirs was a contract. Taking her out to the country should then have no bearing on how the intentions of the accused were understood.[87] Presumably, this was all within the purview of the contract Pamela George made to sell her sexual service and within the limits of her lifestyle.

I suggest that it was difficult for the Crown to disturb the argument of drunkenness and disorderly conduct (as opposed to murder), primarily because of an implicit spatial underpinning which was never challenged and was indeed shared by the Crown. While Pamela George remained stuck in the racial space of prostitution where violence is innate, the men were considered to be far removed from the spaces of violence. She was of the space where murders happen; they were not. The men received support from several white people and were praised for their accomplishments. The RCMP reported that they got along well with the accused and a correctional officer conveyed that he related to Alex Ternowetsky like a father. Counsel received an anonymous note claiming that a juror flirted with the boys.[88] Steven Kummerfield's lawyer reminded the court at sentencing that Kummerfield had often been the most valuable player of the week and that his sports record "is some indication of who he is and more important who he is now and hopefully who he'll be able to become after he pays his debt."[89] At the trial's end, the judge defended his remarks to the jury by noting that the media did not report evidence that was favourable to the accused.[90] As Robinson shows in her review of cases involving hockey players accused of sexual assault, such evidence need hardly be mentioned since white male judges and lawyers alike often share the view that the loss of the young men's hockey career is a greater tragedy than the young woman's loss of her life.[91]

Race rarely surfaced explicitly in the trial but when it did, it was quickly disconnected from whiteness. For example, during a discussion of hair found in the car of the accused, the defence (using a nineteenth-century language of race) discussed negroid, caucasian, and Mongolian hair. The defence lawyer Kovach asked the expert witness on hair whether Kovach, as a Hungarian, would be Caucasian or Mongolian.[92] In this discussion, the word "white" was never mentioned. It was as though white people did not exist, only Caucasians and Hungarians, labels that have less association with racism than the term "white" does. When race threatened to disturb the raceless equivalences that were maintained (George's prostitution and the white men's drunkenness, her addiction and theirs), the attorneys drew attention to their own ethnicity in a bid to represent everyone as equally raced. Following a long exchange in which the expert witness Dr. Aubrey Levin maintained that the language used by the men (language that includes racist slurs but is seldom named as such) indicated their social attitudes rather than their state of inebriation, the defence then asked him whether one's true personality emerged when one was drunk. When Dr. Levin replied that what emerged when drunk was a facet of a person's personality, Kovach once again introduced his own ethnicity and asked:

> So that if one, inappropriately perhaps—and let me use the—we—
> the word Hungarian, because I am Hungarian and proud of it, but if
> one sees six drunk Hungarians, including myself, on the street corner
> and we're being rude to you and drunk to you and aggressive
> towards you, which we might not otherwise be, and if you walked by
> and described us as being six or seven rude, vulgar, drunken what-
> ever, Hungarians in this case, you are saying that that is a true
> description of them, as opposed to how they might otherwise be; is
> that correct doctor?[93]

Hungarians once again replaced white in this exchange where the defence argued that it was unreasonable to consider "rude" conduct while drunk as having anything to do with underlying social attitudes. If the accused uttered racial slurs to Charlene Rosebluff, this could not then be taken as evidence of their racism since racial slurs uttered under the influence of alcohol were not evidence of racism. Instead, as Kummerfield's lawyer Kovach maintained, they were remarks made "out of character."[94] Interestingly, while it was argued that being drunk is out of character for white men, being drunk is more often than not seen as in character for Aboriginal peoples.[95] Alcohol abuse and its accompanying racial and sexual violence were described as temporary aberrant behaviour while Pamela George's "lifestyle" remained a permanent personal characteristic.

It is no small irony that racism, so rarely named during the trial, only emerged explicitly during sentencing. The defence reported that Alex Ternowetsky had taken a course on Native literature while in prison and had written a paper on Aboriginal–white relations that proved that he had "no clear motive of hatred towards someone of a particular racial origin."[96] Racelessness was pursued to the bitter end, however. When there were complaints made against him after the trial, Mr. Justice Malone confirmed (in a letter to Chief Justice Allan McEachern) that race overdetermined the trial, but noted that only a strategy of racelessness (ignoring everyone's race) countered it:

> I suspect the real basis for most of the complaints, including the two that I have dealt with, is the underlying feeling that because the two accused were white and the victim was a First Nations person they received special treatment and the jury's verdict [of manslaughter and not murder] was based on racism. This was certainly the reaction of several First Nations spokesmen and extensive media coverage was given to their remarks in this regard. Furthermore, both accused came from financially secure homes and enjoyed the material benefits associated therewith. Their position in life was in striking contrast to the position of the victim. Every effort was made during the trial by counsel and myself to deal with the case strictly on the basis of relevant evidence and not on the financial and social positions of the accused and their victim or their race.[97]

Here, colour-blindness as a legal approach, the belief that justice can only be achieved by treating all individuals as though they were the same, held full sway.

Race, social position, and, I would add, gender were indeed made to disappear during the trial and in sentencing. The social meaning of spaces and bodies was deliberately excluded as evidence that would contaminate the otherwise pure processes of law, evidence that was not relevant. It was not then possible to interrogate what white men thought they were doing in journeying to the Stroll to buy the services of an Aboriginal prostitute. It was also not possible to interrogate the meaning of consent and violence in the space of prostitution and between white and Aboriginal bodies. Since bodies had no race, class, or gender, the constructs that ruled the day, heavily inflected with these social relations, coded rather than reveal them explicitly. Thus "prostitute" and people of "the street" came to signify the racial Other and the spaces of violence. In contrast, the university, the chalet, the cottage, the suburban home, the isolated spaces in which the men socialized were unmarked. When Pamela George's mother Ina and her sister Denise respectively commented in their victim impact statements, "so what if she was a prostitute" and "it felt she was on trial because she was a prostitute," they were identifying two domains of law—the domain of justice and the domain beyond it.[98] This spatial configuration was explicitly geographical and quite deliberately mapped. It was also explicitly raced, classed, and gendered. Bodies that engage in prostitution and the spaces of prostitution are racialized, as I have argued elsewhere, regardless of the actual race of the prostitute. In this sense, it is possible, as Ternowetsky's lawyer suggested at sentencing, that Pamela George's race made no difference, but only in the sense that any woman engaging in prostitution loses her status as white. What a spatial analysis reveals is that bodies in degenerate spaces lose their entitlement to personhood through a complex process in which the violence that is enacted is naturalized. Even when the trial judge at sentencing acknowledged that Pamela George was the victim of mindless violence and that her murderers "cast her aside as if she were something less than human," these observations did not alter his ultimate position that the accused deserved a punishment of six and a half years, given the time of twenty months already served.[99]

Uncovering this spatialized view of justice helps us to see how race shapes the law by informing notions of what is just and who is entitled to justice. It enables us to see how whiteness is protected and reproduced through such ideas as a contract between autonomous individuals standing outside of history. What would it mean to deliberately introduce history and social context into this trial? In the first instance, we would have to ask questions about the activities of the accused. How did they routinely conduct themselves? What is the role of violence against women in their activities? Who were the women who were seen as targets of the violence? These questions would have to be raised within the historical and social context of Aboriginal–white relations in Regina. Secondly, to appreciate that a person has been brutally murdered, details about Pamela George's life, once again historically contextualized, would have to be on the record to counter the historically produced response to her as a woman whose life was worth very little. Efforts to introduce these two lines of evidence would be thwarted by the notion that prostitution is a contract and not violence, and the notion that individuals must be judged as though they were not embedded in historical and contemporary relations of domination. These approaches would also be resisted by the deeply entrenched notion that colonization simply happened a long time ago, if at all, and that it has ended, without colonizers enacting it and benefiting from it and, most of all, without their continuing to do so. If this exploration of Pamela George's murder trial does anything at all, my hope is that it raises consciousness about how little she mattered to her murderers, their friends and families, and how small a chance she had of entering the court's and Canadian society's consciousness as a person.

CHAPTER 6

The Unspeakability of Racism

Mapping Law's Complicity in Manitoba's Racialized Spaces

Sheila Dawn Gill

The rules of the House apply equally to all members of the House and the privileges of the House apply equally to all members of the House. If this member for The Pas wants to be able to be treated as an equal, then he ought to treat others as equals and not make the kind of discriminatory, inflammatory and irresponsible allegations that he made in this House last evening. . . .

—Gary Filmon, former Premier of Manitoba[1]

I live on a reserve, a reserve that comes from what I call a racist system. I have a number that was given to me by the government. My number is 802. That is racist. My Cree language, my mother tongue, the government also tried to take that away from me. That was the first time I guess my freedom of speech was put into question.

—Oscar Lathlin, Opposition Member for The Pas[2]

There are critical connections that law renders

unspeakable—connections between speech, actions, places, and groups of people—in a racialized, liberal democratic, colonial society. Law can produce and sustain a racial social hierarchy by ruling violent histories of Aboriginal dispossession as being out of order and irrelevant. This chapter analyzes a series of events that occurred in Manitoba's Legislative Assembly between May and November of 1995. At the heart of the inquiry is an apparent contradiction between the law's official and abstract geography of "universal sameness" and an Aboriginal MLA's located geography of radical and painful difference.

On November 1, 1995, members of the Manitoba Legislative Assembly formalized the unspeakability of racism in the House when the word "racist" was codified by the Speaker as "unparliamentary language." The amendment enabled the Speaker to expel Oscar Lathlin, a Cree Member of the Opposition, from the House. Somehow located outside the privileged realm of protected free speech, Mr. Lathlin (representing a northern constituency) was expelled for refusing to retract his use of "racist" from an earlier critique of provincial government policy and programs affecting Aboriginal communities. The Speaker's parliamentary ruling insisted on the performance of a racism-free Manitoba.[3] How was such denial possible in an era when Aboriginal peoples' militancy gained unprecedented mainstream visibility (if little significant support) in Canada?[4] Indeed, what does such denial make possible in a society where racial inequities are normalized, and where the speech of racial outsiders can threaten foundational claims that the dominant society makes about itself, and about the places "we" Canadians call "home."

This chapter challenges the violence of liberal democratic abstraction as it was enacted in the 1995 ruling, picking up where Mr. Lathlin was silenced. My analysis reconnects the legally isolated moment of his expulsion from the white space of the House to the matters at stake in his silencing, and to some of the racialized spaces and bodies invoked by his Aboriginal presence and outlawed speech. To provide a counterpoint to the Speaker's official geography of universal *equality and sameness*, I describe two lesser-known Manitoba geographies—spaces of difference at once symbolic and "real," both imagined and material.[5] The first is northern Manitoba as viewed through the lens of *The Manitoba Hydro Act*.[6] The second is carceral Manitoba, that Other province of jails and prisons that serves as home to a grossly disproportionate number of Aboriginal people, and that is documented in the *Report of the Aboriginal Justice Inquiry of Manitoba*.[7] Such counter-geographies make apparent the socio-spatial relations of dominance that both produce, and are themselves reinforced by, massive denial and misrepresentation in the political sphere of the province.

I divide the discussion of this counter-geography into four parts. In the first part, the events leading up to the November 1st ruling are briefly considered in light of liberal philosophy. I suggest that it is misleading to read Oscar Lathlin's eviction as anomalous, and that within the race-infused liberal paradox, exclusion and separation along racial lines make (dominant) cultural sense.

The second part focuses on former Premier Gary Filmon's intervention of May 29 in the 1995 Throne Speech debate and impassioned rebuttal to the critiques Oscar Lathlin made. Stepping back from the abstract Manitoba of the Speaker's ruling, one sees the Premier performing a *highly specific* geography of the province. In the form of personal tales of youthful adventure in Manitoba's north, Mr. Filmon attempted to (re)centre his "anti-racist" self, and to (re)draw the egalitarian borders of the province in *his* (*not* Lathlin's) image.

The lines of power that bind together the law, "universal" parliamentary space, the elite white male subject, and the objects of imperial desire (most notably, unimpeded access to land and resources), are clearly illustrated in the the *Manitoba Hydro Act*. First passed in 1961, the sweeping colonial geography envisioned and realized by the Act illustrates the spatial networks and racialized order of social relations that enable elite imaginings (and injurious plays of innocence) in the legislature. The Premier's speech and the Act are analyzed in tandem for a number of reasons: first, these texts penetrate northern territories that overlap each other and Oscar Lathlin's Aboriginal north; second, the Premier's travels were roughly contemporaneous with the first decade the Act was in effect; and third, the Premier, a civil engineer by training, travelled north as a forerunner and agent of the hydro electric development that the Act enabled. Going beyond its close association with the Manitoba of Premier Filmon's youth, the Act typifies the colonial relations couched in law that favourably structure life chances (albeit unevenly) for all members of a majority non-Aboriginal "settler" population, at the expense of Aboriginal peoples' economic and cultural survival.

The fourth part of the counter-geography maps the unspeakability of racism from the perspective of the *Report of the Aboriginal Justice Inquiry of Manitoba*. Commonly referred to as the AJI, the Inquiry was formed in 1988 amid long-standing Aboriginal criticism of the justice system, and in response to concerns surrounding two wrongful Aboriginal deaths.

One of these tragedies was the November 1971 abduction and brutal murder of Helen Betty Osborne by four white men from the town of The Pas. The nineteen-year-old Osborne had been living in The Pas attending high school at the time of her death. Sixteen years passed before anyone was brought to trial for the horrific crime. In 1988, when the AJI held its hearings in The Pas, Oscar Lathlin was serving as chief of The Pas band. In 1991, the AJI's landmark *Report* was released, making 293 recommendations for the reform of a system proven to have ill-served, and far too frequently abused, Aboriginal Manitobans. Four years later, not one of those 101 recommendations that were strictly provincial in scope had been put into place. When he was substantiating concerns about racist government policy in late May 1995, Oscar Lathlin made repeated reference to the AJI's sidelined efforts.

The irony of a Cree man's silencing for naming racism in Manitoba is repugnant and painful to anyone cognizant of Canada's colonial past and present. It is all the more painful when the evicted Member's identity is so intimately linked (culturally, racially, and spatially) to the officially documented vulnerability of other Aboriginal bodies, collectively marked and disciplined by law, justice, and cultural practice as the province's and nation's racial outsiders. That Other Manitoba that spoke through the inquiry process—a network of voices and places typically excluded from parliamentary white space—is recovered by highlighting the racialized spaces the law helps to produce, to obscure, and with the judicial inquiry, was called upon to publicly acknowledge.

A critical counter-geography permits the superimposition of racialized and de-linked sites onto a site of elite white power. Recovering those spaces that were excised along with Oscar Lathlin can help make connections that legal and political discourses work hard to disavow. By reconnecting the "race-blind" nation to the violent underpinnings of universality—sites of silencing, eviction, dislocation, dispossession, and assimilation—this chapter demonstrates how the totalizing project of colonialism segregates racialized speech, spaces, and bodies, and effectively locates oppositional agency outside legal and cultural protections of full personhood. And while this chapter is centrally concerned with law's complicity in the production of uneven Canadian geographies (both "imagined" and "real"), it also points to law's pedagogic or educative role.

Law as a privileged and empowered system of moral praxis contributes to the making of normative white Canadian subjects. "We" know ourselves by identifying and separating ourselves from that which "we" are not, and according to the dominant Canadian mythology, "we" are not racist. Moreover, as the Manitoba legislative events of 1995 suggest, the vast majority of these "moral" normative subjects remain unmoved in the face of deeply distressing evidence of injustice. More critically, we are unwilling to know ourselves as benefactors and perpetrators of contemporary colonial relations of dominance, in "our home and native land."

☐ Eviction and the Liberal Paradox

In April 1995, Manitoba's Progressive Conservative Party took the reins of provincial power for a third consecutive term.[8] On May 29, during the Throne Speech debate, the Opposition Member for The Pas brought greetings from "the good people of the riding of The Pas, the town of The Pas, Opaskwayak Cree Nation, Grand Rapids, Easterville, Moose Lake, Cross Lake, Norway House, Cormorant and Wanless."[9] In the speech that followed, Oscar Lathlin used the word "racism" in a broad critique of the government's policy and programs that affect Aboriginal Manitobans. He provided examples to substantiate this fundamental charge. He cited long-standing treaty land entitlement issues; problems with the criminal justice system; recent deep cuts to advocacy, employment, and educational access programs for First Nations people; inadequate Northern infrastructure; and the endemic problem of child poverty.

Central to his critique was naming the problem of "attitude": a problem characterized by the government's lack of accountability for "the deplorable situation that aboriginal people find themselves in." Lathlin claimed that critical matters were consistently dismissed, reduced to federal or provincial hot potatoes: "When it is for [the Premier's] own convenience and the government's convenience, that is the only time that he says, 'I have jurisdiction.' Other times he tells aboriginal people *to go live in the bush* and not bother him." Summing up his assessment of the dominant politic of disavowal, Lathlin maintained that many of the people he represented were in fact "beginning to talk about racism as being central to the policies coming from this Premier and his government."[10]

Points of order were called on both sides of the House when, at the mid-point of his own address, the Premier reacted aggressively to what he called Lathlin's "reprehensible diatribe." Mr. Filmon asserted that he could be "as vicious and as mean" as Lathlin was, by saying that he had "heard oftentimes from people in [Lathlin's] constituency in The Pas that they regard him as a racist." Responding to a point of order from the Leader of the Opposition (Mr. Gary Doer), Premier Filmon replied: "Madam Speaker, I am doing nothing more than using exactly the same language as the member for The Pas used in his speech. If it is inappropriate, then—."[11] And while the Speaker, Louise Dacquay, attempted to bring the House to order, the Premier is alleged to have once again directed insult at the member for The Pas, this time saying from his seat, "you are a racist."[12] Claiming not to have heard these words, the Speaker promised to "peruse Hansard and report back to the House" at a later date.[13]

On June 7, Ms. Dacquay demanded the withdrawal of the offending "unparliamentary language" used on May 29 by *both* Mr. Lathlin and Premier Filmon. It was her "sense that all members of this House would prefer that a word with such negative connotations not be used in this House to describe either another individual or another individual's beliefs, policies or actions."[14] The Speaker made no attempt to distinguish between the members' respective use of the word, even though British parliamentary practice differentiates between charges made against individual members of the House, and those made regarding a collectivity or their actions.

At that time, both men complied with the ruling and withdrew their comments. Mr. Filmon regretted responding "in kind" to the comments that were made by Lathlin. For his part, Mr. Lathlin acknowledged "a lot of difficulty" in doing what was requested of him. He insisted that he had never called the First Minister "directly to his face a racist," and that while he would respect the ruling, he would "continue to do [his] job here as an MLA for The Pas whose riding consists of over 50 percent [of] aboriginal people."[15]

Approximately four months later, on October 11, 1995, Lathlin questioned the Minister of Natural Resources regarding the management of Lake Winnipeg's freshwater fishery. He expressed concern over a policy which, he argued, provided uneven access to the resource, giving twelve non-Aboriginal fishermen from the southern end of the lake "full run" of the lake, an effective monopoly, "while eighty percent of the fishermen in Manitoba are aboriginal people." In the course of this exchange, the Minister went so far as to admit that his government was aware that "there is agony and pain out there in terms of poor fishery in the north basin." Lathlin concluded by asking the Minister if he then considered the policy in question to be "fair, discriminatory, or racist?"

The Speaker immediately demanded the Opposition member "rephrase his question and withdraw the word 'racist.'" But Dacquay's order was put on hold when Steve Ashton, member for Thomspon, raised a Point of Order, counselling the Speaker to rule out of order only those comments ascribing "racism" to specific individuals. He strongly encouraged her not to rule out of order comments regarding "racist policies." To illustrate his point, Ashton provided the House with the notorious example of South Africa's apartheid regime. Adamantly maintaining her stand against "strong language" in the House, the Speaker took the matter under advisement, pending her return at a later date with a definitive ruling.[16]

On November 1, Ms. Dacquay deemed "out of order any use of the word 'racist' when it is used in this House to describe members of this House, another party represented in this Legislature, or a government of this province current or past." Her ruling also foreclosed on any future use of this "unparliamentary language" in critiques of the policies of a government or a political party. However, in elaborating her position, Dacquay did concede "that it should be possible, for example, for a member of this Chamber to refer to apartheid in South Africa as a racist policy." In fact, the Speaker pledged that she "[would] not rule that out of order when used in a similar context when members are speaking of governments and parties outside of this province."[17]

In response to the ruling, Oscar Lathlin maintained that he could not, "in all good conscience, withdraw the remarks that [he] made." Resisting the purifying geography of liberal democratic law, the Cree MLA challenged the eviction of his speech: his embodied, racialized knowing. He asserted a kind of counter-geography by restating his location within his "motherland" of Canada ("I do not have a motherland anywhere else"), a space which the House would agree (in liberal theory) entitles him to "freedoms granted to other Canadians, such as the freedom of speech." At the same time, and within this same imagined territory, Lathlin endeavoured (as he did in his earlier interventions) to re-territorialize both "the motherland" and the immediate ("symbolic"/"real") space of the Chamber, by bringing into the foreground the specific racialized sites of experience that educated and contributed to the production of his outlawed understanding. Lathlin submitted: "I have experienced racism practically all of my life. I have experienced racism in the school, in the workplace. Indeed, I live on a reserve, a reserve that comes from what I call a racist system."[18] When he ultimately failed to comply with the Speaker's request, he was named for disregarding the authority of the Chair, and was expelled from the House for the remainder of the sitting day.

What kind of space is a House that asserts the equality of its members, conferring on them the protection of equal rights and freedoms, only to revoke these rights when evidence of inequality is produced? In the spatial ordering of political relations, what spaces and what subjects can "speak" or be spoken for (and by whom) before anyone has even taken the floor for debate? To answer these questions, it is important to revisit assumptions that are so naturalized they seem to have lost the self-conscious quality of theory.

First and foremost, the House and the liberal democratic nation-space it represents are conceived of as spaces inhabited by abstract individuals who are equal in the eyes of the law. That is to say, by virtue of their "universal sameness" and their distinctly human capacity for reason, all human subjects are *a priori* entitled to the same rights.[19] In this foundational sense, Enlightenment thinking stands in apparent contrast with those earlier times when "natural" and religious hierarchies provided helpful justifications for radical social inequity. Yet in the context of the secular modern and liberal democratic world, a significant problem arises for those who would insist upon the exclusion of certain groups from the new economy of universal equality. In order to accomplish the exclusion of some subjects, without abandoning the now necessary and hegemonic principle of democratic rule, elites and their aspirants were obliged to produce exceptions to the universal rule of human equality. Defining the non-human and unreasonable natures of targeted identities (for example, women and racialized groups in the colonies) thus becomes pivotal to separating out those supposedly unequal subjects: locating them outside the Enlightenment frame of logic and far removed from the range of law's discerning ear and "universally" compassionate eye.

Drawing on an argument made by David Goldberg, Linda Martin Alcoff writes:"the 'universal sameness' that was so important for the liberal self required a careful containment and taxonomy of difference. Where rights require 'sameness,' difference must be either trivialized or contained in the Other across a firm and visible border."[20] On one side of the liberal border are reasonable people who are entitled to equal treatment. On the other are unreasonable people (i.e., the "vicious and mean" Oscar Lathlin) whose unreasonableness disentitles them from equal treatment. Consider the reprimand delivered by Premier Filmon at the beginning of this chapter:

> The rules of the House apply equally to all members of the House and the privileges of the House apply equally to all members of the House. If this member for The Pas wants to be able to be treated as an equal, then he ought to treat others as equals and not make the kind of discriminatory, inflammatory and irresponsible allegations that he made in this House last evening. . . .[21]

Simply by virtue of his Aboriginal presence in the white space of the House (itself enshrining traditions granted to the white settler nation by virtue of its whiteness, its Britishness), Oscar Lathlin insisted upon the existence of disavowed difference. His very body violated the racialized condition of "sameness," encoded as it is within the liberal credo of "universality." Yet even more threatening was Lathlin's commitment (and his capacity) to substantiate claims of racism with compelling evidence. Credible testimonies of difference threaten to rupture Canada's lofty self-image as a highly egalitarian society, and as "the No. 1 place in the world in which to live."[22] In 1995, the Member for The Pas was not willing to allow the "difference" he embodied to be trivialized. Within the bounds of a racist liberal logic, therefore, it became a matter of due course (here, a parliamentary technicality) that a subject who was already an outsider, and who persisted in "unreasonable" ("irresponsible" and less than fully human) behaviour, be evicted from a space demarcated by the firm and visible border of the House walls.

As Alcoff suggests, subjectivity is not only contained in bodies, not only read on the skin. The liberal paradox is ontological (concerned with who is and who is not a true human subject), but it is also inextricably spatial. People and their nations come to know themselves and one another within, through, and across the bounds of place. Radhika Mohanram writes: "Racial difference is also spatial difference."[23] When imbued with political agency the liberal vision demands not only the *embodiment*, but also the painful *emplacement* of hierarchic unevenness. That is to say, liberal democratic nations, built on an ideology of "rights that require sameness," rearticulate inequitable power relations between races as spatial difference.

In the Manitoba legislature, liberal paradox reasserts itself in the form of two distinct microgeographic zones: inside the House, and outside the House. Extending the inside/outside logic to its global limits, the November ruling also defined categorically non-racist zones (Manitoba, Canada) against disordered, racist territories "out there" (epitomized by South Africa). The production of bounded spaces of difference within and without the nation-space normalizes the aggressive policing of borders, and the punishment of bodies ruled "out of place." Alcoff concludes: "the result of these classification practices juxtaposed with liberal ideology [of 'universal sameness'] is a paradox wherein 'Race is irrelevant, but all is race.'"[24]

To this day in Canada, there is a persistent claim from First Nations, Inuit, and Métis people that their land rights have not been respected by either federal or provincial governments. In 1991, twenty-five Manitoba Indian bands were still denied their full land entitlements under the numbered treaties.[25] Edward Said notes that the main battle in imperialism is over land, "who owned the land, who had the right to settle and work on it, who kept it going, who won it back, and who now plans its future."[26] He maintains that this battle has been "reflected, contested, and even for a time decided in narrative." With racism declared an impossibility in official public narratives about the Canadian homeland, race and the effects of its construction within imperial–colonial power relations are also willfully elided. When racism is rendered unspeakable by parliamentary law, elite subjects *will* the erasure of places, communities, and claims that are, in fact, continually marked by racist practice and by resistance to such oppression.

Chief Allan Ross of Norway House told the Aboriginal Justice Inquiry that "Lady Justice is not blind in the case of Aboriginal people. She has one eye open."[27] Indeed, while legal narrative and authority are used to protect homogeneous order in an imagined land of equality, law remains indispensable to the formation of universality's companion landscapes of inequality. Radhika Mohanram reminds us that in the modern world it is the "inscription of land through legal means (such as in land titles or, by extension, the boundaries of nations) [that] functions to ground a community within certain parameters and to legitimize ownership."[28] As of 1991, outstanding land treaty entitlement in Manitoba exceeded one million acres of Crown land. Outstanding land treaty entitlements mean that the government of Manitoba is in debt to the First Nations of the province.[29] What results from liberal law's (apparently) split loyalties is this suppressed geography ("race is irrelevant") that is always about race, always about dominance, and always constructed as a hierarchy of contained, racialized, and bordered places. The sites Oscar Lathlin tried to talk back onto Manitoba's political map in 1995 give us a glimpse of a resistant counter-geography that could bring to the fore such outsider spaces.

In the case of the November 1st ruling, it is with law's customary collusion that the House legitimated an imagined territory of universality, while at the same time legitimately displacing unwelcome difference and reifying the inequality of provincial citizen-subjects. The silencing of Oscar Lathlin, secured by parliamentary law, produces the unspeakability of social relations that are constructed within legal bounds as radical inequality, as domination, and ultimately, as the emplacement of racial violence.

☐ All Spaces and Subjects Are Not Created Equal

Lessons in Elite Geography

During the May 29 Throne Speech debate, Premier Filmon's address deteriorated into the disorder of direct insult against Oscar Lathlin. In this section, I draw attention to the somewhat more restrained moments within the same discourse, to show how firmly the identity of an elite white subject is rooted in the racially "unmarked" space of "universal sameness." I re-enter the Premier's talk after he has made preliminary collegial remarks of welcome to the House. The Premier turned to nostalgic thoughts of Manitoba's past, on the occasion of the province's 125th birthday, celebrated in May 1995. In common colonial-nationalist terms, he described the early days of white settlement in Manitoba as the story of humble people making "a life and a nation built upon hard work . . . a nation that really stood for equality and democracy." In a gesture that recalls Alcoff's "trivialization" as a means of containing the Other, Mr. Filmon adds to this working-class scene of hardship the presence of "welcoming" "aboriginal brothers and sisters who shared all the bounties of this great and beautiful land with [the settlers] when they arrived."[30] And while he continues in this vein for some time (describing settler "gratitude" for indispensable survival assistance from Aboriginals), it is the personal story Filmon tells that roots the vague settler vision of an egalitarian society in the more palpable terrain of a specific (and modern) provincial world.

The following passage marks a shift in discursive gears and directly relates this transition to Lathlin's critical remarks: "I was interested in the comments of the member for The Pas as he talked just prior to my opportunity here tonight because it reminded me of my opportunities to spend time in the North and get to know, on a personal basis and on a friendly basis, many of our aboriginal people as I worked in the North in the summer of 1961 on the Nelson River." A civil engineer by training, the Premier related how he worked with a Manitoba Hydro survey crew that was preparing for the development of several hydroelectric projects on the Nelson River:

> We were, of all things, camped near what was then called Bladder Rapids. I am not sure that it is not flooded out now by one of the projects that was constructed. It was a fascinating summer because, prior to 1989, it was the summer in which we had the greatest forest fires in the history of the province, and they made literally an inferno of much of that area of northern Manitoba. As we stayed in our campsite in tents on the shore of the Nelson River, I might say that I marveled at the ingenuity and the self-sufficiency of the aboriginals who were part of the survey crew in which we were working. [31]

The Premier described at considerable length his northern relationships built on cross-cultural reciprocity. The humble greenhorn, he is taught to use an axe to cut line as they surveyed the area. He received instruction from "the aboriginals" in choosing campsites, and in the storage and preservation of meat. Another expertise he obviously takes great pride in is his ability to handle a canoe in rapids. "Some members opposite have seen me operate a canoe. As a matter of fact, it was part of our commercials in 1990. They [the aboriginals] taught us these things." Gary Filmon explains that, "we," in return, "taught them ultimately during the summer to use the transit and the level and the instruments of survey that we had, and it was a very good relationship, I might say, Madam Speaker."[32]

The imperial travels of Premier Filmon's youth chart routes from Cross Lake to the Grand Rapids forebay, from Cedar Lake to Brochet. In his desire to fashion a depiction of his innocence—a memory to fortify his political stance in the present—the fairly obvious relations of power that structure Filmon's travels are blatantly omitted. The myriad of path-clearing forces (of conquest, colonial, mercantile, state, military, and state "security" interests), the relations of dominance that make Filmon's penetration of the north possible, are obscured in this highly selective mapping of a homogeneous northern space. Instead, he draws on clichés of friendship and co-operation, and in an almost ludicrous image, the Premier describes being in Grand Rapids in 1962, where he worked "hand in hand, side by side" with Aboriginal people while developing hydro-electric projects there. Once again, in 1966, Filmon travelled north, up to the "almost mythical" Brochet and "all along the Churchill River." At that time, he was engaged in his master's thesis research, in which he studied possible alternatives to the (later realized) Churchill River diversion.[33]

Premier Filmon's autobiographical mapping of the province's northlands serves to reinforce, and give comforting content to, the open and abstract free space envisioned by liberalism. His is a nation-place where white bodies (especially white elite male bodies) enjoy unimpeded movement, and find themselves universally at home by means of endearing personal qualities—an openness to friendship and a willingness to labour from dawn to dusk. Although highly personalized, such a mapping finds no fault in the eyes of the law, parliamentary or otherwise. For indeed, the spatial reality of this human does nothing to disrupt the first and universal tenet of the liberal paradox (all "humans" are created equal). Neither does it disturb the workings of the second and contradictory clause, the submerged project of classifying and containing negative difference. In this landscape, the place-bound Aboriginals and their Indigenous "ingenuity" remain safely contained "in the bush," while their subjectivities achieve parliamentary presence only in the guise of the noble savage. Hence "difference" is produced and present, but it is quickly neutralized and assimilated into the imperial/colonial project, like the skills Filmon learned up north. Difference remains in the service of the greater task of provincial economic development.

The Manitoba Hydro Act

To further trace the complicity of law in the production of racialized space, the elite geography reproduced by Premier Filmon's speech can be juxtaposed with the contemporaneous and spatially coterminous landscape produced by law. To do so, I draw on the text of *An Act Respecting the Manitoba Hydro-Electric Board,* commonly known as the *Manitoba Hydro Act*, which was first passed in 1961. The Act granted the Manitoba Hydro-Electric Board (Manitoba Hydro) the right to provide electric power throughout the province. Its sweeping terms authorized an unbridled range of powers, consistent with the dramatic economic, environmental, social, and cultural outcomes it legitimated. Indeed, the devastating consequences of flooding in the north and mid-north areas of the province continues to be felt by those communities disregarded in the development process.

It is significant that most of the power provided by the Manitoba Hydro-Electric Board was generated on the Nelson River,[34] in the region of the province that southern centres conceive of as "northern." Yet, in true imperial fashion, Article 9 of the Act locates the principal offices of the corporation at the opposite end of the province, within the metropolitan area of Winnipeg. Article 15 establishes the "Powers of the corporation" that this metropole is imbued with. The corporation may

> (d) for temporary purposes, and with or without the consent of the owner, enter, remain upon, take possession of, and use, any property, real or personal, and erect, make, or place thereon any structure, installation, or excavation, and flood and overflow any land,[35] and accumulate and store water thereon;
>
> (e) acquire by purchase, lease, license, or otherwise, and hold, develop, construct, use, maintain, repair, operate, and improve, and sell, lease, or otherwise dispose of, any property, including, without limitation, land and works, in each case upon such terms and conditions as the board deems proper;
>
> . . .
>
> (g) enter into agreements and do all things proper or necessary for the due exercise of the powers mentioned in this section.

The rural northern margins, which serve as a primary resource-base to the urban centres in the south, are reproduced under highly partial terms. Even the "normal" implications of individual property ownership (not to mention those of non-Europeans' historical occupation and shared stewardship of the land) are pushed aside. In the face of authority, consent can be rendered optional.

The law is carving out a path for the disembodied agency of the Hydro-Electric Board, of the legislature, and of a majority non-Aboriginal society that stands to profit. Economically speaking, the capital-intensive nature of the electric power industry represents a significant cash cow for many provinces, and for the nation as a whole. The Canadian Electricity Association reports that, in 1995, "provincial electric utilities owned about 83 percent of Canada's total installed generating capacity and produced about 79 percent of total generated electricity."[36] According to their own figures, Manitoba Hydro is the fourth largest electrical utility in Canada.[37] Canada, the world's fifth largest producer of hydro electricity, enjoyed a net revenue of $1,163,401,000 in 1997.[38] It is clear that with imperial-style economic development in the foreground, the path that the law made needed to script northern space as a zone without humans who needed to be consulted or considered. Racialization is the process by which northern Aboriginal peoples are dehumanized and evicted from the liberal conceptual space of universal equality. A stern reflection on the legacies of flooding still borne by Aboriginal communities is found in the *Report of The Aboriginal Justice Inquiry of Manitoba*. Commissioners Hamilton and Sinclair put forward three specific recommendations related to the *Northern Flood Agreement*, a modern treaty perceived by Manitoba First Nations to be deeply inadequate.[39] The agreement was signed in 1977 to compensate five northern bands, and the province shared responsibility with the federal government for its implementation.

In July 1999, speaking to what was believed to be the first protest of its kind in Canada, Fox Lake Chief Mike Lawrenchuk told *The Winnipeg Free Press*, "Since Manitoba Hydro came here to benefit from our resources, we have lived a life of mostly misery and despair."[40] As a sign of protest, the Fox Lake band members (who were not covered under the terms of the *Northern Flood Agreement*) refused to accept federal treaty payment. Even though they had occupied a traditional land base in the Gillam area, the Fox Lake Cree did not have reserve status in the 1960s when people were evicted from their homes to make way for hydro dams on the Nelson River. In the case of Cross Lake (also in the constituency of The Pas), the band had been waiting twenty-two years for the implementation of the Agreement, to which they were signatories. On June 24, 1999, Cross Lake's problems were tragically illustrated by three suicide attempts, one of which resulted in the death of a twenty-six-year-old man.[41]

With the law's complicity, the northern margins and their "unequal" inhabitants are discursively produced as passive. In contrast, the hegemonic centre uses the punitive arm of the law to back itself up. Article 57 of the *Manitoba Hydro Act* describes fines and possible imprisonment for "[e]very person who violates any provision of this Act, or who neglects or refuses to comply with any order, regulation or direction of the board." Thus racialized outsider space is divided off from elite white space by means of "firm and visible borders," once again recalling the Goldberg–Alcoff formulation of the liberal paradox. One is reminded of the legal disciplinary measures of policing and punishing speech that put walls between Oscar Lathlin and the rest of the House. Without recourse to any "illegitimate" measure, the democratic locus of control can render itself nearly impenetrable to direct opposition.

Meanwhile, the corporate body that makes itself within this uneven grid can literally become the body that sits as a member in the legislature. Article 8 overrides the *Legislative Assembly Act* and permits a member of the Legislative Assembly, "who may also be a member of the Executive Council," to be a member of the board. This individual "may accept from the corporation salary or remuneration under this Act; and he does not thereby vacate or forfeit his seat, or incur any of the penalties imposed by the Legislative Assembly Act for sitting and voting as a member of the Legislative Assembly." Article 13 clarifies the limits of accountability:

> Neither the chairman of the board nor any officer, member, or employee of the corporation, nor anyone acting under the instructions of any of them or under the authority of this Act or the regulations is personally liable for any loss or damage suffered by any person by reason of *anything in good faith done*, caused, permitted, or authorized to be done, or omitted to be done, by him or them, pursuant to, or in exercise of, or supposed exercise of, the powers given by this Act or the regulations. (Emphasis added.)

Dominant identities escape the loss, damage, or suffering related to unequal access and unequal exercise of power. Unlike the subjects upon whom their decisions fall, elite identities are kept secure behind a shield of *good faith*, a principle used defensively in legislative and legal discourse. *Good faith* surfaces time and time again as the legal and cultural lynchpin in the construction and enactment of violating, and often violent, civic in/actions.

Members of the board are not held accountable, and the text simultaneously disassociates them from their progenitor, the provincial legislature and its House of representatives. Article 56 describes "the intention of the Legislature [as] being to give independent effect, to the extent of its powers, to every enactment and provision of this Act." At the same time, the "Ancillary powers" of Article 55(2) give the independent corporation or board the power "to do, or enforce the doing, of any act or thing":

> (a) all such powers shall be deemed also to be given as are necessary to enable the corporation or the board to do, or enforce the doing, of the act or thing; and
>
> (b) if the doing by the corporation or the board of any such act expressly authorized is dependent upon the doing of any other act not expressly authorized, the corporation or the board, as the case may be, has the power to do that other act.

In the first place, the corporation or board gains an individual autonomy in keeping with the template of the abstract, universal citizen governed by Reason (here, the board). In the second place, this corporate "individual" roams freely across social space and is given *carte blanche* access to Aboriginal spaces, not unlike the surveying Premier Filmon and the settlers before him. Finally, the text empowers the board or corporation with unlimited freedom of choice in terms of its *modus operandi*.

I want to make one final point with respect to the unbounded nature of power in this legal text. Throughout the fifty-eight articles of the Act, the powers described never appear to lack the capacity to "extend." Article 53(2) provides for the retroactivity of "any order, approval, or authorization, given to the corporation" as directed by the Lieutenant Governor in Council. Article 54 deals with other legal spaces and, by implication, with potential resistance from marginalized spaces by means of law, no doubt a concern for some of the legislators in 1970: "In case of conflict between this

Act and any other Act or law, this Act prevails unless expressly otherwise provided in any such other Act." In combination, these two articles bear resemblance to the Speaker's ruling on the word "racist" in November 1995. Both impose strict parameters on permitted debate (limits proper to a specific set of interests), and extend protection to this sacred discursive space through the law's mastery over time. In the Speaker's ruling, the future is reined in; in the *Manitoba Hydro Act*, the past is brought under elite white control.

I do not claim this to be a legal or even quasi-legal analysis of the *Manitoba Hydro Act,* but it is nevertheless important to understand the specific and entirely legal methods by which discriminatory practices secure themselves within a framework of liberal democratic right. The text in question puts into action a comprehensive, hierarchic, and prejudicial system of spaces marked as more or less "human"; populous places versus seemingly "empty" spaces; sites practised as differentially accessible; and zones produced as audible or inaudible, speakable or categorically unspeakable. Political and legal language remake the landscape through an Act, which operates as a point of transfer. By moving the power of "legitimated" racial privilege outward from the site of articulation in the legislature, through the disciplinary grids of public institutions (seen by some to benefit all citizens), a disembodied "universal" will circulates with impunity, in a network devoid of accountability. Manitoba's commodified and racialized spaces absorb and contain the harmful affects and effects of colonial race (economic, class, and gender) privilege in action, while they give literal and symbolic sustenance to the national (and deeply personal) dreams of innocent white subjects.[42]

These are the kinds of spaces the Member for The Pas tried to represent to the House in 1995. As Lathlin told the Speaker on May 30, "I can handle a lot of things, but when I have to listen to the Premier belittling me, calling me a racist, trying to turn things around—he first blames aboriginal people for coming into the city and creating havoc with his child poverty statistics—and then he goes on, when I ask questions, to call me a racist."[43] The law of the land expends considerable energy attempting to incarcerate its racialized subjects in places the law produces as peripheral, politically consigning them to "go live in the bush." The law is thereby complicit in protecting the sanctity of white privilege, and the places where privilege stakes its multiple claims.

☐ Rupturing "Universal" Space with Race

The very "out of place" quality of Oscar Lathlin's (not-white) Aboriginal body in the House introduced a kind of undertow into the democratic discourse of a provincial political performance. The outlawed Aboriginal body and the racialized places it signifies rupture the firm borders of liberalism's universal body politic, threatening and obliging a moment-by-moment reconstitution of the colonizer's identity and that of the colonial nation-space itself. In the May 1995 Throne Speech debate, Premier Filmon *needed* to fashion a non-racist identity in response to Oscar Lathlin's critique of his government. The Speaker's November ruling *needed* to fortify the image of a non-racist province, in order that political, cultural, and racial dominance (which is still the objective) be maintained in a highly legitimate and enlightened fashion.

On the other hand, as a body out of place—as a minority made visible by racism—the member for The Pas carried within himself traces of the places that have un/made him and other Aboriginal people in Manitoba. If he was to resist the purifying liberal geography of the House, the contingency of his identity as a racialized, colonized subject could position him for, and compel him to be, a certain kind of representation to the legislature. In direct contrast with the Premier's "autogeography," Oscar Lathlin's travel stories were not coterminous with his abstract universalist mapping of the province. Lathlin's Manitoba was made up of the lived spaces of the reserve and the residential school, the latter being a site of colonial silencing *par excellence*.[44]

☐ Looking through the Aboriginal Justice Inquiry

On May 30, Mr. Lathlin rose to address the House on a Matter of Privilege. He moved that the Premier be asked to withdraw and apologize for comments concerning himself made the previous day. Lathlin revisited issues he had raised during the Throne Speech debate, highlighting matters that substantiated his "unparliamentary" suggestion that the provincial government exhibited a racist attitude towards Manitoba's Aboriginal people:

> I said last evening that I could go on and on. I mentioned the AJI-293 recommendations, 101 of which do not need federal government

authority. One hundred and one recommendations of the AJI are strictly provincial. The provincial government could have gone ahead and implemented some, if not all, of the 101 recommendations in the AJI.[45]

Lathlin again referred to the Aboriginal Justice Inquiry (AJI) when he described the role he played as Chief of The Pas band, at a time when the Inquiry hearings were held in the town of The Pas (October 1988) and on The Pas Reserve (January 1989). In his intervention, however, the Premier chose to focus almost exclusively on defending a broad range of government cutbacks critiqued by Lathlin. He chose to completely disregard the repeated references to the AJI and its 101 provincial recommendations. The Premier closed with assertions regarding his government's strong track record in working closely "with the people of the North, with people of all backgrounds."[46]

The Aboriginal Justice Inquiry was created in response to the outcry surrounding two specific incidents in late 1987 and early 1988. The first was the controversial November 1987 trial of two men for the 1971 murder of Helen Betty Osborne. The second was the death of J.J. Harper, executive director of the Island Lake Tribal Council, following a March 9, 1988 encounter with a City of Winnipeg police officer. Detailed discussion of these events is contained in volume two of the AJI *Report*.[47] The controversy surrounding the Osborne and Harper cases, coupled with long-standing "harsh and pervasive" Aboriginal criticism of the justice system, led to the creation by Order-in-Council of the "Public Inquiry into the Administration of Justice and Aboriginal People" on April 13, 1988.

The mandate of the Inquiry was "to examine the relationship between Aboriginal people and the justice system, and to suggest ways it might be improved."[48] Associate Chief Justice A.C. Hamilton and Associate Chief Judge C.M. Sinclair (Manitoba's first and Canada's second Aboriginal judge) were appointed to head the Inquiry. Making a meaningful revision of the dubious naming by Order-in-Council, and later by provincial statute (a naming that suggests Aboriginal people are "administered" along with Justice), the commissioners themselves referred to their project as "The Aboriginal Justice Inquiry."

The shift in perspective that resulted from the commissioners' efforts went well beyond a renaming of their task. Commissioners Hamilton and Sinclair established a number of juridically unorthodox, informal methodologies that enabled them to effectively gather Aboriginal communities' perceptions.[49] Non-Aboriginal persons were also encouraged to make presentations. Representatives from various levels of government, police forces, and social agencies participated. Yet the significant feature of the Commissioners' approach was their commitment to hearing directly from Aboriginal people. This commitment led the Inquiry to visit over thirty-six Aboriginal communities, approximately twenty of which were accessible only by winter roads and air travel. In addition, they held hearings in seven other Manitoba locations, including extensive hearings in the City of Winnipeg, and in five provincial correctional institutions. Appendix III of the commissioners' report lists these other hearing locations, like Cross Lake, Grand Rapids, Norway House, Brochet-Barren Lands, The Pas Reserve, Shamattawa, Tadoule Lake, and Stony Mountain Institution.[50]

The authorization of these spaces in the essentially epistemological work of the Inquiry is important. The Inquiry created an institutional space for a critical process of oppositional and situated knowledge-production. A map of the hearing locations included in Volume One of the Report illustrates the subversive potential of such an exercise. Political and cartographic convention is subverted here, as every hearing location is given the same visual presence on the map. The small communities of Pukatawagan and Moose Lake, for example, are marked with dots equal in size to the one locating "Winnipeg."

At the community hearings alone, the commissioners heard presentations from approximately one thousand people in Manitoba, and travelled more than 18,000 kilometres to do so.[51] The collective knowledge of these subjugated lived spaces reflects highly inequitable raced social relations in the province, relations which are obscured in dominant political and juridical narrative. The testimonies and submissions, coupled with the research results of the Inquiry, bring to mainstream attention a law of the land dramatic in its systemic racism. Perhaps the most evocative geography of injustice explored by the Inquiry is that of Manitoba's carceral spaces. At these sites, the boundaries that locate and limit universal rights and freedoms stand in stark and shocking relief.

In 1989, the superintendent of Stony Mountain federal penitentiary provided the Inquiry with an overview of federal incarceration rates for Aboriginal people in Manitoba. The percentage of Aboriginal inmates in federal custody in the province had climbed from 22 per cent in 1965, and

33 per cent in 1984, up to an even 40 per cent in 1989. The Manitoba Department of Justice told the Inquiry that 47 per cent of the Headingley provincial jail population was Aboriginal. At the Portage jail for women, 67 per cent of all admissions were women of Aboriginal descent. As of October 1, 1990, Aboriginal youth accounted for 64 per cent of the inmates at the Manitoba Youth Centre and 78 per cent of the admissions to the Agassiz Youth Centre.[52]

Even more shocking, bail and pretrial detention figures (according to the AJI's analysis of Provincial Court data) revealed that more than 90 per cent of female young offenders held on remand in the province were Aboriginal.[53] By 1989, the Aboriginal population of all provincial correctional institutions in Manitoba was 57 per cent. The Aboriginal population of federally and provincially administered institutions combined was 56 per cent.[54] In 1991, Aboriginal people represented 11.8 per cent of Manitoba residents.[55]

Commissioners Hamilton and Sinclair condensed their observations as follows: "Aboriginal people, depending on their age and sex, are present in the jails up to five times more than their presence in the general population. Moreover, 'the full extent of the problem is not known because statistics underestimate the extent of Aboriginal representation in the . . . correctional system.'" Indeed, today the commissioner's 1991 report is statistically outdated. According to a 1999 Elizabeth Fry Society fact sheet, Aboriginal people nationwide are nine times as likely to go to prison than are the majority of the non-Aboriginal population in Canada.[56]

Clearly there exist radical, yet forcibly suppressed, contradictions within Euro-Canada's view of the equalizing "scales of justice." Grand Chief David Courchene summarized the matter at one of the public hearings held in Winnipeg:

> The overwhelming evidence coming before you from our people is that the fairness and equity of the Canadian justice system do not apply to us. In relation to Canadian First Nations, the system is profoundly unbalanced. More often than not, we do not experience, nor do we see, justice being done; nor do our families and neighbours; nor did our parents and grandparents. This Inquiry cannot fail to note, like a sinew, or thread, linking the testimony of our people, not so much anger as profound disillusion; a hardening, a deepening, an increasing, loss of respect for the Canadian justice system.[57]

Significantly, when Oscar Lathlin argued the legitimacy of his use of the term "racist" to describe systemic injustices—including those apparent in the justice system—Premier Filmon and the House majority rejected his claims. This disavowal came in the face of a commissioned report that insisted otherwise, and which drew on the wisdom of over one thousand provincial citizens. Playing a complex shell game, the parliamentary law of the House closed its ears to the testimony that law itself delivered via judicial inquiry, a testimony to injustices in which law found itself complicit. In this paradoxical yet "legitimate" manner, the Premier (and the province) may with impunity take no action on the injustices named by Lathlin and documented in the *Report of the Aboriginal Justice Inquiry of Manitoba*.

If disillusionment links the testimonies of Aboriginal people—betrayed, marginalized, and sometimes brutalized by the justice system—to zones of social marginality, and segregation, then shared social and economic privilege link elite speakers to the legislature, the symbolic and "real" hub of provincial political power. It is revealing to note, as Oscar Lathlin did,[58] that in 1995 Premier Filmon was the member for Tuxedo, one of the most affluent Winnipeg neighbourhoods. In 1990, the Manitoba Bureau of Statistics reported that residents of Tuxedo had median household incomes of $40,000 "and over." Deputy Premier Jim Ernst represented the constituency of Charleswood, the popular suburban neighbourhood west of Tuxedo. Charleswood residents also earned median incomes in the $40,000 "and over" bracket.[59] Compare these figures with the median household income in Lathlin's riding of The Pas, listed between $21,000 and $26,000.[60] No income figures are available for the residents of Headingley jail, located outside Winnipeg, fifteen minutes west of Charleswood on the Trans-Canada Highway.

Carol LaPrairie observes that "the provinces with the highest levels of unemployment, the lowest levels of education and income for both on-reserve and off-reserve registered Indians (Saskatchewan, Alberta, and Manitoba) also have the most disproportionate incarceration levels." She suggests that with "high off-reserve migration and permanent residency of aboriginal people in these settings, inner cores of some western cities show signs of becoming entrenched aboriginal-ghetto areas."[61] Winnipeg economist John Loxley estimated, in his study commissioned by the Royal Commission on Aboriginal Peoples, that Aboriginal people represented about 84 per cent of Winnipeg's inner-city population in 1993. The incidence of poverty among Aboriginal families in the city was in the region of 60–70 per cent, compared with the (1989) rate for Winnipeg families in general, which was at 18.9 per cent. In 1991, 61 per cent of all Aboriginal adults in the city were without work.[62]

As these figures suggest, Lathlin's Manitoba is a drastically different homeplace than the one in Premier Filmon's imagination. Clearly, if one wishes to challenge the abstract rules of liberal universality, it is important to acknowledge not only the specificity of the body speaking but also what kind of homeplace they are speaking from. A conscious analysis of race and space affords just such a grounded perspective. We are able at once to reconnect race-blind liberal orderings of the House to intimate (lived and imagined) realms of protected whiteness, *and* to those racialized spaces and subjects *by legal means* are both actively produced, and vehemently disavowed: contemporary colonial power relations in action.

Oscar Lathlin was silenced and expelled from the House on November 1, 1995, only four years after the publication of the AJI *Report*. Ironically, November 1995 saw a momentary revival of mainstream interest in the issues championed by the Inquiry. Aboriginal women and men initiated public actions across the province. For example, accompanied by members of a women's wellness circle, Justine Osborne carried out an 800-kilometre March for Justice that began in Norway House on November 13 and culminated weeks later on the steps of the Legislative Building. The women were protesting the upcoming full parole of the only man convicted in the murder of Osborne's eldest daughter, Helen Betty.[63]

That same November, thirty people from the Pukatawagan reserve were going into their thirtieth day camped out in teepees at the Forks of the Red and the Assiniboine Rivers in the centre of Winnipeg. Minutes away from the provincial legislature, the group of primarily women and children occupied an open snow-covered space to protest the critical housing shortage in their northern reserve community, a situation forcing an average of ten to twelve people to share a residence. According to the Aboriginal press, the housing crisis in Pukatawagan was seen as a major factor contributing to the spread of tuberculosis and other disease in the community. Social and health conditions there were further aggravated by substandard drinking water (related to a botched Indian Affairs sewage project), and by the legacy of a fuel spill that had contaminated about one-third of reserve land with cancer-causing agents. The spill was caused by a former hydro diesel generating station.[64]

How can the elites of Manitoba's legislature be so sure that *their* House, and *their* province are in no way connected to the racialized territories invoked by Oscar Lathlin? Within a broader national and international context, how can Manitoba (or the rest of the nation, for that matter) consider itself to exist somehow outside the racist architecture of uninterrupted imperial and colonial history? Judging by the November 1st ruling, it is clear that they (and "we") are by no means sure. Would not any "reasonable" person find it strange that Louise Dacquay's ruling on the word "racist" does not collapse in upon itself, confronted as the province was in the early 1990s with the explicitly racist geography detailed in the AJI *Report*? By the same token, Dacquay's reference to South Africa, the infamous, distant place Manitobans and Canadians can turn to for confirmation of our anti-racist goodness, simply cannot contain all contemporary racism, when countered with more proximate geographies of colonial dominance.

Oppositional geographies like the one produced by the AJI and reproduced in critical, political mobilizations of its meanings, repatriate to Manitoba and to the Canadian nation as a whole a disavowed landscape of racialized violence. Without the words "racist" and "racism," and without an understanding of these concepts as they are manifest within today's colonialism, there is no language to describe what shaped the sacrifice of Aboriginal land, lives, and lifeways to one vision of economic development. There is no language to comprehend the ways in which our justice system continues to systemically oppress and marginalize Aboriginal people. To aggressively separate out and legislate what can be perceived and named as "racist" from what must remain concealed from the exclusive purview of a consensual dominant society is itself a racist practice. Tracey Lindberg, an Aboriginal law student, protests: "This is my personhood, and we are dismembering it. Its main organs are taken out: the facts, the issues, and the ratio."[65]

David Goldberg maintains that "it is not just that the limits of our language limit our thoughts; the world we find ourselves in is one we have helped to create, and this places constraints upon how we think the world anew."[66] AJI Commissioners Hamilton and Sinclair recognize "that Canadians know relatively little about Aboriginal history and culture. Few Manitobans have had the opportunity to learn about their fellow citizens of Aboriginal background."[67] In 1995 the punitive mapping of "universal sameness" over resistant assertions of unspeakable, racialized difference proves that the chasms dividing us are great, and further, that liberal democracy encodes within itself an enduring desire for such incommensurability. How, then, will the excision of the word "racism" from official public talk remedy these gaps in our knowing of one another, particularly when the problem is not only a matter of language but also one of spatialized and embodied racial and cultural privilege? Quite clearly, it will not. Unless we protest the silencing, the world we find ourselves in is the inequitable one we have helped to create, and this places constraints upon how we think—and on how we may enact—the world, ourselves, and each other, anew.

Kathleen Kirby tells us that

> part of the function of mapping . . . is to ensure that the relationship between knower and known remains unidirectional. The mapper should be able to "master" his environment, occupy a secure and superior position in relation to it, without it affecting him in return. This stance of superiority crumbles when the explorers' cartographic aptitude deteriorates. To actually be in the surroundings, incapable of separating one's self from them in a larger objective representation, is to be lost.[68]

Oscar Lathlin's re-territorialization of provincial space sought to reverse the relationship between knower and known—a reversal that would turn the November 1st ruling (the House, and the nation) on its head. Making "speakable" the evidence of colonial racism threatens the liberal subject not only with being lost, but also with the very loss of a dominant sense of self in local and national space. Such claims force that subject into a new and disordering proximity with an environment that calls for accountability, and with a world in which she or he has already been enmeshed. By resisting the stance of dominance desired by imperial cartographers and contemporary legislators alike, this chapter follows Lathlin's lead. It calls for analytic practices that make visible not only the evidence of legally normalized race-based oppression, but also the lines of accountability that link conditions of racialized marginality to the social systems, groups, institutions and actors who stand to benefit from an undisrupted status quo. As the Manitoba case demonstrates, this transgressive task remains paramount for those who would challenge "a nation of people who decided that their world view would combine agendas for individual freedom and mechanisms for devastating racial oppression."[69]

CHAPTER 7

Making Space for Mosques

Struggles for Urban Citizenship in Diasporic Toronto

Engin F. Isin and
Myer Siemiatycki

On October 2, 1995, several hundred

Muslims "stormed out" of a meeting of the then East York Council. The Toronto area municipal council had just rejected a proposal to establish a mosque in a vacant factory building because the mosque was twenty-six parking spaces short of the required 130 spaces. "Let's get out of here," some reportedly declared. "This is a racist vote."[1] Even after East York Council finally approved a scaled-down version of the mosque, the experience of securing space for prayer in East York still pained mosque president

Mr. Abdur Ingar, who believed "there are huge double standards that are preventing Muslims from having the same access to their religious freedoms as others."[2]

The East York saga lurched from impasse to accord and back again over the next year. Searching for a permanent site to replace rented facilities serving East York's large South Asian Muslim community, the Islamic Society of Toronto (IST) had purchased an unused low-rise industrial site. Places of worship (of diverse faiths) are commonly located in Toronto's post-war suburban industrial landscape. Deindustrialization has made these properties available and relatively affordable. Typically, these sites are well served by road and highway access, which is significant for mosques whose congregants might travel to prayer services several times a day from their places of residence, work, or study.

The primary concern raised against the mosque by East York's Planning Department and some of its politicians was that mosque occupancy would cost the municipality over $90,000 in lost taxes due to the tax-exempt status of places of worship. Yet churches are commonplace in East York's business districts, and places of worship are now permitted in industrial zones across Toronto.[3] The mosque's strongest champion on council, Mayor Michael Prue, argued that the lost taxes were minimal compared with both the municipality's $60-million budget and a religious group's right to practise its faith.[4] *Toronto Star* columnist David Lewis Stein argued that a municipality so desperate for $90,000 that it would deprive a group a place to worship had "outlived its usefulness."[5]

In July 1995, East York Council reversed an earlier planning committee decision to approve the mosque in principle by a close vote of five to four. Three months later, the mosque was stymied by a six-to-three council vote on the grounds that insufficient parking was made available, despite a report to the contrary from a prominent transportation planning firm acting for the mosque. Yet at least four churches in East York had succeeded in gaining exemptions from similar parking requirements that were more stringent than those prevailing in most other Toronto area municipalities.[6] Newspaper editorials and Catholic and Jewish leaders supported the Islamic Society of Toronto in condemning the council's decision. Stein suggested that, for some members of council, "quibbling about parking is just a means to keep the mosque out of there [altogether]."[7]

In the winter of 1996, East York Council finally approved the mosque after the Islamic Society of Toronto agreed to reduce the site's worship space and demolish part of the factory for added parking. While East York finally had a mosque, many of its worshippers suspected that their faith had singled out their proposal for undue scrutiny. This specific struggle was one of many for Toronto's growing Islamic population seeking appropriate places of worship. Yet, as we shall argue, the issues in the struggle were deeper than finding a place of worship to practise religious freedoms and faith; they also involved the articulation of Muslim groups in a way that recognized their presence both symbolically and spatially. These forays into civic politics by Muslims represented their first collective claims to urban citizenship and belonging through rights to urban space. The responses of Toronto area municipalities reveal that the fate of newcomers to the city and the city's own identity as one of the world's most cosmopolitan cities are entangled. How do we interpret these conflicts that are simultaneously about space, identity, faith, and fate and that are increasingly visible in urban politics? This chapter examines three additional case studies of mosques struggling to make space for themselves in the Toronto area and incorporates the issues of citizenship, racialization, identity, and space. We would like this chapter to be a contribution towards understanding what Jane M. Jacobs aptly names "the complicated politics of the production of urban space."[8]

☐ Diaspora Groups in Toronto

Global migration during the late twentieth century has dramatically changed Toronto's demographics. The city has transformed, in less than a generation, from an overwhelmingly white Christian society to a multiracial, multi-faith society. While commonly referred to earlier in the century as "the Belfast of the North," following the 1998 municipal amalgamation, the newly established mega-city of Toronto adopted the phrase "Diversity is our Strength" as its official motto. (In 1998, the Province of Ontario imposed municipal amalgamation on the six municipalities of Toronto, York, East York, North York, Scarborough, and Etobicoke.) The amalgamated city's new slogan certainly captured Toronto's current status as one of the world's most cosmopolitan immigrant destinations. During the 1990s, four out of every ten immigrants to Canada settled in the Greater Toronto Area (GTA), which included the City of Toronto and surrounding suburbs. By the end of the decade, immigrants made up 48 per cent of the City of Toronto's population.[9]

The countries of origin of immigrants coming to Toronto have changed dramatically over time. Before 1961, Toronto's immigrant population was composed almost exclusively (92 per cent) of people born in the United Kingdom and Europe. Since the 1960s, the number of European-born immigrants in Toronto has steadily decreased, representing just 17 per cent of those settling in Toronto (with Poland as the most common European country), while the number of immigrants from Asia and the Middle East, Central and South America, the Caribbean, and Africa steadily increased. By 1996, six out of ten new immigrants living in Toronto were born in Asia and the Middle East, with Hong Kong, Sri Lanka, and the People's Republic of China being the most frequent countries of origin.

In the print and visual media, as well as in official discourse, Toronto appears to have harmoniously "integrated" these groups into the "mainstream culture." The federal policy of multiculturalism gives them legitimacy, yet underneath these representations of harmony and commitment to multiculturalism lurks a more problematic reality. Many diaspora groups in Toronto occupy a marginal and racialized position in the city's social space.[10] A recent study of socio-economic conditions in Toronto found that racialized immigrant groups in the city suffer extraordinarily high levels of poverty, severe levels of unemployment, overrepresentation in low-skill jobs, and low home-ownership rates. As author Michael Ornstein concluded, Toronto is a site of "pervasive inequality among ethno-racial groups."[11] In a 2001 study focusing on integrating diverse communities in Toronto, the authors reported that "Toronto continues to display a surprising tolerance for inequalities rooted in identity."[12] Citizenship—defined not only as a legal status but also as participation *and* influence over the city's economic, social, cultural, and political spheres—has eluded many members of racialized groups.

It is useful to make a distinction between legal (formal) and sociological (informal) spheres of citizenship. The latter includes, among other things, those practices of immigrants that claim public space as their own to foster the formation of new group identities. Records of street parades, demonstrations, media presence, and park and civic square permits portray diaspora groups actively staking claims in their new urban milieu. Yet an examination of immigrant group involvement in formal and institutional arenas of citizenship suggests a more marginal experience. For example, immigrant participation in both municipal elections and the debate over the amalgamation of the constituent municipalities of Metropolitan Toronto into the Greater Toronto Area reveals a more tenuous attachment to Canadian society.[13]

New critical urban research on immigrants rejects the earlier mainstream urban research that focuses on immigrants as the Other, or as subjects of integration and assimilation. Instead, the new research is concerned with how diaspora groups make and re-make space to assert their citizenship rights through articulating strategic differences that draw upon their religion and culture. This research has expanded to include the relationship between citizenship rights and cities. It is in that sense that urban citizenship has become the main arena in which new rights are claimed and existing rights are maintained and redefined.[14] How Muslim diaspora reshapes urban space by strategically articulating certain needs and how it encounters equally strategic resistances is the subject of this chapter. We explore the intersections of identity, citizenship, and urban space in diaspora Toronto, critically examine the emerging literature on immigration and metropolis, and explore its implications and usefulness for empirical research and urban politics in the global era. We then focus on the conflicts arising when Muslim groups attempt to build mosques across the GTA, and the symbolic and material resistance they have had to overcome to do so.

☐ Making Muslim Space: What is Urban Citizenship?

Today, ethnic, racial, ecological, and gender groups are making new demands for group-differentiated citizenship rights. In many Western nation-states, for example, women are fighting to expand their citizenship rights to include reproductive control, access to childcare, pay equity, and safe cities. Similarly, gays and lesbians are struggling to claim rights already extended to heterosexual couples, such as spousal benefits and common-law arrangements.[15] The struggle for recognition and social justice revolves around new claims to inclusion and engagement with the polity in which groups seek membership in a qualitatively different way. Yet Muslim groups and the strategies they articulate for claiming rights to citizenship encounter particularly intense resistances and become the subject of intense scrutiny. To put it another way, while the discourse of citizenship invokes universal entitlements available to all, some "strangers" may be cast into the role of outsiders by the dominant culture. This has been the experience of Muslim groups in North American and European cities. Edward Said contends that "[f]or decades in America there has been a cultural war against the Arabs and Islam."[16] But in Europe this orientation has been even more intense than in America. In France, notes Sophie Body-Gendrot, the mantle of the allegedly unassimilable and undesirable immigrant has been transferred to Muslims. "Muslim populations," she observes, "are now ascribed the stereotypes which had been attributed to Jews, Italians and Poles in the French cities of the 1920s."[17]

There are two reasons for the resistance that Muslims have encountered in the West over the past decade that merit a brief discussion. First, since the collapse of the Soviet Union and the end of the Cold War, the emergence of political Islam in the Middle East, Southeast Asia, and Africa has been received with a moral panic in the West. Current tensions ostensibly between Islam and the West are now viewed not only as a global threat but also, given the significant presence and growth of Muslim groups in the West, as a potential domestic threat. Images of past clashes between Christians and Muslims are conjured up and linked to the alleged incompatibility between Islam and democracy and citizenship.[18] These images reinforce the possibility of an impending Islamic threat, which in turn shapes attitudes towards Muslim groups in Western cities.

North America and Europe have both experienced new waves of Muslim immigration from Asia, Africa, Eastern Europe, and the Middle East, making the assimilation of Muslims a particularly contentious issue. The presence of significant Muslim groups challenges established norms of citizenship through symbolic struggles such as women wearing the veil and burka and the construction of mosques. While Muslim groups in Western Europe and America increasingly face a combination of anti-Muslim racism and xenophobia, these orientations are grounded on systemic racialization of Islam. Thus, the continuing struggles of Muslim groups over questions of immigration, identity, citizenship, and the recognition of Muslim rituals and practice confront immanent strategies of racialization that are based on centuries of white Christian domination.[19]

Yet, and this is the second reason Muslim groups encounter resistances, it would be a mistake to assume that Muslims in Western cities are simply seeking accommodation. Although Muslims find themselves in countries that vary demographically, socially, and juridically, their shared experiences have produced some commonalities in their engagement with the Islamic tradition and their modalities of creating Muslim groups. They have not struggled for recognition and negotiated for rights in isolation:

Muslim groups today are tied together globally through a range of institutions and media that further suggest that the dispersion of Muslim groups must be seen as a diaspora. To put it another way, while it is important to resist strategies of racialization that constitute Muslim groups as a domestic threat, it is equally important to see the increasing presence of Muslim groups as another challenge to universal liberal citizenship.[20]

Admittedly, the resources Muslims draw upon for the formation of their identities are not isolated, dispersed, and accidental but are connected and shared with other social groups. In that sense, Muslim groups invoke, mobilize, and assemble strategies of group formation that have been invented by various social movements in the last few decades, for example the civil rights, women's liberation, and environmental movements, and even some movements of the Christian Right.[21] However, encounters and enactments such as building mosques, adoption of certain dress codes, differentiated gender roles, claims for education rights, organizing fundraisers, and marches and events all constitute strategies of group formation that require analysis and discussion to better highlight the specific and general aspects of the Muslim diaspora's challenge to liberal universal citizenship.

For these two reasons our investigations of the formation of Muslim groups move us beyond calls for multicultural citizenship, differentiated citizenship, or multi-layered citizenship.[22] Notwithstanding their differences, these calls consider citizenship as a bundle of rights that are progressively expanded to accommodate claims by various social groups. We consider how Muslim groups destabilize citizenship in a more fundamental way, calling into question citizenship's racialized and orientalist grounds. We show how the universal sameness of liberalism produces a containment of racialized Others across firm and visible borders that are both symbolic *and* spatial. Our focus is on spatial strategies that Muslim groups use, especially the building of mosques. The issue of space is particularly significant for Muslim groups because it is well known that Islamic conception of space is unique. As Regula Burckhardt Qureshi argues, Islamic discourse assumes that Muslim space in essence is where Muslims prevail. For Muslims the mosque is *any* place where Muslims pray—a restaurant, a gathering place, or a home can become a place of worship. The "multiplicity of purpose and flexibility of space" is a pervasive theme in Islamic discourse. For Qureshi, this multiplicity marks the history of Islamic "built space" for the people's use, which cannot be reduced to meaning visual and accessible to reification, as it is interpreted in Western scholarship. Rather, "Islamic praxis transcends local space primarily by aural, not visual, communication."[23]

Similarly, Barbara Daly Metcalf argues that it is ritual and sanctioned practices that are a priority and it is these practices that create "Muslim space," which does not require juridically claimed territory or formally consecrated or architecturally specific space. For Metcalf, Muslim ritual requires no "sacred place." Thus, there is no formula of consecration or deconsecration of a site of worship. Historically, mosque sites have been used not only for praying but also for everything from doing business to mobilizing community. It is not surprising, then, that among North Americans, the term mosque is often used to describe a group of people uniting for worship, rather than to describe a building.[24] While Qureshi and Metcalf isolate a significant aspect of the uniqueness of Islamic space, empirical evidence from different cities indicates that mosque-building has been a crucial strategy of identity formation for Muslim groups.

John Eade argues, for example, that the appearance of mosques and community centres in London, England, has visibly reminded non-Muslims of the expansion of Muslim groups in certain urban neighbourhoods. "The construction and use of these buildings has been part of a process of making new demands upon public space, a process that has become embroiled with non-Muslim concerns over a visible and audible Muslim presence."[25] In Eade's interpretation, mosques have clearly become places not only for prayer but also for representation of the Muslim presence. The mosques in London's East End have, in this regard, stimulated a wide-ranging debate. The debate implicitly addresses the symbolic significance of Islamic buildings in a predominantly non-Muslim country. Whether using a historic building or using an all-purpose centre, Muslims have found themselves severely constrained by resistances beyond their control. Yet they have succeeded in creating mosque congregations and, in the East London Mosque, a site that physically and audibly asserts the Muslim presence.[26]

In American cities, the demand for what is seen as visual authenticity in a mosque intensified in the 1990s. Muslim groups in the U.S. have increasingly bypassed the "melting pot" and have asserted a Muslim identity as a better alternative. These groups see themselves as part of the diaspora; they have a sense of identity and linkage to the *umma*, or worldwide Muslim community, which they use as a strategy for resisting the racialization and marginalization they encounter in their spatial settings. Now that some Muslim groups have started to express "dome and minaret envy," it is important to document and investigate how this expression mobilizes resistance to racialization.[27] In the Toronto area, as we will see, attempts to build mosques with a distinct Islamic architectural design have engendered and exposed deep-seated neighbourhood resistance.

While Qureshi and Metcalf are right to emphasize the unique Islamic conception of space, it is misleading to conclude that Muslim groups in Western cities transcend space and do not want to enact themselves spatially. On the contrary, spatial strategies are crucial to helping Muslims constitute themselves as social groups and make themselves present in civic and political space. That mosques acquire a symbolic and material significance and meaning in the process is all the more important not because Muslims reproduce an essentialized conception of space or of mosques, but because they use strategically appropriate Islamic symbols—among which the mosque is the most potent—to articulate their group rights. So while citizenship bespeaks an affirmation of rights, these rights must contend with the resistances they encounter. In that sense, the use of spatial strategies is no different from other social movements. As David Goldberg argues, racialization "becomes institutionally normalized in and through spatial configuration."[28]

Muslim attempts to create space for mosques in Western cities thus become part of what Jane M. Jacobs describes as "the racialized politics of differentiation."[29] The Canadian Muslim identity is constructed by the dominant culture as both a religious and a racialized minority—with its predominant South Asian, African, and Middle East composition. This outsider image constitutes a resistance to Muslim citizenship claims. It is also a critical sphere of engaged citizenship as Muslims resist their collective exclusion from the urban space.

☐ Muslims' Struggle Over Space

There is a growing recognition that land use conflicts have become particularly acute flashpoints of tension for racialized diaspora groups in global cities. "Products of hyper-mobile capital and complex human migrations," Leonie Sandercock observes, "perhaps the most visible characteristics of these cities are struggles over space, which are really two kinds of struggle: one a struggle of life space against economic space, the other a struggle over belonging. Who belongs where and with what citizenship rights, in the emerging global cities?"[30] These struggles over space, however, are simultaneously cultural and political because globalization ensures the presence of large immigrant groups who are subjected to various forms of racialization for the functioning of the global city. Thus, the claims of racialized immigrants to citizenship are fought on the terrain of the city, which can be interpreted as "rights to the city."[31]

Struggles over space have been the most recurring conflicts between immigrants and local governments in the Greater Toronto Area. To be sure, other municipal issues and services such as policing (particularly police shootings of visible minorities) and schooling (notably streaming and heritage language programs) have periodically mobilized various immigrant groups. But the issue that has recently troubled more racialized diaspora groups in the municipalities of the Greater Toronto Area has been land use and zoning.

The centrality of urban space as a site of conflict emerged from a survey we conducted in 1997 of the senior administrative staff of all thirty-five upper- and lower-tier municipalities then comprising the GTA. The questions asked whether there had ever been conflicts between diaspora groups and their municipal government; the responses indicated that seventeen of the thirty-five municipalities had experienced at least one such dispute. Conflicts were recorded in the lower-tier municipalities of York, East York, Scarborough, North York, Etobicoke, Oakville, Mississauga, Brampton, Vaughan, Richmond Hill, Markham, and Oshawa as well as the upper-tier municipalities of Halton, Peel, York, and Metropolitan Toronto. In fourteen of these seventeen municipalities, the conflicts (more than one in some municipalities) involved zoning disputes over land use: conflicts over attempts to establish or enlarge mosques occurred in at least nine municipalities; conflicts arose over the character of Chinese retail malls or the location of funeral homes in five municipalities; and conflicts arose over the location of Jamaican community centres in two municipalities.

Why have land use and zoning been a source of conflict for immigrants in the Greater Toronto Area? There is a variety of factors that contribute to these conflicts. Land use in cities has proven inherently political and contentious. Owners of property can be counted on to object to new land uses they feel will undermine the enjoyment or value of their property. Planning laws entrench neighbouring property rights in a variety of ways. Nearby residents and property owners must be notified of proposed land use changes and invited to offer their opinions at public municipal meetings. The criteria established by provincial statutes for assessing whether intended spatial transformations are appropriate often emphasize conformity with existing uses, official plans, bylaws, and avoiding undue negative impact on neighbouring properties.

When it comes to urban space, then, the stakes (both in lifestyle and finances) are very high and the decision-making process is very public. As Mohammad Qadeer has noted, this can be a recipe for confrontation. "Ironically," he writes, "the very participatory procedures meant to give citizens a voice in planning provide the convenient means for some local groups to resist the accommodation of others' divergent needs and tastes. Public hearings on planning regulations have often turned into the tools of NIMBYism and ethno-racism."[32] Clashes over public space sometimes embody different conceptions of citizenship and raise the question, Who belongs, and on what terms?

Modern urban planning often combines economic, fiscal, and technocratic "governmentalities"; the dominant rationalities guiding land use decisions typically embody the aesthetic, political, economic, and moral mentalities of the dominant groups in any given city. Immigrants, along with other groups marginalized by urban planning such as women, gays, lesbians, the disabled, and the elderly, have recently taken to "asserting and demanding respect and space for their 'difference.'"[33] Therefore, clashes over land use have occurred between diaspora groups and Toronto municipalities when newcomers seek to claim their urban citizenship rights spatially. Significantly, the most heated conflicts have arisen over attempts by immigrant and minority groups to establish *collective, cultural expressions of their identity* in places of worship, commercial environments, recreational facilities, and community centres. Urban space and planning, therefore, are able to embody a group's identity in ways that other municipal services typically geared to *individual* residents or clients do not. For all these reasons urban space has become a battleground of citizenship rights in the Greater Toronto Area.

Muslim groups have grown rapidly in the GTA in recent decades. Immigration from South Asia, the Middle East, Somalia, South Africa, Turkey, and Bosnia has given rise to a population estimated at between 150,000 and 250,000.[34] The *Muslim Guide to Canada*, published in 1997 by the Muslim World League's Canadian Office, places the number at 200,000—almost half the total for all of Canada. (A precise count will be available from the 2001 census as religious affiliation was not surveyed in the 1996 census.) Muslim groups are broadly dispersed across the GTA, with significant settlements in all parts of the recently amalgamated City of Toronto, as well as the other GTA municipalities of Mississauga, Markham, Brampton, Ajax, Oshawa, Oakville, and Burlington.

Identifying the number of mosques in the GTA is prone to imprecision. As Qadeer notes, Islamic congregations typically progress through three stages in their places of worship: "In the beginning, someone's living room serves as the gathering place for weekly prayers, which leads to renting a hall or buying an unused church for congregational gatherings, and finally to the stage of building a new mosque."[35] Prayer rooms at places of work or study constitute other emerging sites of worship. Through interviews conducted with community leaders, estimates of the number of mosques now operating in the GTA range from twelve to over fifty; the *Muslim Guide* identifies twenty-nine.[36] Muslims are called to prayer five times per day, with the most significant (and widely attended) service being the *Jummah* (Friday) early afternoon service. Our research identified twenty-six full-service mosques across the GTA holding five prayer services per day: five in the former central city of Toronto; four in North York; three in Scarborough; three in Etobicoke; one each in York and East York (for a total of seventeen in the amalgamated City of Toronto); three in Mississauga; and one each in Ajax, Brampton, Burlington, Oakville, Oshawa, and Vaughan. Most of these sites were established in the 1990s.

During the summer of 1998, twenty-four of the twenty-six full-service mosques responded to a survey we conducted regarding their location and experience securing zoning approvals. Eight of the twenty-four reported that they had encountered zoning or planning difficulties in establishing the facilities to meet the religious needs of their group: two in North York and one each in Brampton, East York, Etobicoke, Mississauga, Scarborough, and York. Opposition to the mosques from municipal officials or local residents, or both, was expressed as "technical" concern over the site location, the size, or parking. For their part, however, members of the Muslim groups applying for zoning permits have been left with feelings of discrimination and stigmatization. Three other Muslim struggles over space in the GTA proved particularly contentious and merit closer examination. Unlike East York's case, however, none of these disputes was resolved within the confines of their municipal councils. Rather, all were the subject of contentious appeals to the Ontario Municipal Board (OMB), a provincially appointed quasi-judicial body empowered to review municipal land use decisions.

Talim-Ul-Islam Mosque

In North York, members of the Talim-Ul-Islam Mosque purchased an abandoned site for their place of worship. Their attempt to secure zoning approval for the site from North York Council led Dr. Muhammad Ibrahim of the Canadian Islamic Congress to conclude, "There is one set of laws for everyone else and then there's another for Muslim communities. There is no fair and equal treatment for everyone."[37] In 1995, North York Council revised its bylaws dealing with places of worship. More on-site parking was required for places of worship in all zones, limits were placed on their maximum size in industrial zones, and no more than one place of worship could be located per block or within 500 metres of another place of worship on lots in an industrialized zone which stood within 500 metres of a residential area. These bylaws were clearly intended to defend local residents' interests from the intrusion of worshippers.[38]

The Talim-Ul-Islam Mosque had occupied its site since 1993, when it purchased the property on the assurance that it would be used as a mosque. On this basis, members of the mosque had never applied for zoning approval, but under the terms of the revised 1995 places of worship bylaws, the mosque now required grandparenting exemption. The mosque, like other existing places of worship, was in non-compliance with the new bylaw because it lacked the new standard of required parking spaces, and because there were three churches and a Sikh temple within a radius that was no longer permitted. Council rejected the mosque's application for exemption from the new bylaw in 1995, pending clarification of the renovation plans for the mosque.

In 1997, the mosque applied to North York's Committee of Adjustment to expand its washroom facilities and secure exemption from the 1995 bylaw provisions on the grounds that the deviation from the bylaws was minor and inconsequential. A resident and a local municipal councillor, who complained of parking problems and disorderly behaviour by mosque worshippers, opposed this application. Given their religion's restrictions of alcohol consumption, mosque members were particularly offended by the allegations that they were responsible for drunken behaviour, urinating on lawns, and littering the neighbourhood with alcohol bottles.[39] In December 1997, the Committee of Adjustment denied the mosque's application on the grounds that its variance was not minor, not within the intent of the 1995 bylaw, and not an appropriate development of the property.[40] Of the three nearby churches and the Sikh temple, then, only the mosque was labelled an illegal use of space.

The mosque appealed the verdict to the Ontario Municipal Board and was vindicated. OMB adjudicator Ronal Emo ruled that the parking provision was indeed adequate, that there were no undue traffic problems in the area in which the mosque had been situated for the past five years, and that the mosque was prepared to undertake several design measures to buffer it from nearby homes. Perhaps most important was a point of historical comparison that Emo cited in his ruling. He noted that all immigrants, dating back to Ontario's first European settlers, made a priority of establishing places of worship in their new land. However, early Anglican immigrants had been privileged by the designation of Clergy Reserves—space specifically set aside for churches. In the absence of state-provided worship space, Emo observed that recent immigrants had to be more "entrepreneurial and resourceful," and Talim-Ul-Islam's use of a vacant industrial building was making good use of space that might otherwise be empty and derelict.[41] For these reasons, Emo approved the mosque in its location, concluding that it would be unjustifiably arbitrary to reject it simply because of its proximity to other places of worship.

Canadian Islamic Trust Foundation Mosque

In their ruling on the Mississauga mosque review, OMB adjudicators noted that the Canadian Islamic Trust Foundation's (CITF) application to locate a mosque in an industrial site had been "vigorously opposed by the City of Mississauga and many residents in the area."[42] Since its incorporation in 1974, as an amalgamation of several long-time independent towns immediately west of Toronto, Mississauga has experienced massive population growth. From 1981 to 1996, the city's population almost doubled to 546,186 making it by far the largest municipality in the GTA after the City of Toronto. Much of this growth was the result of global migration: immigrants represented 43 per cent of Mississauga's population in 1996, led by newcomers from India. Yet the city's political culture continued to reflect an outdated demography. Thus, while residents of British ethnic origin constituted about 15 per cent of Mississauga's population in the mid-1990s, politicians of British origin held nine out of ten seats on city council. Mississauga was also one of the very few municipalities in the GTA without a special committee (typically identified as a race relations or equity committee) to enhance communications with racialized diaspora groups.[43]

The Canadian Islamic Trust Foundation's effort to locate a mosque in Mississauga reflected one immigrant group's desire to secure space for their collective expression of identity. In October 1995, the CITF selected a site for a new mosque in a vacant industrial area just off the Queen Elizabeth Way, the highway that connects Toronto with its westerly metropolitan sprawl. The site fulfilled all the CITF's criteria: it enjoyed highway access to an existing building on seven acres, which could be renovated to provide prayer space and parking to accommodate eleven hundred worshippers per week. Constructing a place of worship in an industrial area was permitted, yet given its cost, the site was only feasible if it could include revenue-generating facilities such as a social hall, travel agency, and the Toronto area's first private Islamic high school. The CITF assumed the latter addition could be secured through rezoning, since the adjacent Catholic Iona High School had recently been built within the same industrial zone.

A fundraising ad for the mosque in *The Toronto Star* in early March 1996 provided the first public notice of the CITF's plans. The nearby residential community's concerns over traffic and parking surfaced immediately (much as they had earlier over the new Catholic school in the area). Yet Muslims believed that opposition to their plans was in fact "based on considerations other than planning considerations," that is, they were not wanted in the area by residents of the nearby suburban enclave.[44] Veteran Mississauga Mayor Hazel McCallion called a meeting for late March to discuss the CITF's plans: one city planner who was present recalls it as the largest turnout ever to discuss a zoning application. The message from the Islamic group was, "This is something we've dreamed of all our lives, that there would be a big, beautiful mosque in Mississauga. This is something we really want. We are peace loving. We don't drink. We're not violent." The planner went on to note, "It was almost like they were defending themselves and yet they weren't really being accused. There were some people on the other side, on the residents' side, who were probably not too happy with the [Muslim] group but basically they did use land use reasons for not supporting it—that is the traffic or the parking, hours of operation, that kind of thing."[45]

Explicit motivations behind neighbourhood opposition to a development like this are difficult to establish. To be sure, there were already long-standing traffic problems in the area that residents feared the mosque would exacerbate. As well, concerns over parking spilling onto neighbouring residential streets needed to be addressed in all applications for places of worship. Yet at least one seasoned observer of the interplay of religion and space across the GTA believes that mosques come in for particular scrutiny. Rick Gosling served as executive director of North York's Office on Race and Equity Relations. "It's always the same," he believes. "Churches, synagogues have cars lined up and down the streets [and] no one says a word or even thinks about it, but when a mosque comes in and you've got cars parked down the street everyone goes 'what the heck are we doing here, we're bringing in all these strange people.'"[46]

Two factors suggest that the Islamic nature of the place of worship may have been a factor in this case. First, the city's Planning Department saw fit to investigate the operation of another mosque in the city and found worshippers there making use of an adjacent park on weekends to the dismay of local residents. As a Mississauga planner describes it, residents in that area felt "displaced because they cannot use their local neighbourhood park because people have kind of taken it over. So there was a lot of comparison between that situation and this [CITF] proposal."[47] Would the use of the park by a church group have caused as much neighbourhood discomfort? Would the city have studied the impact on neighbouring areas as scrupulously when assessing an application from a new church? These are questions that define the nature of struggles for citizenship rights in the cosmopolis.

Second, residents who opposed the mosque at hearings before the OMB "spoke of the need to preserve the character of the residential neighbourhood." This prompted the Board adjudicators to doubt that a mosque would affect the character of the neighbourhood any more than its existing churches or community centre.[48] It appears unlikely, then, that issues of citizenship and identity were absent from this attempt to establish a mosque in Mississauga.

At the March 27, 1996 public meeting, the CITF was informed that neither the mayor nor the local councillor regarded the proposed site as appropriate, and that the mayor was prepared to assist in finding an alternative location. After the Muslim group decided to proceed in closing the deal on purchasing their site, a more surprising setback ensued. The CITF now learned from the city's Planning Department, through a bylaw provision just uncovered, that contrary to everyone's assumption a place of wor-

ship could not be located on this site as it was one of three "prestige industrial" zones in Mississauga. In the end, Mississauga council voted seven to
two against the CITF's rezoning bid to establish a mosque and related community facilities on the site.

The CITF turned to the OMB for redress, and they were not disap-
pointed. The two Board adjudicators acknowledged the urgent need for
additional Muslim prayer facilities in Mississauga. Equally important, they
rejected this industrial site's "prestige" designation since it already contained a school, a small church, a gas station, and retail outlets. What
remained to be established was whether the CITF's proposal was appropriate to accommodate traffic and parking. The Board found the area's road
network capable of absorbing the additional traffic, with any congestion
likely limited to no more than thirty minutes every Friday mid-afternoon.
In the adjudicators' opinion, this did not constitute "an unacceptable
impact on the residential area." However, the Board did scale back the
project to avert undue parking pressure on residential streets: the mosque's
prayer space was reduced from a capacity of eleven hundred worshippers
to under nine hundred, and the social hall was not permitted but additional parking required to be built in its place. The Board's decision, then,
was designed to establish a mosque that would "eliminate the possibility"
of detrimental impacts on neighbouring residential streets.[49]

Predictably the ruling played to mixed reviews. Pat Mullin, councillor for the ward where the site is located, complained, "It is very disap-
pointing that an unelected body can determine what is appropriate development in a 30-year-old 'community.' It appears the hearing wasn't about
land use or transportation issues, but about the need for the Islamic community to have a place for worship."[50] Conversely, the ruling left the CITF's
Muhammad Ashraf prouder than ever of his new country, "I am very grateful for the OMB. Canada is a great country where there are a series of
checks and balances. The system is very fair where the public has a right to
plead its case. The OMB overturned the decision by the City."[51]

Yet this redress has come at a cost. Dr. Ashraf estimates that community and municipal council opposition cost the mosque two years of delay
and $350,000 in legal and consultant fees, amounting to exactly 25 per cent
of the cost of purchasing the disputed property. Perhaps more damaging
was that twice, within weeks of the OMB's decision, swastikas were
painted on the building purchased by the Canadian Islamic Trust Fund. On
a more hopeful note, students from the nearby Catholic school joined

Muslim students to remove the offensive spray-painting, and calls of support for the mosque came in from some local residents.[52]

El-Noor Mosque

The case involving the El-Noor Mosque in the former City of York (now part of the amalgamated GTA) may well be the most contentious dispute over a mosque in the GTA to date. Michael Melling, the OMB adjudicator hearing the appeal, began his ruling by observing, "What this decision will likely do is mark the end of a lengthy, fiercely-contested and emotionally-charged dispute. What it will not likely do, for reasons that will become apparent, is resolve the parties' fundamental conflict."[53] The dividing lines in York had indeed been starkly drawn; yet even here, symbolically at least, differing perspectives and traditions could indeed be reconciled.

In 1986, the El-Noor Mosque purchased a small Protestant church in a modest residential neighbourhood of post-war bungalows and converted it to a mosque with minor and modest renovations. A decade later, with a growing congregation of several hundred worshippers, the mosque was ready to expand. Renovation plans called for transforming the original structure in two ways. First, enlarging the worship space by extending the ground floor and basement, and adding a second storey. Second, redesigning the second storey to architecturally reflect traditional mosque appearance, complete with dome and minaret. The dome would allow building a new roof without interior columns, and the minaret steeple symbolically represented the calling of Muslims to prayer.

Once again, neighbourhood residents objected to both the enlargement and redesign of the mosque. The mosque won round one in January 1996, when the City of York's Committee of Adjustment approved the mosque's plans as an acceptable minor variation of the existing zoning bylaw, requiring only that the minaret be scaled down from a proposed height of 80 to 60 feet. Round two was fought at the OMB. Two hundred and fifty-two residents signed a petition opposing the mosque's expansion, and eighty-five neighbours raised $16,000 to finance the appeal of the Committee of Adjustment's decision. The hearings before the OMB proved unusually heated and protracted, and Board adjudicator Michael Melling evicted one resident for profanity, noting in his judgement "that ten-day hearings of minor variance appeals are relatively rare."[54]

The most prominent complaint the residents made was about parking. They complained that their streets were constantly filled with worshippers' cars, which were sometimes illegally and recklessly parked.[55] Board adjudicator Melling accepted the legitimacy of the complaint but he noted that parking problems were common for places of worship located in older residential areas. He also noted that the mosque was striving to impress on its congregants the importance of observing street parking rules. Melling commented on what he described as the residents' overly proprietary sense of their neighbourhood space. He rejected what he termed their "explicit suggestion that the Mosque's congregants are improperly appropriating legal parking which 'belongs' to the residential neighbours. This is simply not so. The evidence is uncontradicted that street parking in this area of the City is *public;* that is, it 'belongs' to no one. It may be used equally by the neighbours, the Mosque's patrons, and the customers of the stores on Eglinton."[56] Neighbourhood in other words could not be invoked as a claim to exclude newcomers from what is public space.

Some residents were even more direct in objecting to the mosque's proposed architectural makeover. Long-time resident Fred Lindsay was one of the mainstays who mobilized the neighbourhood, becoming particularly concerned once he learned of the plans for the dome and minaret. "There is no comparison to that kind of building, here in Canada," he felt. "It was going to be a foreign, exotic building."[57] As Lindsay also told the press, "We feel we don't want to see a minaret or dome in this neighbourhood. If they put up this minaret and dome, it will act like a calling card for the whole community." The result, he told the OMB hearings, would be lower property values in the neighbourhood as only Muslim congregants would be interested in moving in.[58]

In his ruling, Michael Melling approved the mosque's renovation but imposed several minor modifications to minimize its impacts on the neighbourhood. The original manse (cleric's home) on the site would be demolished and replaced by parking, the library was not to be used as a prayer site, and the minaret would be reduced from 60 feet to 55 in height. The issue of awarding costs was also raised, with the mosque calling on Melling to assign their costs to the residents. This Melling declined, stating that while the residents "certainly mounted a comprehensive and occasionally hostile attack on the [mosque's] plans," their conduct did not meet the test required for awarding costs for being frivolous, vexatious, or clearly unreasonable.[59]

Transforming a Presbyterian church into a mosque had indeed unleashed strong antipathies. Mosque supporters believed the residents simply did not want them in the neighbourhood, and some residents felt their neighbourhood rights were sacrificed to the Muslim need for a place of worship.[60] Symbolically, at least, the mosque's design may afford some reconciliation, even integration, of the distinct traditions and identities at play here.

☐ Imprinting an Identity

Struggles for recognition provide tangible, visible evidence of a cosmopolis in the making. In large cities inhabited by people from many different countries and cultures, Leonie Sandercock observes, "citizens wrest from space new possibilities, and immerse themselves in their cultures while respecting those of their neighbours, and collectively forging new hybrid cultures and spaces."[61] But, as we have argued, these struggles for recognition are much deeper than the wresting of new possibilities from space; they involve resisting, subverting, and exposing strategies of racialization that are enacted through space. The redesign of the El-Noor Mosque (shown at the beginning of this chapter), represents a step towards cosmopolis for Toronto.

Ironically, the best tribute to the new design came from a retired planner living in the neighbourhood who appeared before the OMB to oppose the redevelopment. Contending that the site was simply in the wrong place, he nonetheless acknowledged the design by award-winning architect Zak Ghanim to be "a beautiful structure," which would transform a "plain" church into "a different cultural idiom." More evocatively, he noted that the redesign represented "completely crossing cultural lines from the historic, simple Protestant idiom to the exotic, romantic, eastern design."[62] Cities often open themselves to the world one building at a time. A building can be a symbol of citizenship and identity for new immigrants. Bilal Abdullah, an observer of the York saga, noted that there was a message of citizenship embedded in this use of space. He wrote to the Toronto news weekly *Now*: "The erection of the dome and minaret would signal that the city of York is a tolerant, multicultural place, a place where all are welcome to live and contribute to the cultural and economic life of the region."[63]

Yet these buildings may raise new questions. By inscribing themselves in space, are Muslim groups really able to call into question let alone transform and change racialized strategies oriented towards them? To put it another way, by building mosques, do Muslim groups really provide a fundamental challenge to the liberal definition of universal citizenship as being the same as the other? It may be argued that Muslims as racialized immigrants are being compelled to act as virtuous citizens, reproducing the dominant ways of being a citizen rather than issuing a fundamental challenge to the racial and orientalist foundations of citizenship. Bonnie Honig argues that the valorization of immigrants as the founders of settler nations often lead to a backlash against them when they conduct themselves in ways that are not acceptable to citizenship: "the liberal xenophilic deployment of the foreigner as the truest citizen (because the only truly consenting one) actually feeds the xenophobic backlash against the non-consenting immigrant—the illegal alien—to whom we supposedly do not consent and who does not consent to us."[64]

Although it is important to question images of the immigrant that mobilize the virtuous citizen, it is a mistake to draw a sharp distinction between immigrants as consenting citizens and illegal aliens as non-consenting citizens. For immigrants also engage in practices that dissent from accepted norms and question these dominant images. While building mosques may seem an insignificant practice without wider and broader effects on dominant strategies of racialization, we would like to highlight four reasons why that is an inadequate interpretation.

First, the significance of claims on urban space as a strategy, which has most frequently and passionately drawn Muslims into public engagement with the civic political process, cannot be underestimated. As Muslims have articulated a symbolic and material need for places of worship, they have not only mobilized themselves as "active" urban citizens but also articulated the necessity of building a space for themselves as a condition for making themselves a group with rights and claims.

Second, while opposition to mosques was typically articulated in technical planning terms (with concerns over parking and traffic dominating), in each case there was evidence of unusual scrutiny or objection to the mosque relative to non-Muslim places of worship. In other words, struggling over spaces of everyday life, Muslim groups increasingly exposed, revealed, and disclosed that the dominant groups are just as strategic in resisting or blocking the formation of Muslim groups as social groups in the social space.

Third, it is noteworthy that elected local politicians tended to be less supportive of new mosques than the appointed adjudicators hearing land use appeals on the Ontario Municipal Board. This may suggest that the public sentiment influencing local politicians in these issues has not been sympathetic to new mosques. But it may also suggest that the legal and administrative authorities can be provoked to practise liberalism. Fourth, the specific terms of resolution in these cases bear an uncanny compliance with David Goldberg's proposed remedy of "principled pragmatism" as the most apt resistance to exclusion. Each case ended with the establishment of a mosque, yet each required the provision of additional parking spaces and a reduction in the site's size. This may be regarded as evidence that compromise and openness to difference are important elements of Toronto's civic culture. But it equally illustrates, as Ruth Fincher and Jane M. Jacobs have written, "the ways oppressed groups can, through a politics of identity and a politics of place, reclaim rights, resist, and subvert."[65]

We have argued that the presence of large Muslim communities in the cosmopolis moves us beyond calls for multicultural citizenship. Rather, it stretches Western citizenship in a more fundamental way, calling into question the racialized and orientalist grounds of citizenship. Toronto's democratic cosmopolitanism and its depth in recognizing strangers and outsiders as citizens are bound up with claims such as the Muslim struggle to establish mosques. To put it differently, there is both a temporal and spatial dimension to citizenship. To be sure, citizenship is about making a place, about identifying with markers, boundaries, and identities of a place, but it is also about investing in the fate of that place, inscribed and materialized in space as memory.

Being a citizen or practising citizenship means having a stake in the fate of a polity to which one wants to belong and imprinting an identity on that space that, for many newcomers, begins with politicizing their faith. The articulation of Muslim citizenship claims in a Western cosmopolis, therefore, constitutes a challenge to rethink the universal figure of "Western man" as the universal bearer of citizenship rights and obligations, just as other social movements have called into question the male, heterosexual, white, able-bodied, and propertied man as the universal exemplar of citizenship rights.

In the aftermath of the September 11, 2001 events in New York City and Washington, the prospect of advancing Muslim citizenship claims in Toronto—as elsewhere in Western societies—has become significantly more problematic. Symbolic and physical violence have been inflicted on Muslims and mosques. Racial profiling has increased, as has discrimination against Muslims in such spheres as travel and employment. Anti-terrorist laws and campaigns have abandoned civil liberties and due process. Additionally, from both within and beyond Muslim groups, there have been interrogations of whether Islam is compatible with Western liberal universalist principles. Both within and beyond Muslim communities, the extent to which some mosques in the diaspora have been sites of anti-Western mobilization has been interrogated. All this has exposed more visibly than ever before the fault lines for creating a genuine diasporic urban citizenship.

CHAPTER 8

The Space of Africville

Creating, Regulating,
and Remembering
the Urban "Slum"

Jennifer J. Nelson

There is a little frequented part of the City, overlooking Bedford Basin, which presents an unusual problem for any community to face. In what may be described as an encampment, or shack town, there live some seventy negro families. . . .

The citizens of Africville live a life apart. On a sunny, summer day, the small children roam at will in a spacious area and swim in what amounts to their private lagoon. In winter, life is far from idyllic. In terms of the physical condition of buildings and sanitation, the story is deplorable. Shallow wells and cesspools, in close proximity, are scattered about the slopes between the shacks.

There are no accurate records of conditions in Africville. There are only two things to be said. The families will have to be rehoused in the near future. The land which they now occupy will be required for the further development of the City.[1]

This chapter traces a series of events that

demonstrate how the space of Africville, Nova Scotia, was legally regulated by the City of Halifax throughout its existence. This space remains a contested site—a reminder to the city that burial of past injustice requires diligent maintenance. Through exploration of several events over time, it becomes clearer that the notion of a united black community, which exists on its own terms and is subject to the same rights and freedoms as the greater white community, was and remains inconceivable. The dislocation of Africville residents from their land and community was more than an isolated, finite project; on the contrary, the process has been one of ongoing eviction, suppression, and denial.

The role of a spatial analysis becomes clear in three ways throughout the discussion. First, the legal regulation of space governs what can and cannot happen within it, in ways that may not be obviously defined as racist in law itself, nor perhaps to a community not directly and negatively affected by such regulation. Second, the regulation and limitation of spaces of resistance are easily masked as a necessary measure to protect the public, a reasonable and equitable measure that applies equally to all

The Monument to Africville Settlers,
Seaview Memorial Park, Halifax, 2001
[TONY COLAIACOVO]

citizens, rather than targeting any specific group. Third, the violence inherent in the regulation of racialized space is rendered invisible when law is conceived as being a product of consensus of liberal social values. The inequities can only be heard when the differing stories of those involved are allowed to emerge. Thus, this chapter makes an argument for context-specific considerations of wrong-doing that go beyond an assumed consensus of "fairness" to a series of legal actions that were planned and carried out by one group against another.

While there are many elements to the Africville story that tell a tale of spatial and racial discrimination, for the purposes of length and poignancy, I have selected a few key moments from a broader and ongoing struggle to demonstrate the inconceivability to a racist society of an enduring communal Black presence.

As a white writer, I believe it is important to make clear my choices in directing the study's conceptual bent towards whiteness-as-dominance, rather than attempting to replicate "the black experience" of Africville, a story which is not mine to tell. While not intended to alienate or exclude, I acknowledge that this form of analysis and the conclusions I make embody a critique directed to the white community, which people of colour may not find to be "new" or illuminating. Further, I do not mean to suggest at any stage of analysis that resistance and opposition were absent among Africville residents themselves. Certainly, organization against the city's plans took place at the time of Africville's forced dislocation, and various events and projects that seek justice, encourage remembrance, and celebrate resistance have been underway ever since. I am merely choosing here to focus on the dominant players whose governance made resistance insufficient to save Africville. It is the practices of the dominant group that we must critically examine if we seek to educate for change among a white community that is accountable for things done to Black communities.

☐ A Story of Un/settlement

. . . consideration of this or any other urban development must recognize the significance of its prior occupancy and revisit the colonial past to retell some of the histories of initial dispossession of the land involved. . . .The issue is not only one of initial invasion, but of ongoing dislocation and exclusion.[2]

To "begin at the beginning" draws one into a complex history of Black settlement in Nova Sotia in the eighteenth century, a history too detailed to fully discuss here. Briefly, the means by which Black residents of the province came to form the community of Africville must be regarded in the context of a history of the displacement and enslavement of Black people by whites in North America, of hostile reception upon settlement in Nova Scotia, complete with a worldview that demanded their containment and denial, and of a young nation struggling to form its identity through the predominantly British colonial enterprise.

Although slavery was never legally instituted in Nova Scotia, some whites held slaves at the time the City of Halifax was founded in 1749 and throughout the next fifty years. The practice failed to reach the proportions of American plantation cultures, due more to a paucity of arable farmland than to widespread public opposition. The number of slaves following the arrival of slave-holding Loyalists is thought to be around fifteen hundred. While officially frowned upon by the courts at a relatively early date, Nova Scotia's "slave culture" was undermined as the labour of incoming free Black and white Loyalists could be had for little more than the price of keeping slaves.

Soon-to-be Africville residents were among the wave of refugee Blacks who arrived after the War of 1812 and who were allotted space in rural regions, particularly present-day Preston, where rocky, inadequate soil made survival off the land impossible. The Africville site on the shores of Bedford Basin, not far from today's city centre, held the hope of diminished isolation, better employment and living conditions, and other economic opportunities. Having purchased the properties in the 1840s from white merchants, founders William Brown and William Arnold established the boundaries within which Africville would develop. Along with other early families, they established a church congregation and elementary school, a postal office, and a few small stores. Although land conditions for farming were no better than on their former plots, a few head of livestock were kept, the Bedford Basin offered a steady supply of fish, and the new location held the increased chance of obtaining waged labour in the city.[3]

Throughout the community's approximately 120-year history, Halifax's development, particularly in the industrial and disease- and waste-management sectors, encroached on Africville land. In addition to the construction of railway lines, which required the destruction of several Africville buildings, an oil plant storage facility, a bone mill, and a slaughterhouse were built. Encircling these establishments were a leather tanning plant, a tar factory, another slaughterhouse, and a foundry. Shortly after the settlement of Africville, the city established Rockhead Prison on the overlooking hillside; about twenty years later, the city's infectious diseases hospital was placed on this hill, and the open city dump was located about one-and-a-half miles away. Additional construction of railway lines to different factories dislocated more Africville families. Destruction of many surrounding industries following the Halifax Explosion of 1917 resulted in new facilities being built in their places. For decades, this waterfront region was the target of much discussion regarding expropriation for industrial expansion by the City of Halifax, a plan which became solidified in the 1947 rezoning of the city. In the early 1950s, the city dump was moved directly onto Africville land—350 feet from the westernmost home—and two years later, the city placed an incinerator only fifty yards beyond its south border.

Throughout Africville's existence, building permits to improve homes were increasingly difficult to obtain from the city government. Requests for water lines and sewers, which would bring sanitation and quality of life closer to the standards for the rest of the city, were refused. Police and fire protection and garbage collection on par with such services received by the rest of Halifax were denied. Living conditions were ironically described by city officials as intolerable and unsanitary—in short, as justification for the inevitable dismantling of the community and eviction of its four hundred residents. Discussion of the dismantling continued, until finally, in the 1960s, the threat became a more serious reality. By the end of the decade, despite avid resistance and organization on the part of Africville residents themselves and in concert with other community groups, Africville was expropriated by the City of Halifax for the purposes of industrial development, as well as for the alleged benefits of "slum clearance" and "relocation" of the residents.[4]

Due to an informal system of handing down properties and housing within families and between in-laws over the years, many residents were unable to prove legal title to their land; thus, they had little recourse when faced with the proposition to sell or be evicted. Due to historical, social, and economic conditions, residents had no formal community leadership that would be seen as legitimate political representation and little access to the legal and bureaucratic bargaining tools of the municipality. Most were forced to accept the city's small compensation, or to settle for low prices offered for homes they had not been permitted to maintain and improve, located in what was defined as "the slum by the garbage dump."[5] In a seeming mockery, when moving companies refused to be hired, city garbage trucks, which had never serviced Africville, were sent to carry away the residents' belongings.

The last Africville home was bulldozed in 1970. Most of the former residents had to adjust to living in public housing facilities, struggling to pay rent for the first time in their lives, while those who owned their own homes would suffer financial difficulties in the near future. Separated from friends, family, and their strong sense of community, many Africvilleans were left with the insufficiency of welfare dollars and the meager $500 compensation they had received—defined as a "moral claim"—from the benevolent city.

☐ Stage 1: Inducing Illness

Of particular interest to a critical geographical race analysis is the manner in which the control of space and the control of bodies through control of space become tools for defining a community's physical and metaphorical boundaries, its character, and how individuals or groups will be determined through such understandings and associations. David Goldberg writes,

> The slum is by definition filthy, foul smelling, wretched, rancorous, uncultivated, and lacking care. The *racial* slum is doubly determined, for the metaphorical stigma of a black blotch on the cityscape bears the added connotations of moral degeneracy, natural inferiority, and repulsiveness . . . the slum locates the lower class, the racial slum the *under*class.[6]

In denying the community of Africville essential services that would facilitate its health and its development within the larger metro area, the city produced the community, in the "outside" public mind, as a place of dirt, odour, disease, and waste. These associations, which came to be manifested as the conflation of Africville with degeneracy, filth and "the slum," justified the further denial of essential services on the basis of how Africville had come to be known. Working from a basic assumption that the use and characterization of space is socially determined, and that the ideologies surrounding race are socially produced, it is possible to speak of a socio-spatial dialectic wherein "space and the political organization of space express social relationships but also react back upon them."[7]

   In the formation of Africville, and its regulation over time, we see an extension of this dialectic in the relationship between power–dominance and the creation of the slum. Particular race relations in this context produced certain space as a repository for all that the dominant group wanted to contain and distance itself from. In the self-fulfilling prophecy—that is, Africville becoming exactly what it was set up to become in the eyes of the outer white community—the slum legitimates dominance by offering a concrete example of filthy, intolerable conditions, a notion of helplessness and a lack of self-determination that are seen as inherent to its inhabitants. The origins of the conditions in question and the absence of choice for the residents must be conveniently forgotten, and this forgetting is accomplished most easily when the dominant group can achieve an axiomatic yet unspoken association of blackness with inevitable demise. As Barnor Hesse discusses in terms of "diasporic outside/inside," the internal Other, as opposed to the colonial Other overseas, poses a particular problem in western societies:

> . . . temporal nativization of the "other", outside/inside the West is accompanied by a spatial nativization in which people are compressed into prefabricated landscapes, the ghetto, the shanty town, and undergo a process of "representational essentializing" . . . in which one part or aspect of people's lives comes to epitomize them as a whole. . . .[8]

At the same time that we see that observable concrete realities of poverty and deprivation exist, we see in the creation of the racial slum a set of knowledge-making practices that serve to legitimate all that we must believe about Africville in order to dominate it. As Henri Lefebvre writes:

> Space is not a scientific object removed from ideology and politics; it has always been political and strategic. If space has an air of neutrality and indifference with regard to its contents and thus seems to be "purely" formal . . . it is precisely because it has been occupied and used, and has already been the focus of past processes whose traces are not always evident on the landscape. Space has been shaped and molded from historical and natural elements, but this has always been a political process. . . . It is a product literally filled with ideologies.[9]

The ideologies produced in the making of Africville-as-slum involve narratives about raced bodies that are tied to, but must not be conflated with, the spaces they inhabit. Take, for instance, the moving of the dump into Africville: this act was received by Africvilleans in the only way they saw possible—to make use of it, to salvage the things that others threw away, repair or clean them, and go on with life:

> . . . we try to make the dump work for us. . . . There's all kinds of scrap metal in there that you can collect and sell. . . . There's ways of tellin' good stuff from bad. . . . We got fellas here who can get [car] parts off

the dump and make the worst lookin' wreck in the world run like new. . . . You know what really gets up folks' behinds out here? When those newspapers talk about us "scavenging" food and clothes off the dump. People read that stuff and think we're runnin' around diggin' week-old tomatoes and nasty rags out of that messy dump. Any fool knows you get stuff off the trucks *before* they throw it on the dump . . . by the time the ladies out here get through workin' on second-hand clothes with their needle and thread, you'd never know they were bound for the dump. Some folks say the dump was put here to try to drive us out. If that's true, things kind of backfired, didn't they?[10]

The dump, although smelly and distasteful, becomes incorporated into social practice as a means of survival. At the same time, from "outside," Africville becomes characterized more strongly than ever as a space of garbage, of the waste of the white community. The use of the dump can be viewed as proof that the Black community is indeed comfortable being associated with dirt, that it is natural for them to live off the waste of others. Spaces are manufactured in ways that dictate what sorts of activities can and will take place in them. Life practice, then, determines both insider and outsider perceptions of identity: from within, perhaps, emerges a sense that the community can survive against unfair odds. Black identity in the outside white public discourse becomes intimately bound up with space/place in a negative sense—they are no longer simply people who live near the dump; they are "scavengers."

To see Others as recipients of your garbage, as *desiring* your waste, constitutes a very particular kind of relation and belief system about their place, their culture, their "peoplehood," on a dramatic level (as well as, very intimately, a belief system about your own place, culture, personhood). Dominant group members are not required to see how these relations are formed; on the contrary, "common-sense" views engender and support a sense that they are natural, that some people simply live "this way."

Many space theorists have described the way in which both marginalized groups and peripheral space signal an existence "beyond" society, apart from civilized norms, and as separate space in which undesirable activities could take place in order to preserve the purity of dominant, ruling space.[11] Essentializing the people and the space of Africville becomes apparent in the notion of the community as a site "outside" the rest of society, metaphorically and spatially. As Peter Marcuse makes clear in his concept of the *residual city*, racial minority spaces frequently come to house the wastes of society, be they pollutants from industrial manufacturing, sewer systems and garbage disposal areas, or houses for others deemed undesirable, such as AIDS victims or the homeless.[12] This means that undesirable places and practices are located across a boundary that is rarely crossed, or crossed for specific purposes that are "outside" the purity of the white middle-class home—for instance, the treatment of disease or exploring the red light district.[13] Specific to Africville would be the acts of buying liquor illegally[14] or disposing of waste. (Garbage, by definition, is material that is useless, has been thrown out. It is not a legitimate part of your space. It *must* be taken away from where you live, to another place.)

David Sibley's research on gypsy communities has been influential in pulling together many factors, discourses, and social sanctions that enable the construction of a marginal community as "separate," inferior, and slumlike. He speaks of the problematic of perceived "disorder," particularly in travelling communities, whose borders are never clear and require strict regulation.[15] Despite its more than one-hundred-year history and long line of founding families, Africville residents were frequently thought of as a group of transients. In her essay on "the homeless body," Samira Kawash explores how the absence of place, while socially constituted, is seen as highly problematic and in need of legal and social systems of order-making and containment.[16] Although the Africville population was not seen in quite the same light as the homeless, their image as being outside society, undeserving of "place," and as threats to the place of the rest of the community, I believe, form some similar conceptions in the dominant public mind. Narratives of disorder become clear as well through references that are made in news reports and in the original relocation study to the community's criminal element, its potential for disease, and to the possibility that its population was composed mainly of squatters.

Goldberg discusses the making of the slum as periphractic space, characterized by "dislocation, displacement and division" from the rest of society. He concludes that this is "the primary mode by which the space of racial marginality has been articulated and reproduced."[17] At the same time, he notes that periphractic space is not physically marginal to the urban centre, but, quite the contrary, is usually central, promoting a constant surveillance of its inhabitants and conditions. He refers to Vancouver's Chinatown and other similarly positioned communities, as functions of "that set of historical categories constituting the idea of the project: idealized racial typifications tied to notions of slumliness, physical and ideological pollution of the body politic, sanitation and health syndromes, lawlessness, addiction, and prostitution."[18]

These notions help to fuel an anachronistic sense of Africville's Otherness in time and space. Consider, for instance, the quotation at the beginning of this chapter from the provincially commissioned Stephenson Report: Imposing on land coveted for "development of the city" and threatening the city's borders (even though it was there first), Africville becomes *not* part of the city. The representation of an "encampment" connotes an axiomatic impermanence, antithetical to progress and development of "society," which is already understood to be *not*-Africville. The abrupt solution proposed does not take into account the desires or needs of the residents themselves from their own perspectives. His sweeping disregard for any possibility of the community's survival is achieved in one brief and conclusive paragraph in a lengthy report that devotes detailed analysis to the upgrading of many other areas of Halifax, some of which are identified as exhibiting "the worst" conditions in the city.[19]

The depiction of Africville as "an unusual problem for any community to face,"[20] suggests who is considered to be—*and not to be*—"the community." One might also question what, exactly, was "unusual" about a peripheral, underprivileged, and neglected Black population in a North American urban centre with a dominant white majority. To see the situation as an isolated case sidesteps a critical interrogation of the systemic causes of racial oppression. In any case, Africville's "life apart" begs the question, "Apart from *what*?" The answer can only mean some combination of society-community-nation-progress-time-space-history. Indeed, this view must be fundamental to the description of a place as "little frequented," although four hundred people were living there.

Interestingly, as the City of Halifax justified its forced dislocation of Africville residents through reference to land use and the need for industrial development, Sibley points out how outsider societies are understood to be contrary to, even the antithesis of, "development."[21] The wild and untamed lifestyle connoted in Africville's "private lagoon" was easily imagined as an outdated freedom, as an intolerable privilege of inhabiting valuable harbourfront space. Space that had to be made white.

☐ Stage 2: Euthanasia

... we knew all about segregation. But we didn't look at ourselves as a segregated community. We just looked at ourselves as a community. And when the people from the Progressive Club and others like them held out integration like some kind of Holy Grail, we told them we weren't sure exactly what integration could do for us as a community.

And the fact that we would raise doubts about it—well, that kind of shocked 'em.[22]

To solidify the ideologies produced around the space of Africville, the project of racial desegregation enabled an appearance, to many whites, of good intent that relied on a mode of imposed euthanasia—that is, the necessity of putting the community out of its misery.[23] When suffering is seen as "obvious" and incurable, destruction can be looked on as a form of rescue. Investments in the inevitability of this solution are so strong that it is extremely common for white people to ask, upon hearing of this issue, what Roger Simon might call the obscene question, "Why wouldn't they just leave?"[24] This question relies on a learned arrogance that assumes the solution being offered, in this case, to live among white people, is superior, and that the notion of free choice based on a common understanding of the experience exists. The many outsider narratives surrounding the slum construct a background against which implicit and explicit understandings of the (invisibly white) self and community as legitimately dominant are formed. The logic of the slum is productive in its own death, making common-sense knowledge of the fact of its dependence and inevitable need of an outside solution.

What, then, are we to make of the role of law in carrying out the solution in question? Not surprisingly, there was little space for Africville residents to contextualize their claims within a history of poverty, racism, and colonialism inflicted upon them by the same dominant group enacting the current violence. I have struggled with the problematic of identifying the precise legal (illegal?) moves made by the city—in all the accounts I have read the destruction of the community was simply "carried out." There are no references made to specific legal rulings or principles in the historical accounts, other than the mention of a more recent law passed to prevent certain forms of public protest. Nowhere in city reports from the time of relocation have I found expressions of doubt that Africville *could* be removed. Nor does there seem to exist a concern with justifying the removal through official channels. Instead, a common-sense logic prevails, composed of interwoven themes of understandings to which "we," as rational, race-neutral beings, are assumed to adhere. I soon felt forced to realize that it may be precisely the legality of the process that is so strikingly violent. This violence of the legal process is an integral thread in the common-sense discourse of relocation that, from a relatively privileged perspective, is easy to miss. In his discussion of liberal discourses of desegregation, as applied in various contexts, Goldberg summarizes well what I felt to be the imprecision of the legal process:

> . . . law's necessary commitment to general principles, to abstract
> universal rules, to develop objective laws through universalization,
> is at once exclusive of subjectivities, identities and particularities. . . .
> So when law in its application and interpretation invokes history the
> reading is likely to be very partial, the more so the more politicized
> the process becomes. And race, I am insisting, necessarily politicizes
> the processes it brackets and colors.[25]

I have seen no legal opening for demonstrating, for example, that to be black, poor, displaced, and faced with the threat of physical removal from your home, in a segregated city in Nova Scotia, is not the same thing as to be white, professional, and arguing that the new mall's parking lot should not be placed in your backyard. There is little framework in place within which to claim that "relocating" in this context is different from simply "moving to a new house," hoping you'll soon get to know the neighbours. Such assumed neutrality of experience in the eyes of the law is extremely imprecise and misleading, while attempts to understand injustice are made difficult when context does not come into play. As Sherene Razack demonstrates in her analysis of the murder of an Aboriginal woman working as a prostitute in the Canadian West, any attempt to suggest a context in which race, gender, white male violence or discourses around the bodies inhabiting racialized, degenerate zones, is seen to bias the case. She illustrates how this renders particular identities invisible: "Since bodies had no race, class or gender, the constructs that ruled the day, heavily inflected with these social relations, coded rather than revealed them explicitly."[26] More than a matter of having "the wrong information," which can then be corrected, the discourses that define what white individuals in positions of power can hear about the subordinate group allow a self-concept of innocence to continue. Elsewhere, Razack writes, "Storytelling as a methodology in the context of law runs up against the problem of the dominant group's refusal to examine its own complicity in oppressing others. The power of law's positivism and the legal rules that underpin it are willing accomplices in this denial of accountability."[27]

To acknowledge complicity in histories of oppression and violence would be to give up an individual and collective sense of self and place. To ensure that this toehold is intact, the appearance of accountability can be manufactured through such venues as the $500 "moral claim" given to those residents who could not prove title to their homes. Take for instance the 1994 letter from R. J. Britton, the Halifax director of Social Planning, to City Council, reviewing the options that were perceived to be available at the time: "The City can use its statutory powers to remove the blight and at the same time, temper justice with compassion in matters of compensation to families affected."[28] Britton goes on to pronounce the "official story" that is to be known about Africville in public consciousness. This includes clauses assuring city officials that the aggressive bulldozer approach taken in the 1960s was simply the accepted method of "relocation" at the time, that the utmost compassion was given at various stages of negotiation, and that, since the actual cost of relocation was in the end approximately nine times the estimated cost, they can be assured of their benevolence. (On the contrary, it could be seen as their mistake and as evidence that rehabilitating the community might have been possible after all.) Compensation is cited as "at least very fair and perhaps generous." In this telling of the official story, historical distance excuses what are seen as minor glitches in the project of "relocation," and officials are permitted to feel good about their current perspectives and their predecessors' conduct. Moreover, as the "official story" ends, these leaders move beyond compassion to a sense of friendship and celebration: "The City of Halifax does need to recognize the reality of Africville in its history, celebrate the contributions the Africville people made to the City, and to continue to seek and help in their full participation in the life of the City."[29]

It is clear that within the governmental discourses surrounding Africville, officials define their innocence based on the absence of a legal structure that would hold them accountable in any way. What is perhaps most astounding is the absolute investment in legality as a moral foundation. This investment and the uninterrogated belief in its epistemic assumptions strike one as almost childlike in their simplicity: "If something is illegal, it is *wrong*; if something is legal, it is *correct*; if something is not our legal obligation but we offer it anyway, this makes us *good*." Not only are questions of accountability erased, they are made to seem unequivocally absurd when dominant subjects can believe they have kindly gone "above and beyond" their responsibilities. What is forgotten is that Africville's residents had no part in defining what would constitute these moral parameters, nor in constructing what was a legal or moral way of thought that made racism invisible.

What are the theoretical tools that might interpret the city's intended "slum clearance" or "industrial development" as processes that had, and continue to have, consequences for a poor black community? It is clear that straightforward *evidence* of racism, or even of what is definable as harm, will not be forthcoming. Richard Thompson Ford offers a detailed study of the manner in which segregation upholds itself even when legislative policy seeks to disband it. Were racial segregation banned, he posits, the structures in place to maintain people's links to specific areas, networks, services, and survival mechanisms devised by various communities, regardless of their differing socio-economic statuses, would see that desegregation remained extremely difficult at best.[30] Similarly, Goldberg traces the discriminatory and regulatory consequences of seemingly race-neutral legal rulings. He cites examples from South African apartheid, under which landlords could refuse to rent property to families with more than a certain number of children.[31] It so happened that Black families tended to have larger than average numbers of children, thus the areas in which they were permitted to live could be "raced" without having to name this intent.

As Africville residents were moved, some were targeted by similar policies, having to give away some of their children or break apart families, forming household structures that differed from those they had known for generations. In some cases, single mothers were required to marry the fathers of their children in order to qualify for the new housing projects,[32] thus removing their power of choice to live as they pleased and implementing a value system based on the centrality of the nuclear family, rather than on Africville's sense of community and co-operation among extended relatives and friends. There are lawful ways in which to invoke "universal" values to bolster regulatory measures, as Goldberg points out:

That the State in the name of its citizenry insists on overseeing—
policing—the precise and detailed forms that housing must take for
the poor and racialized suggests that we really are committed to the
kinds of disciplinary culture that inform current practice. The principle of agent autonomy so deeply cherished at the core should not,
it seems, extend to the periphery; the racially marginalized should
not be encouraged to exercise independence (least of all with public monies).[33]

In "relocating" them to their new homes, the municipality hoped,
perhaps assumed, that Africville residents would melt into their new
neighbourhoods, establishing the appearance of a desegregated city
regardless of the hostility they might experience from white neighbours
and regardless of the great psychic expense they might suffer—an expense
that would make it only too apparent "why they wouldn't just leave."

☐ Stage 3: Burial

Drawing on Heidegger and on architectural theory, David Harvey theo-
rizes the *genius loci*. Taken from the Roman, *genius* refers to a "guardian
spirit" which determines the essence of one's identity. Harvey expands this
to explore the essence of identity and community as it is associated with
specific central locations. He speaks of how buildings and places absorb
relations that occur within them, that these variant relations—to environment, history, physiology, sociality, psychology—become embodied in
meanings that are projected onto the *genius loci*. In part, this reading practise begs the distinction of space from "place." As I intend it, space is the
more general term, referring to any conceptual or actual space, including
place. Place depicts a space upon which identity is founded. While either
may be political, I see place as automatically so, referring to and incorporating notions of "home," collective history, and social location in reference
to an identified group or individual. Place is the more precise term, encompassing the particular meanings embedded in spaces that are of significance to those who occupy them.

Harvey describes place as having a quality of "permanence." He
studies a wealthy, walled community, which insulates itself against the
outside world's perceived danger and degeneracy, as an example of place-
making. His "place," and that of Heidegger whose work he engages, is inti-

mately bound up with identity, roots, belonging, continuity, and readings onto space of particular memories.[34] I do not believe that *genius loci* is limited to a connotation of positive or negative meaning-making, but that, depending on how it is used, it can incorporate the violences, inequities, or comforts of how we come to understand our "place" in the world. Harvey's walled community shifts focus to the way in which dominant subjects make their place in the world through rigid boundary-maintenance designed to keep degeneracy at bay.

In a similar vein, Kathleen Kirby examines the mapping of space as fundamental to the formation of the "Cartesian subject."[35] Speaking of the necessity of establishing identity through the mastery of unknown places, she notes how space, for the privileged newcomer, is studied and "known" while space itself is not actively permitted to "know," to act back upon, the dominant subject. When this relationship shifts, such disorder is profoundly disturbing to the privileged (usually) white male subject who "explores" and, through mapping, conquers and reformulates space into something felt to be his own. It is in the project of this expropriation, with its concomitant distancing from the environment, that dominant subjects come to know themselves. While Kirby's theory is set out among "New World" explorer narratives, a greatly similar mechanism is at work in Africville, where white panic over the possibility of an enduring black presence is played out in a continual project of re-examining, rezoning, and reformulating the environment, making it clear who is in control and who may not achieve this subjugation of space.

A new stage in this project began in the 1980s when the city established Seaview Memorial Park on Africville's former site. Named after Seaview Church, which was destroyed before the rest of Africville, the park lies under a major bridge between the cities of Halifax and Dartmouth and winds for several acres along a stretch of waterfront. Landscaped as a gently rolling green space, the park provides benches overlooking the water and gravelly walking trails. A paved parking lot has replaced the oily dirt roads former residents have described. When the park was opened in 1985, the city's mayor announced plans to build a swimming pool there—on this site where Africville had been denied the installation of water lines throughout its existence.[36] A reunion with several hundred former Africville residents or descendants and their families takes place there each summer. In 1988, a monument was built near the park's entrance, engraved with the names of the area's first Black settlers. This monument is the only visible evidence that Africville once existed, and even its tribute does not tell the story of the destruction of this community.

Standing in the park attempting to feel some semblance of connection to my project, I was struck by the manufactured ignorance and erasure available to someone like myself—born after Africville's destruction, white, never having been taught this element of my province's history. Attempting to map the images in photographs and stories onto the site was futile. The land is not the same shape; it is not the same colour; its contours have been altered. It could easily be seen as a park where Halifax proudly honours a founding Black family and a community that happened to blend silently into the city's past. Unless one knows, nothing in sight speaks to the history of this space.

To read the park as *genius loci*, I believe, helps to situate it as a site of evidence with multiple meanings that can be read onto it, or onto the monument itself, depending on the histories and awarenesses people bring to it. As much as the monument shapes memory and dictates how we are to remember the story it depicts, it is important to remember that socially made preconceptions interact with our interpretation of what is being presented. Obviously, those who enter Seaview Memorial Park as their "place," or as a grounded symbol of continued resistance, will define this locale differently from those who remember driving to Africville to dump their garbage. Different still are the definitions of those who have never been to the city before, who visit as tourists or newcomers and "receive" a history that has been laid out for them, even as they bring specific conceptual tools to its interpretation. For them, the space says nothing of the violence that has been enacted upon it. It is in this act of burying the true story and dramatic transformation of the land that forms a poignant link in the chain of events that evicted Africville from its own space.

In the compression of time and space embodied in the monument and in the park, what might prevent us from seeing space as possessed of a history, of seeing the land we stand on as intimately problematic? What is *buried* beneath this symbol of remembering, or what truths does it hold down? It seems that the emptiness of space, here, is another form of *genius loci* for the Cartesian subject, who is complicit or silent in Africville's dislocation. In hiding the evidence where the community once stood, the city continued to produce an ongoing regulation of space to serve the purpose of memory-making. It predetermined how the space was to be received—as recreational land, a "neutral" greenspace open to "anyone." As non-Black outsiders, we can imagine little more than a mythic existence of a Black community, either romantic or slumlike, well in the past. In knowing ourselves through its reclamation and subjugation, we return to our "place" and know that it is *not* that place, which existed only as a site of intolerable disarray awaiting our inevitable intervention and organization.

The monument and park may foster a collective white belief in a sense of innocence or, in what Jane Jacobs has called "reconciliation." Tracing the effect of "Aboriginal walking tours," which display Aboriginal cultural artworks alongside traditional colonial monuments in the urban space of Melbourne, Australia, Jacobs explores the narrative of reconciliation that underpins this public positioning of histories. In its attempt to unite historically colonized and colonizing groups under a common national identity, reconciliation "attempts to bring the nation into contact with the 'truth' of colonisation—and this includes the attendant emotional 'truths' of guilt, anger, regret and hurt—in order that there might be a certain 'healing.'"[37] The anxieties this discourse raises among non-Aboriginals as to their understandings of their past and their place in the nation's history are, in Jacobs's view, rekindling a more overt racism imbued with a sense that Aborigines now possess too much power and privilege.

Would this sort of defensive hostility result from attempts to retell the truth of Africville's history in the public forum? Do the monument and park, along with more recent acceptance of memorials in the form of plays, music, and art displays, incur a sense of reconciliation among white Halifax residents, a sense that they have gone far enough in paying tribute to "unfortunate" events of the past? Informally expressed regret, combined with the more common-sense notion that Africvilleans are "still bitter" and should "put the past in the past," fail to expose personal and collective complicity, much less to ignite a strong public legal move towards material compensation. Further, they allow a sense of personal achievement in having come to a point of understanding, of believing we relate to what happened, that we regret what those before us did, while remaining distinct from the whole mess. As in the Australian case Jacobs describes, we have seen heightened resentment against Africville residents who are making demands at the government level, while many white residents assert that the city has been generous and compassionate where there was no racism to begin with.

How might the way in which the Africville story is "told" enable a dominant, privileged audience to receive a message of complicity and responsibility? As Lefebvre writes, "Monumental space offered each member of a society an image of that membership, an image of his or her social visage."[38] To usefully explore the social visage of a community that forced the dislocation of others, it is crucial to understand the way we remember or forget, but we also must look further to determine the historical understandings and memories we bring to the Africville monument. When these remembrances are disconnected from the actual space, as they are in most white public consumption of the story, the story may retain a mythic quality, like an entertaining but "unreal" war narrative from ancient history. The potential of a physically grounded analysis, in which we can hear the story from the perspectives of former residents and connect it to their space, is lost.

☐ Silencing the Ghosts

In 1994, there was a resurgence of municipal panic when two brothers, former Africville residents, occupied Seaview Memorial Park. They were protesting the lack of compensation and demanding renewed claims on Africville land. The Carvery brothers, teenagers when they left Africville, set up camp in Seaview on the site of their former home for over a year, getting through a cold winter with only a tent and a few survival implements. The authorities failed in their repeated threats and attempts to evict them, which included locking the park's only public washroom.[39] Their protest took place at the same time that the city was preparing to host the G7 summit. To allow the ghosts of Africville (though in reality very much alive) to seep through the carefully managed fabric of a well-tended burial would cause Halifax worldwide embarrassment—whether over a failure to manage "its blacks" or over leaked knowledge of its injustices is not clear.

News reports during this time reflect a daily concern with the presence of the Carvery brothers in the park and cite complaints from Halifax residents who claimed the Carverys' protest "took away from their enjoyment of the park."[40] A few months before the summit, despite widespread protest from the Black community, a law was passed that forbade citizens to camp in public parks overnight. Mayor Fitzgerald, who earlier claimed his government had "bent over backwards" in attempt to negotiate with Africville protesters, cited the new ordinance as falling under the *Protection of Property Act*. In contrast to two days earlier, when the city had had no legal recourse against those sleeping overnight in a city park, he was able to announce that "people are in the park illegally and we want them off."[41] The Carverys eventually moved their protest just outside the park's border, to an area that did not fall under municipal jurisdiction. As the city alone could not evict them without provincial and federal consent, they maintained their campsite for several more years.[42]

The city's destruction of Africville was the culmination of a moral panic at the possibility of an independent, sovereign blackness. The nation makes itself not through exclusionary practice alone, but, to borrow Sibley's term, through "geographies of exclusion."[43] Through the desecration of space as black, the appropriation of space as white, the suppression of the story of this violence and the denial of accountability, the life of Africville is grounded upon a geography of racism and its discursive organization. Like the proverbial lie, once told, the story necessitates the telling of a chain of "maintenance fictions," complete with the management of space in such a way that the fictions prevail intact and that oppositional stories remain buried. For the purposes of demonstrable racist harm, it will never suffice to engage in a strictly information-based investigation, for it can never be proven within such a paradigm that Africville was destroyed because a black presence was disdained.

The legal, social, and historical logic of "relocation" tells us that the city's actions were unfortunate but necessary, humanitarian, compassionate, non-racist, integrative, progressive, and, perhaps above all, innocent. A conceptual analysis of the regulation of space over time helps us look beyond this, perhaps because it asks as many questions as it answers: Why was industrial development *not* carried out? Why was "empty" recreational space created instead? Why didn't this take place in a white neighbourhood? Why is there no dump in the city's prosperous south end? Why does the city still speak of "black areas" in derogatory ways? For it appears that the discourse of integration, never realized, is more a discourse of erasure from sight and site.

Africville's story does not begin in 1962; it does not even begin in 1862. It begins in slavery, in Preston, in the founding of Halifax and the nation, in the hunting of the Mi'kmaq by British settlers.[44] In short, our perceptions of what functions as "evidence" must shift to allow the building of a context of ongoing oppression that may inform the way such issues are approached in law, to re-examine common key assumptions about fairness and equity which, by design, will serve the case badly. Our framework must shift from one of innocence or pity to one of justice.

Legal decision making follows social histories that include poverty and racism. Such histories rely upon complex narratives of blackness that operate in the making of the slum. In turn, legal policy is producing further histories that perpetuate racist practice. These phenomena operate as threads knotted together; to remove any one would make the story of Africville qualitatively different. To discuss any one in isolation is to belittle and betray any attempt at truth or justice. In drawing continuities along a chain of evictions, burials, denials, and complicities through time, their logical sequence becomes evident: depriving the community of essential services; defining the community as slumlike based on the conditions this deprivation promotes; dislocating both persons and space, claiming the inevitability of destruction; altering the space and redefining its purpose and use by opening a park; installing a monument to suggest a sense of reconciliation; suppressing the true story when it resurfaces, and legislating restrictions on protesters who resurrect it.

As I have tried to demonstrate, the legal moves inherent in Africville's history as a degenerate site become clearer when a spatial analysis is permitted to trace and broaden the scope of what are considered to be regulatory measures. If we want to resist the official story, we must insist that history be alive and visible, and look at Africville's destruction not as a segment of the past but as fabric in the history of the present.

CHAPTER 9

Delivering Subjects

Race, Space, and the Emergence of Legalized Midwifery in Ontario

Sheryl Nestel

The first Canadian legislation establishing

midwifery as a state-regulated and state-funded health profession was passed into law in Ontario on December 31, 1993. Hailed as a "victory for women," the enactment of midwifery legislation has been viewed as a triumph of grass-roots feminist organizing and as part of the ongoing struggle for gender equity and female reproductive autonomy.[1] There can be no doubt that the midwifery model of practice as developed in Ontario has much to recommend it over a medical model of maternity care that has been documented as consistently overly interventive and frequently misogynistic.[2] However, the benefits resulting from the legalization of midwifery have been very unevenly distributed. Indeed, the Ontario midwifery movement is indistinguishable from many other Western feminist projects which, having failed to inquire after the differential impact of their political strategies on women positioned unequally in the social field, unwittingly reproduce global and local structures of domination and subordination.

The role of law in creating racialized subjects has been crucial in this process. While the legislation itself distinguishes between, and creates the categories of, "legal" and "illegitimate" midwives, the relatively unmarked character of these classifications has been transformed in the process through which the *Midwifery Act*[3] has been implemented. Those empowered by law to develop the disciplinary framework of the profession made decisions early on which served to attach racialized bodies to the "illegal" category. In the province of Ontario, immigrant midwives of colour who possess considerable professional skills, competencies, and credentials have found themselves largely excluded from access to the newly legalized midwifery profession.[4] The devaluing of non-European

Jamaica Birth
is a division of 5 Star Training Center
North Miami Beach, Florida, USA.

◆◆◆

- home
- the hospitals
- the birth center
- contract
- midwifery education
- questions & answers
- articles
- jamaica
- past trips
- donations
- contact jamaica birth

5 Star Training Center
★★★★★

Jamaica Birth strives to offer a variety of hands-on educational opportunities to midwives and apprentice midwives while providing Jamaican hospitals with needed equipment and supplies.

Jamaica Birth trips are designed to enhance the individual's practical skills through observing and working with Jamaican midwives, a group of women experienced with normal, natural birth in addition to routinely managing complications including breeches and twins.

NEW **Ask about our volunteer program for RN/LMs!** NEW

home | hospitals | birth center | contract | midwifery education
q & a | articles | jamaica | past trips | donations | contact jamaica birth

Web Site Advertisement for "Hands-On"
Midwifery Educational Opportunity
[<WWW.JAMAICABIRTH.COM>, DECEMBER 4, 2001]

experience, credentials, and training, the deployment of inferiorizing discourses surrounding "immigrant women," a tenacious adherence to forms of feminist organizing that reinforce normative whiteness, and numerous acts of "everyday racism"[5] have converged to create a largely monoracial midwifery profession in a geographic space whose multiracial character is one of its most frequently invoked social signifiers.

Discriminatory licensing policies, which are not confined to midwifery, work together with various forms of racist exclusion to guarantee that highly trained professionals from "Third World" countries are effectively deskilled and subsequently slotted into subordinate spaces in the labour force.[6] For a number of complex reasons, including the decimation of local health-care systems by policies of structural adjustment, female health-care workers from "Third World" countries have been significantly affected by processes of globalization and have come to occupy spaces in the North American health-care labour force abandoned by white women increasingly able to climb the ladder of occupational mobility. The interrelationship between white women's progress in the North and global forces that play havoc with the lives of "Third World" women is the topic of this chapter.[7]

Ontario is a space significantly shaped in the last two decades by the global migrations that followed the collapse of formal European rule in Africa, Asia, and the Caribbean. These racially exclusionary dynamics reflect not only histories of colonialism but also contemporary relations of domination where the local and the global are so thoroughly intertwined that their ontological positioning as oppositional categories can no longer be defended.[8] Liberatory movements are not exempt from the processes that keep "dominated societies secure within the wider sphere of neo-colonial influence, definition and assessment."[9] Indeed, the movement to legalize midwifery in Ontario offers a practically paradigmatic example of this. Like many feminist projects of the nineteenth and twentieth centuries, it occupies a "historically imperial location,"[10] deriving material and discursive benefit from an engagement with "Third World" women.

While midwifery policies and everyday practices in the province have discouraged the entry of immigrant women of colour into the lucrative and newly prestigious profession, travel to the "Third World" and access to the bodies of birthing women there have played an indispensable role in the implementation of midwifery legislation by helping midwives achieve professional status. Such a process attests to the recent claims of critical human geographers that subjectivities are constituted in and through space.[11]

The co-construction of metaphorical and material space is evident in the process by which these travels are rendered benign and even benevolent through epistemological claims about women's shared identity. Such an epistemology paves the way for an unproblematic commodification of "Third World" space and those who occupy it. In this schematization, travels to border or "Third World" midwifery clinics are viewed as an example of "First World" women's sisterly magnanimity and not as the very grounds of their social advancement and dominant racial identity. In this essay, I examine the global economic conditions and representational practices that have enabled "midwifery tourism"[12] and how "First World" women who engage in this form of travel rationalize, justify, and name their overseas experiences in ways which gloss over unequal relations of power.

As a white[13] anti-racist educator with an extensive background in childbirth reform activism and prenatal education, I had become increasingly aware of how racial dominance functioned in ostensibly liberatory projects such as childbirth reform and how seamlessly the relations of power that saturated hegemonic social formations were reproduced in movements for social change. I was able to recognize my own use of racist discourses in the service of childbirth reform as a painful case in point. Intending to promote humanized childbearing and to emphasize that most women give birth without the help of medical interventions, I embraced, and for years enthusiastically articulated, a central expression of racism: the use of visual and discursive representations of racialized women as idealized childbearers. Such representations had suffused the re-emergence of midwifery in Ontario and elsewhere in North America, and I began to probe more extensively into the racialized dimensions of this widely lauded feminist initiative.

I was only vaguely aware of training programs in the South that catered to North American midwives before 1995, when I began work on a doctoral research project which sought to explain racist exclusion in the midwifery movement in Ontario.[14] The dissertation adopted a contrapuntal methodology, cataloguing exclusionary policies and practices related to the re-emergence of midwifery and counterposing these with the narratives of exclusion of twenty-three immigrant midwives of colour residing in the province. Not all those who had been excluded, however, had been immigrant women of colour; some white women had also faced barriers as they attempted to enter midwifery practice.

Those midwives who, in the pre-legislation period viewed midwifery neither as primarily a political crusade nor a public profession, but as an extension of their spirituality and of their legitimate social roles as wives, mothers, friends, and neighbours were regarded by some colleagues as a political liability. Indeed, by clinging to traditional motherhood, spirituality, iconoclastic dress, and other behaviours, some white midwives threatened the construction of midwifery as a respectable bourgeois female profession by rejecting the image of the scientific-rational practitioner, which key midwifery activists believed to be fundamental to the creation of pro-midwifery sentiment among physicians, nurses, and the childbearing public. It is from interviews with this group of white women that the narratives used in this article are taken. That the image of the respectable midwife is produced through its differentiation from racialized representations of midwives is a point to which I return below.

☐ Midwifery as a Feminist Project

In this century, North America physicians have exercised a near-monopoly over the provision of care to pregnant and birthing women. They have done so within a medical model that regards human childbirth as an inherently pathological process. While childbirth-reform activists have long argued that many standard obstetrical procedures are both inhumane and clinically ineffectual, such practices have been slow to disappear.[15] One response to the North America's medicalization of childbirth has been the revival, over the last thirty years, of community-based midwifery—the provision of services to birthing women outside of the conventional medical institutions. The practice of "lay midwifery"[16] was, with a few exceptions, largely eradicated in Canada early in the twentieth century, but in the 1970s it began to be embraced by middle-class white women.[17] These empirically trained midwives acquired the skills necessary for the provision of reproductive care within a framework that promoted informed choice in the birthing process, appropriate use of technology, and the recognition of birth as a psycho-social as well as a physiological event. Central to this form of midwifery has been the belief that while choice of birthplace is a fundamental right, a woman's home is the birthing venue most likely to provide the optimum conditions for the achievement of these goals. Decidedly white and middle class, the midwifery movement in Ontario grew from these roots while incorporating aspects of feminist and traditional women's health movements,[18] counterculture lifestyle practices, and long-standing efforts by white, British-trained midwives to have their skills recognized within the health-care system.

The achievement of legal status and state funding for midwifery in Ontario required more than sophisticated political strategies. Crucial to midwives was the acquisition of a politically efficacious subjectivity in a socio-political context where a powerful medical profession was largely opposed to the legalization of midwifery.[19] Negative representations of midwives have been used liberally in both recent and past campaigns to eliminate the midwife in North America. In the U.S., the midwife was a racialized figure throughout much of the twentieth century and represented in a number of discursive contexts as "primitive and dirty."

Such representations found their way into Canadian anti-midwifery discourses. Despite evidence demonstrating that midwifery is safe and cost-efficient, some physicians and consumers still see it as an archaic and discredited form of maternity care or as a primitive practice surviving only in "underdeveloped" regions.[20] As one recent study shows, the *Canadian Medical Association Journal* only ceased publishing articles that represented midwives as atavistic relics after midwifery legislation was passed in Ontario.[21] In their evocation of the dangerous midwife, opponents of the re-emerging midwifery practice in Canada invoked some racist discourses but relied mainly upon arguments that conflated the obsolete and the feminine. The task for midwifery activists, then, was to reconfigure the midwife in the public imagination as respectable—that is, knowledgeable, modern, educated, and Canadian/white.

While some Ontario midwives[22] had acquired formal midwifery credentials abroad, most had learned the profession through intensive self-study and apprenticeship. However, opportunities to gain and exercise a wide spectrum of clinical skills were rather limited in the period prior to proclamation of midwifery legislation. Barred from practising in hospitals, midwives could use their full expertise only at home births. The twenty-six midwives who were practising in Toronto, for example, attended the home births of one thousand and one women between 1983 and 1988.[23] In a period critical to the establishment of midwifery's credibility, a Toronto midwife had, on average, complete professional responsibility for fewer than eight births per year.[24] Obtaining clinical experience became a matter of some importance for women who wished to devote their professional lives to the practice of midwifery.

For midwives practising in the legal limbo,[25] which characterized the pre-legislation period, obtaining wider clinical experience was crucial to increasing public confidence in the viability of midwifery care and to stemming physician opposition to the burgeoning practice. Such experience took on even greater significance with the advent of legislation when obtaining a licence became a basic requirement. In 1986, the Ontario government accepted the recommendation of a Health Professions Legislation Review that midwifery become a regulated profession and appointed a provincial task force to develop implementation strategies. The Task Force for the Implementation of Midwifery made clear in its recommendations that attendance at a substantial number of births would be required of currently practising midwives seeking to be "grandparented" into practice in the province.[26]

Responding to the need for its members to acquire maximum clinical experience in the minimum time possible, the midwives' professional organization, the Association of Ontario Midwives, scrambled to find clinical sites where midwives could gain experience. Lacking institutional midwifery credentials, most Ontario midwives had no access to American or European clinical settings where midwifery was the standard of care. While some midwives found placements in rural areas in the Philippines and in Guatemala, Haiti, or Jamaica, the vast majority of those who travelled enroled as interns at independent midwifery clinics in the U.S.–Mexico border zone. In these clinics, they could pay a fee and attend Mexican women who for a variety of reasons crossed into the United States to deliver their babies. An Ontario midwife, whom I interviewed and who had spent time at one such clinic in the late 1970s, was able to name more than twenty colleagues who had also done so in the years prior to legislation. Evidence suggests that nearly one-third of those who practised midwifery before legislation and who were "grandparented" into practice in 1994 had received some portion of their training in "Third World" or border sites.[27] For these women, Canadian nationality and white skin served as passports to unmolested border crossings and instant authority in the border spaces made available to them through this midwifery tourism.

What follows is an account of how encounters with "Third World" women, made possible because of the flow of transnational capital and ongoing practices of racist representation, have been central to the con-

struction of a respectable midwifery subject in Ontario. Travel was one c
the strategies Ontario midwives used to reverse the professional illegiti-
macy that plagued them in Ontario. Inspired by a widespread belief among
natural birth advocates that "Third World" women possessed birthing
knowledge uncorrupted by civilization, Ontario midwives' travel to geopolitical spaces—where, in Norma Alarcon's words, "the 'Third World' rubs
against the first."[28]—created the discursive and material conditions for professional status back home. Not the least of these was the acquisition of the
requisite number of births for participation in the pre-registration program
that would produce the province's first group of practising midwives.[29]

Midwifery tourism has operated for more than two decades, and
continues to provide both Canadian and American midwifery aspirants
access to clinical experience and professional credibility. Below I describe
the global conditions that make this travel possible and analyze some of
the travelogues I have gathered from "midwifery tourists." These travelogues explore both violence and benevolence as well as innocence and
complicity, but above all, they demonstrate how feminist projects that rely
on unexamined notions of "global sisterhood" reproduce unequal relations
of power between women.

☐　Travel and the Female Subject of Modernity

As postcolonial theorist Lata Mani has observed, colonized space has frequently served as a "theater of social experimentation" wherein Europeans
have sought to critique and reconfigure the social relations of "home."[30] In
the previous two centuries, European women's ventures into such space
have allowed them to claim social identities unavailable to them under
Western patriarchies. This area of inquiry has been a fruitful one, with fem-
inist/postcolonial historians and theorists crafting a burgeoning "cultural
retrospection of empire"[31] aimed at untangling European women's role in
the establishment and consolidation of empire. In colonized locales, Western women were frequently able to act outside of the restrictive gender
roles available at home because cross-gender bonds of race in the colonies
were far more important to the maintenance of colonial hierarchies than
upholding the gendered social organization of the metropole.

Scholarship that explores the historical relationship between feminism and imperialism can be useful in understanding contemporary social
relations, because the contours of the imperial world and the very categories

and spatial boundaries that it created and policed continue to hold sway.[32] In a recent study, Barbara Heron has demonstrated how white Canadian women who participate in overseas development work are able to enjoy a "release from the strictured constructions of white femininity" within largely masculinist development projects. "Faced with the numerically overwhelming physical presence of the Other," Heron explains, the "response of whiteness seems to entail extending a degree of insider status and white power relations to women development workers albeit in gender specific ways." Heron's interview subjects emerge from their development experiences with a "new narrative of self," reflecting a subjectivity that approximates that of the modern bourgeois subject—free, unfettered, and able to act in the world in ways unrestrained by hierarchical gender norms.[33] Like that achieved by their historical counterparts, this contemporary feminist re-coding of the self accomplished by development workers and other white female travellers, such as Ontario midwives, requires (and subsequently reproduces) the colonial context.

☐ Why Midwifery Tourism?

"Tourism," rather than "travel," best characterizes the process by which white women from Ontario engaged in encounters with providers and consumers of birthing care on the U.S.-Mexico border. The term "travel," as Inderpal Grewal has noted, implies a "universal form of mobility,"[34] and consequently elides contemporary population movements that are inherently coercive—that is, movements of people as the result of war, interethnic conflict, forced migration, or the decimation of social and economic structures wrought by policies of structural adjustment. "Tourism," on the other hand, connotes a largely voluntary form of travel available to those whose citizenship status and financial resources permit them access to locations and populations deemed desirable.

While an appetite for the exotic has long fuelled the modernist tourism enterprise, some of its newest forms claim to offer the tourist something more morally uplifting than the pursuit of pleasure through the consumption of difference. In a context of widespread anxiety in the West around social degeneracy and planetary decline, initiatives such as eco-tourism and cultural tourism promise the Western tourist access to those spaces not-as-yet destroyed by capitalism's excesses. Indigenous cultures are fantasized in this schema as the repositories of health and wholeness and both land and people, represented via a "revitalized primitivist stereo-type," become seductive objects for tourist consumption.[35] Construed as an inherently ethical and mutually beneficial engagement with the Other, these forms of tourism promise a fundamental transformation of self in which the tourist's implication within neo-colonial relations of power are rendered moot. What cultural tourists seek, argues Griselda Pollock, is to "refuse the space and time of their own cultural deaths while inflicting it on everyone else." [36]

"When the past is displaced, often to another location," explains Caren Kaplan, "the modern subject must travel to it."[37] It is to this "ana-chronistic space,"[38] a place that exists in the real world but lacks syn-chronicity with modernity's teleological march, that cultural tourists are drawn. And while the broad outlines of cultural tourism's appeal have been traced above, midwifery tourism is driven by a desire for a very specific Other: the "Third World" mother, mythologized widely within natural childbirth discourse as possessing innate feminine birthing knowledge as yet uncorrupted by western medical practices. From American anthropolo-gist Margaret Mead in the 1940s to British childbirth reformer Sheila Kitzinger in the 1990s, primitive subjects have been referred to as a way of decrying the impaired childbearing capacities of women in the West.[39]

Indigenous Latin American women have been awarded a particu-larly revered iconography in natural childbirth literature. Bridget Jordan's *Birth in Four Cultures* is a scholarly ethnography of childbearing "with the assistance of family and friends" among Maya Indians in Yucatan, Mexico. Once impossible to find, it is currently in its fourth printing and is being widely used, by the author's admission, "in the ongoing enterprise of changing the American way of birth."[40] For many years, the U.S. publica-tion *Birth*, a medical journal devoted to clinical reform of maternity care practices, has featured Latin American birth art from reproductions of Mix-tec geneaological-historical manuscripts to a contemporary painting enti-tled *Homage to the Mothers of Latin America*. In Canada, the image of a Nicaraguan *partera* (midwife) is emblazoned on a poster promoting the Association of Ontario Midwives, and a film produced in 1979 in a Brazilian maternity ward has been enthusiastically screened for more than twenty years, proof that childbearing women in the West have lost the innate abil-ity to birth naturally while those in the "Third World," frozen in time, have retained it.[41] Indigenous Latin American childbearing women can be con-structed as particularly authentic through links to iconographic figures such as Quiché Indian activist Rigoberta Menchú, as well as through popular representations of the forest-dwelling suppliers of raw materials to The Body Shop, touted as having access to the secrets of natural health through substances unknown in the West.

Midwifery tourism is a material practice involving travel from one place to another, the exchange of money, the performance of medical acts, and the issuance of certificates of completion. However, its materiality is inextricably interwoven with, indeed produced by, discursive constructs. A discourse of authenticity makes the "Third World" woman a desirable object of engagement because she is a "full representative of . . . her tradition."[42] However, it is the discourse of global sisterhood that allows midwifery tourists to defer any implication in the North–South relations of global inequality. As one midwife told me about her experience on the U.S.–Mexico border, "There was something that went beyond borders, in terms of midwifery care and terms of caring for each other as women. It was such a common bond that it didn't matter who you were at that point. . . . I felt you were just 'with woman' and all you had to be was a woman to make that happen." Framed within discourses of borderlessness and benevolence, midwifery tourism allowed Canadian women to produce themselves as respectable professionals while rationalizing both the specific relations of violence experienced in the border clinics and the global violence that produces the geopolitical spaces in which those clinics have thrived.

☐ **The U.S.–Mexico Border as Transnational Space**

The U.S.–Mexico border zone is a space characterized by histories of colonial conquest, dramatic demographic shifts, and aggressive economic incursions by multinational corporations. According to Chicana theorist Gloria Anzaldúa, the border is a "1,950 mile open wound."[43] The proliferation since 1965 of scores of maquiladoras, or export-processing factories, which are largely U.S. or Japanese owned, has dramatically altered the population of northern Mexico, drawing residents of central and southern Mexican states northward to border regions such as Matamoros/Reynoso, Ciudad Juarez/El Paso, Calexico/Mexicali, and San Diego/Tijuana.

Factories employ Mexican workers at low wages—typically the peso equivalent of between $40 and $50 U.S. per month—which inadequately support an individual worker, much less an entire family.[44] The largest concentration of maquila workers in Mexico is to be found in Ciudad Juarez, bordering El Paso, Texas. These workers, Debbie Nathan explains, put in "forty-eight hour weeks soldering electronics boards, plugging wires into car dashboards, binding surgical gowns and sorting millions of cosmetics discount coupons mailed by North Americans to P.O. boxes in El Paso."[45] In the Matamoros/Reynoso maquiladoras, the organization of work has been described as "reminiscent of 19th century U.S. sweatshops . . . Tayloristic and authoritarian, with detailed division of labor, repetitive simple tasks and piecework wages."[46] Mexican labour from this border space makes possible the consumption of low-cost consumer goods and other commodities that contribute to the high standard of living in the West.

As elsewhere in the globalized economy, employment in the maquiladoras has a distinctly gendered dimension. The proliferation of export-processing plants in Free Trade Zones around the globe has created unprecedented employment opportunities for women who are considered to be a dexterous and docile, apolitical, and endlessly replaceable workforce. A decade ago, 75–85 per cent of Juarez's maquiladora workers were women; in recent years, this number has been reduced to 50 per cent of the total workforce. Increasing militancy by female workers has rendered their employment less desirable to the managers of export-processing plants. At the same time, the devaluation of the peso has reduced the cost of labour, making maquila production even more profitable for transnational corporations. Under these conditions, the recruitment of male labour has become a practical necessity. For the young women who do enter the maquiladora workforce, hiring is conditional on a negative pregnancy test, and pregnant workers can be summarily dismissed. Employee turnover is exceedingly high and most workers have less than one year's seniority on the job.[47]

For women displaced to the north of Mexico, but unable to sustain employment in the maquiladoras, domestic labour across the border in the U.S. offers a viable employment option. In El Paso, at least fifteen to twenty thousand homes hire domestic help, the majority of whom are women from Ciudad Juarez, employed as both daily maids and live-in household workers.[48] At both the personal and the global level, "Third World" women's labour translates into "First World" privilege.

Undocumented Mexican migrants are the targets of border surveillance in an increasintly "militarized border zone," and the focus of a discourse that points to them as a drain on the public purse.[49] Unwanted as citizens, Mexican residents and migrants are indispensable as transnational consumers in border cities like El Paso. These cities are economically dependent on Mexican shoppers who spend $22 billion a year on consumer goods, pay $1.7 billion in taxes, and generate some four hundred thousand jobs. By some estimates, six thousand medical service jobs in El Paso are underwritten by Mexican nationals willing to pay for medical services, including prenatal, intrapartum, and postpartum care delivered by direct-entry midwives in out-of-hospital birth centres on the U.S.–Mexico border.[50]

White midwives and Mexican women are at the nexus of several transnational processes. Displaced to the north by the promise of employment in export-processing plants and largely impoverished, Mexican women who become pregnant require cheap and competent perinatal care. Poor or inaccessible services on the Mexican side of the border and tightened controls over services to undocumented migrants on the U.S. side of the border (coupled with fears of deportation if they seek care in state-funded institutions), prompt some Mexican women to deliver their babies in out-of-hospital clinics run by predominantly Anglo, direct-entry midwives. More than a cheap or convenient individual solution, for some Mexican women giving birth in the U.S. can arguably be construed as an act of resistance that challenges arbitrary border delineations and creates a transnational Hispanic community through the children's U.S. citizenship.[51]

A widespread practice, cross-border childbirth has gained the attention of public-health researchers hoping to improve maternal-infant health status on both sides of the border. At least two studies have shown that approximately 10 per cent of border-dwelling Mexican women cross into the U.S. to deliver their babies, frequently without having received prenatal care there.[52] While some of these women give birth with nurse-midwives in church-funded Catholic maternity homes, many receive care from direct-entry midwives. While only 0.3 per cent of all births in the U.S. (approximately twelve thousand births) are attended by lay or direct-entry midwives, 75 per cent are conducted in birth centres located on the U.S.–Mexico border and the majority involve Mexican or Mexican-American women as clients.[53] "The great demand for this service," boasts one clinic's promotional pamphlet for potential students, has resulted in El Paso being "the heart of midwifery in the United States."[54]

☐ Border Clinics and Tourist Schemes

There is little in the way of historical documentation about the midwifery border clinics, but their founding is largely contemporaneous with the installation by transnational capitalist enterprise of export-processing industries in the north of Mexico. Although numerous alternative midwifery training schemes have arisen in North America since the early 1970s, most direct-entry midwifery training has been based on attendance at home births which, according to available statistics, did not, in the last decade, exceed 0.7 per cent of total births in the U.S.[55] Border clinics have, for the last twenty years, been a significant training site for those unwilling or unable to pursue long apprenticeships in the few available programs. The clinics have been popular because they enable direct-entry midwifery students to attend large numbers of births within a relatively short time frame.

The Maternidad La Luz clinic in El Paso, Texas, for example, promises that students will attend approximately twenty-five to thirty-five births in a three-month "quarter," nearly enough to fulfil the requirement (depending on the student's role at the birth) for attendance at the forty births required to sit the North American Registry of Midwives qualifying examination. More recently, self-study programs have offered direct-entry midwifery students short-term "externships," primarily to impoverished Jamaican hospitals but also to American-run birth clinics in the Philippines and Guatemala. Students can garner the requisite number of births to acquire the designation "Certified Professional Midwife" granted by the independent Midwifery Education Accreditation Council.[56] Both the border clinics and the travel schemes are contingent on transnational processes that make "Third World" women's bodies available for "First World" women's educational and professional needs.

The training programs last from eight days (hospital stint in Jamaica) to fifteen months (missionary midwifery training program in the Philippines). Costs vary from $1,850 U.S. for the shortest trip to more than $12,000 U.S. for the training program in the Philippines. A popular three-month internship at one Texas midwifery clinic costs $3,750 U.S. Internships at the border clinics typically involve didactic/academic training in the form of classroom education and immediate hands-on experience. Most border clinics do not require previous midwifery experience and yet students can expect to attend twenty-five to thirty-five births in a three-month period. The Jamaican trips offer a much higher volume of births to the prospective student, who, according to one information letter, can expect to deliver between two and five babies per shift and assist at another four to six even if she has had no previous training.[57]

Promotional materials for the clinics and related trips use an unmistakably touristic framing to depict the sites as exotic and desirable. Topographies that have been ravaged by the incursions of transnational corporations are portrayed as whole and unblemished. The following description of the El Paso Maternidad La Luz Direct is offered from a border where the poorest residents on both sides find themselves "breathing the same particulates from open fires, smoke stack emissions, automobile exhausts, burning tires, road dust, and construction sites and sucking water from the same briny depleting aquifers beneath a surface polluted by raw sewage, pesticides and toxic wastes":[58]

> El Paso is situated in the Chihuahuan desert in the western corner of Texas, on the Texas, New Mexico and Mexico borders. It is very hot and dry in the summer with balmy mild winters; sometimes it even snows. The city is bisected by the Franklin Mountains, which is at the tail end of the Rocky Mountain chain. This creates a diverse scenery, including spectacular sunrises and sunsets and beautiful mountain views.[59]

In a place where both space and identity are subject to frequent and often violent contestation, human interaction, too, is discursively costumed in the garb of a contented co-existence:

> The term "bilingual and bicultural" come[s] to life in practically every day-to-day activity in El Paso. With a combined population of over two million, El Paso and its sister city of Cd. Juarez are the largest cities on the U.S./Mexican border. The constant interaction between the two cities adds up to over a million border crossings per month over the four bridges which connect the U.S. and Mexico.[60]

More than geography, however, is re-imagined by the narratological strategy used to promote and sustain midwifery tourism. Indeed what is most successfully re-coded is the relational positioning of the "tourists" and the "natives." Here, cautious comparisons can be made between midwifery tourism and another form of tourism in which transnational movements and racialized and gendered processes of representation collude: the sex tourism industry in Asia. Ample care must surely be exercised in such a comparison. As will be described below, brutal treatment of Mexican women was witnessed by some Canadian midwives in the border clinics, but sex tourism exposes the women who are its objects to far more grievous forms of sustained violence, including physical assault, HIV/AIDS infection, and involuntary confinement.[61]

What links these two forms of tourism, however, is that in both cases "Third World" women's bodies are viewed as a natural resource. As Ryan Bishop and Lillian Robinson put it, "customers lured by an appealing conflation of natural, social and cultural forces are themselves represented as inherently desirable."[62] Bishop and Robinson have demonstrated in the case of the heterosexual sex trade in Thailand that the conditions of globalization, which thrust Thai women into prostitution, are thoroughly obscured through Thai women's representation in tourist literature as naturally desirous of sexual commerce with white men—a representation which also serves to explain the low cost and easy availability of these women for paid sexual encounters.

The identical discursive dynamic can be viewed in the midwifery tourism pamphlet quoted above. Having rendered neutral the harsh environmental and social realities of the border, indeed having performed a magical disappearance of the entire colonial system, promoters of midwifery tourism can argue that Mexican mothers freely choose midwifery care in the clinics because it is an "affordable and desirable alternative" and not because it is a survival strategy in an environment that offers few options. As in sex tourism discourse, midwifery tourism's key selling points are the abundance of desirable bodies and promises of pleasure for the consumer. A brochure from Casa de Nacimiento for potential interns guarantees, in proto-pornographic language, access to "a lot of beautiful Mexican Mamas" and promises that the intern can "expect to palpate and listen to more bellies than you ever thought possible . . . But most of all you can expect to have fun!"[63]

Although they position themselves as the generous benefactors of women eager and grateful for contact, both sex tourists and midwifery tourists reap rewards well beyond those gained by those who service them. Western (male) heterosexual sex tourists return to a privileged existence, their white masculinities secured through sex with brown women. Midwifery tourists, on the other hand, come home endowed with an enhanced respectability that allows them to claim a relatively lofty slot in a workforce segmented by race and gender. These women who made these rewards possible, however, merely survive. This unequal exchange is at the heart of transnational logic. "Whether the gift is worth the price for which the receiver has to pay," Minh-ha T. Trinh has commented, "is a long term question which not every gift giver asks."[64] To do so, I would argue, would unveil the reigning "mystique of reciprocity,"[65] revealing that these tourists' innocence is no more than an illusion.

☐ Narrating the Innocent Tourist

The discursive enticements to midwifery tourism promise a fair exchange, an act of benevolence and a moral project, all of which secure the traveller's innocence, rather than reveal her collusion with the violent effects of globalization. However, real-life encounters in the border clinics threaten to undo this. Indeed innocence is fundamental to midwifery subjecthood in Ontario, where it is narrated through a frequently reiterated heroic tale—a story of meritocratic achievement by a determined and dedicated group of women who endured both legal jeopardy and personal sacrifice to create "not just another profession, but a tool to gain community-based woman-defined care."[66] Some of the challenges threatening the univocal timbre of this narrative have been rehearsed in this essay, but it is the "forgetting" of marginalizing processes that allows the tale to be told and enables midwives to assume a subjecthood which is unassailably moral and unproblematically unitary. If, as Teresa de Lauretis has argued, subjectivity is not a "fixed point of departure or arrival from which one then interacts with the world,"[67] but is produced through our social interactions and our shifting positionalities within those interactions, then it cannot be the case that experience is something that individuals "have." Rather, experience is the grounds upon which our very subjecthood is articulated. It is how midwives rationalize their contradictory experiences in the border clinics in order to preserve their status as innocent subjects.

Subjectivities, as I have noted, are produced in relationship, however they need to be articulated clearly so that they are intelligible and serviceable. Narratives impose a coherency on the unruly strands of a story by discarding those threads that threaten to disturb the desired pattern of the weave. But the sequencing of this weave, as Hayden White has pointed out, always assumes a moral ordering.[68] How, then, do midwifery tourists, through the stories they tell about their experiences in the border clinics, reclaim a moral self by reordering the threads of a narrative that includes participation in forms of care which, at best, are antithetical to an articulated Ontario midwifery philosophy of female benevolence and multicultural sensitivity and, at worst, unmistakably violent and dehumanizing?[69]

A common thread running through the midwives' narratives of the border experiences is the language barrier between themselves and the Spanish-speaking women they attended. In the promotional materials for the Maternidad border clinic, "a thorough understanding of English" is required for admission but only a basic understanding of Spanish is deemed necessary. This, despite the fact that 85 per cent of the clientele are unilingual Spanish speakers. In the Casa de Nacimiento clinic, Spanish is "recommended but not required."[70] Most communication between Ontario midwives and Spanish-speaking women in the clinics was through non-verbal forms of communication, which, for the tourist, can be yet another exotic attraction "to be felt·internally, recognized and enjoyed as a private and intensified 'object.'"[71] The Ontario midwives were convinced of the authenticity of their interpretations of the communication conducted through non-verbal cues and improper Spanish usage and, as demonstrated below, communication gaps were frequently construed as benign. I suggest that such a construction serves to rationalize the contradiction inherent in Ontario midwives' providing care under inferior communicative conditions when education and counselling, shared decision making, and informed choice are the hallmarks of midwifery care in the province.

Ineffective communication between Spanish-speaking women and their Anglo/Canadian caregivers is a theme repeated again and again in the interview narratives as a humorous event. "They're amazing people actually," remarked one veteran midwife, referring to the women she cared for. "They're so warm in terms of being accepting especially of students who speak poor Spanish. They used to laugh at me all the time." Another midwife told me, "I would make a lot of those Mexican ladies laugh their heads off all night long listening to me attempt to speak Spanish. It was really good to help them open up [dilate]. They thought it was really funny." In this quote, communication barriers are not just amusing, they are therapeutic as well. Another midwife found it "hilarious" to be working in an environment that was Spanish-speaking when she spoke only a rudimentary form of the language.

Whether care in a border clinic is benevolent and humane (as it frequently is) or tinged by violence (as in the experiences described by some of those interviewed), the relationship between Mexican women and white midwives is embedded in a transnational and local racial hierarchy. For

Mexican women using the border clinics, compliance and laughter might represent a spontaneous display of mirth, but it might also be an indispensable survival strategy they learned in a hostile border space. Cross-cultural communication, argues Ophelia Schutte, is often received in fragments and it is frequently the most important part of the message that is discarded because its accurate reception would require "the radical decentring of the dominant Anglophone speaking subject."[72]

In at least one study of Latina women's childbearing experience in the U.S., laughter was not the response the researchers encountered when women relayed the impact of language on their maternity care. Rather, Carolyn Sargent, and Grace Bascope report that when interviewing Spanish-speaking women in hospital after childbirth, "several women cried upon realizing that the interviewer spoke Spanish, expressing their desperation to find someone with whom they could communicate."[73]

Two Ontario midwives described witnessing events in the border clinics that transformed their experience from a demonstration of their dedication to the profession to a test of their moral and physical resolve to gain midwifery experience. The women are clear about their objection to what they witnessed but still attempt to resolve the contradictions between the unnerving realities of the border internships and their own benevolent self-conceptions. Their strategies range from constructing a subtle narrative that distinguishes the witnessing student from the guilty perpetrators of the violence, to constructing a blanket rationale in which the repellent elements of the training are justified by the acquisition of valuable midwifery experience.

In the following quote, one of the midwives describes her astonishment and disgust at the violent treatment a Mexican woman receives, but quickly elides that violence by recoding herself as a victim of her colleagues' vicious behaviour. In this way, she manages to justify both her self-imposed silence and her continued stay at the clinic:

> The hardest part for me was, after being there for two weeks, seeing the director kind of say to women (harshly spoken), "Get up on the bed" . . . getting really impatient with this women (shouting), "Open your legs, ahh aah ahh!!!" And I just thought . . . what am I doing here? This is awful! I've got to speak to this. So we're sitting around the table afterwards chewing the fat and I just [said] . . ."You know, I feel that it's really important . . . I don't feel that any woman in labour

should ever be treated unkindly." "Oh," says Connie, "Uh-hmm." "Oh," says Rita, the other intern. Silence. Then they decided they were going to blackball me, kick me out of the program. How dare I critique the program? So, very early on, I got my threat, you know? And I never ever opened my mouth about anything that I couldn't stand there.

The other Ontario midwife describes the behaviour of a clinic employee whom she knew ocassionally worked as a prostitute. She emphasizes the clinic midwife's unrespectable status by referring to her as a prostitute and a biker and masculinizes her by describing her behaviour in the language of sexual violence (the birth is characterized as a "rape"). As the narrative describes the "prostitute woman," it simultaneously constructs, by contrast, the femininity, innocence, empathic character, and bourgeois sensibilities of the speaker, masking her complicity in the violent scene:

> You know the rape began and the woman in the Harley-Davidson T-shirt, the prostitute woman . . . put her feet up against the wall and her knee in the woman's belly to push the baby out, and the blood flowed and her mother-in-law came with her Kleenex to cry and mop up the blood. It was just awful. There was this sort of camaraderie, this sort of rough camaraderie afterwards, "Oh, did you see her mother-in-law was praying?" Gross stuff, gross stuff.

Several of the Ontario midwives infused descriptions of their border experiences with a deep sense of ambivalence. One woman returned with a "real sense of experimenting on people," and others described being profoundly disturbed by the lack of respect and absence of choice that characterized the care in which they participated. Another was particularly disturbed by the transformation of a woman in delivery into a spectacle. She reported that up to ten people would pile into a labour room to observe the final moments of birth. "Sometimes, it's kind of like a 'crotch on a plate,'" she told me. They'd be in the room, she said, and what would they see? A woman giving birth? No. They'd see a baby come out. However ambivalent they felt about their stays in the border clinics and "Third World" practice sites, all the midwives considered their experiences to be invaluable. They were described as "good," "great," and "inspirational." Those who had witnessed the most violent incidents were adamant that even if they had known beforehand what it would be like, they would still have gone to the clinics.

☐ The Rewards of Midwifery Tourism

Ontario midwives were unanimous in their recognition of the material and discursive value of the experience. During the early years of the midwifery movement in Ontario, travelling to border clinics increased midwives' credibility not only among peers and clients but among other medical professionals as well. A recent study of the midwifery movement in Ontario notes that "rewards and actual leadership status [were] given in the early days in the Movement in Ontario to those who had very early begun learning about birth through 'life experience' the traditional way midwives used to learn. 'Third World' experience was especially held in high esteem."[74] One midwife who had apprenticed with physicians in the 1970s talked about the importance of her lengthy stay at a border clinic:

> The significance was that I was considered by the doctors that I worked with when I came back as someone now who had experience, a lot of experience. And most doctors . . . just absolutely assumed that I had my equipment . . . (and that) I would catch the baby at birth. So it gave me a certain kind of ability, expertise, understanding. I learned a lot, I thought a lot. I dealt with stuff down there, postpartum hemorrhage [for example,] that was unbelievable [and] that I'd never dealt with here.

Exposure to complicated maternity cases was key in obtaining a degree of medical expertise and credibility. Such experiences would have been impossible to acquire in Ontario where midwives managed only medically uncomplicated births. In an oddly contradictory way, the clinic experiences allowed Ontario midwives to claim both medical and midwifery authenticity through their experience with "Third World" women whose birthing capacities are ambivalently marked as both "natural" and pathological in the descriptions. Border experience even served as a tool for convincing hostile Canadian physicians of midwives' professional skill. Venturing into what must have been exceedingly hostile territory, pro-midwifery Toronto physician Brian Goldman published a 1988 article on home birth in the *Canadian Medical Association Journal* in which the described border experience of the midwife and of her exposure to abnormal birth are used as evidence of her competency.[75] More recently, the border clinic experience allowed one aspiring midwife "to see a lot of things that I wouldn't see here because of numbers. I mean I saw a prolapsed cord, I saw babies going, I saw a lot of hemorrhages, this and that." For another midwife, "Third World" women provide a constantly renewable source of expertise: "And what I find . . . I've always done is I go back to developing countries to refresh my skills on doing breeches and twins and some of these complicated cases here."

Midwifery tourism is a particularly transparent example of how "First World" feminists make use of imperial subject positions in their struggle for localized forms of gender justice and of how identity is made in and through space. And while midwifery legislation did not directly compel midwives to travel abroad for experience, the conditions for its implementation made midwifery tourism a necessary strategy for some white women seeking to become registered midwives in the province. The enticements and incentives that make these travels desirable and the rationalizations that render them benevolent demonstrate the numerous ways in which white "First World" subjects, even those with relatively little power in the transnational scheme of things, continue to find racialized Others a useful tool for constructing dominant identities. Little, if any reward, however, accrues to the women whose availability as objects of study is predicated on globalizing processes of uneven development. Furthermore, when "Third World" women appear in the West, they are not recognized as agents in their own rights but as reified objects of a primitivist discourse.[76]

Feminist projects that capitalize on the results of global conditions of subordination both at "home" and in the "Third World" can have little moral purchase on "global sisterhood." Whether "the emancipatory impulse of feminism can only become possible through the construction of unequal subjects"[77] is a question we must continue to ask. Western feminists must, in the meantime, insistently oppose the entanglement of our projects with cultural and economic inequities in their numerous transnational manifestations.

Notes

Introduction: When Place Becomes Race

1 *R.v.Hayden,* Manitoba Court of Appeal, Monnin C,J,M., Hall and Philp JJ.A. Judgment delivered by Hall J.A. *Western Weekly Reports* [1983] 6 W.W.R. at 659.

2 Michael Ignatieff, *The Rights Revolution* (Toronto: House of Anansi Press, 2000), pp.123–4.

3 Anne McClintock, *Imperial Leather: Race, Gender and Sexuality in the Colonial Contest* (New York: Routledge, 1995), p.130.

4 Dara Culhane, *The Pleasure of the Crown: Anthropology, Law and First Nations* (Burnaby: Talonbooks, 1998), p.48.

5 Carl Berger, "The True North Strong and Free," in Peter Russell, ed., *Nationalism in Canada* (Toronto: McGraw-Hill, 1966), p.5; Robert Shields, *Places on the Margins: Alternative Geographies of Modernity* (New York: Routledge, 1991), p.162.

6 Berger, "The True North Strong and Free," p.5.

7 David Goldberg, *Racist Culture: Philosophy and the Politics of Meaning* (Oxford: Blackwell Publishers, 1993), p.186.

8 Ignatieff, *The Rights Revolution*, p.10.

9 "Government of Canada Introduces *Anti-Terrorism Act*." *Department of Justice Canada.* <http://canada.justice.gc.ca/en/news/nr/2001/doc_27785.html>. November 13, 2001.

10 Sherene H. Razack, "'Simple Logic': Race, the Identity Documents Rule and the Story of a Nation Besieged and Betrayed," *Journal of Law and Social Policy* 15 (2000), pp.181–209.

11 Richard Phillips, *Mapping Men and Empire: A Geography of Adventure* (New York: Routledge, 1997), p.143.

12 Steve Pile and Michael Keith, eds., *Geographies of Resistance* (New York: Routledge, 1997), p.6.

13 See, for example, N. Smith and C. Katz, "Grounding Metaphor: Towards a Spatialized Politics," in Michael Keith and Steve Pile, eds., *Place and the Politics of Identity* (New York: Routledge, 1993), pp.67–83, discussed in David Morley, *Home Territories: Media, Mobility and Identity* (New York: Routledge, 2000), pp.7–8.

14 Edward W. Soja, *Postmodern Geographies: The Reassertion of Space in Critical Social Theory* (London: Verso Press, 1989), p.247.

15 Julie Kathy Gibson-Graham, "Postmodern Becomings: From the Space of Form to the Space of Potentiality," in Georges Benko and Ulf Strohmayer, eds., *Space and Social Theory* (Oxford: Blackwell Publishers, 1997), p.307, discussing N. Smith and C. Katz, "Grounding

Metaphor: Towards a Spatialized Politics," in Keith and Pile, eds., *Place and the Politics of Identity*, pp.67–83.

16 Henri Lefebvre, *The Production of Space*, trans. Donald Nicholson-Smith (Oxford: Blackwell Publishers, 1991), p.7.

17 Eugene J. McCann, "Race, Protest, and Public Space: Contextualizing Lefebvre in the U.S. City," *Antipode* 31,2 (1999), p.169.

18 Goldberg, *Racist Culture*, p.198.

19 Lefebvre, *The Production of Space*, p.39.

20 Samira Kawash, "The Homeless Body," *Public Culture* 10,2 (1998), p.323.

21 Ibid., 329.

22 Ibid., p.325.

23 Ibid., pp.332, 337.

24 Michel Foucault, "Space, Power, Knoweldge," Interview with Paul Rabinow, trans. Christian Hubert, in Paul Rabinow, ed., *The Foucault Reader* (New York: Pantheon, 1984) p.252.

25 Foucault, "Madness and Civilization," in Rabinow, ed., *The Foucault Reader*, p.124.

26 Ibid., p.131.

27 Ibid., pp.181–2, 184, 189, 191.

28 Kathleen Kirby, "Re:Mapping Subjectivity: Cartographic Vision and the Limits of Politics," in Nancy Duncan, ed., *Body Space: Destabilizing Geographies of Gender and Sexuality* (New York: Routledge, 1996), p.44.

29 Ibid.

30 Ibid., p.48.

31 Radhika Mohanram, *Black Body: Women, Colonialism, and Space* (Minneapolis: University of Minnesota Press, 1999), p.4.

32 A bricoleur undertakes odd jobs and is a jack of all trades. Since the term as used in Lévi-Strauss has no English equivalent, it is usually not translated. Lévi-Strauss uses bricolage to describe a characteristic feature of mythical thought. David Macey, *The Penguin Dictionary of Critical Theory* (London: Penguin, 2000), p.52.

33 Mary Louise Pratt, *Imperial Eyes: Travel Writing and Transculturation* (New York: Routledge, 1992).

34 Mohanram, *Black Body*, pp.11, 14, 15; Alfred W. Crosby, *Ecological Imperialism: The Biological Expansion of Europe, 900–1900* (Cambridge: Cambridge University Press, 1986).

35 Phillips, *Mapping Men and Empire*, p.60.

36 Mohanram, *Black Body*, p.167.

37 Phillips, *Mapping Men and Empire*, p.68.

38 Barbara Heron, "Desire for Development: The Education of White Women as Development Workers" (Ph.D. diss., University of Toronto, 1999).

39 Arjun Appadurai, "Putting Hierarchy in Its Place," *Cultural Anthropology* 3,1 (1988), pp.36–49. See also Mohanram, *Black Body,* p.11, for a discussion of Appadurai.

40 Sherene H. Razack, "From the 'Clean Snows of Petawawa': The Violence of Canadian Peacekeepers in Somalia," *Cultural Anthropology* 15,1 (2000), pp.127–63.

41 See, for example, Erica Carter, James Donald, and Judith Squires, eds., *Space and Place: Theories of Identity and Location* (London: Lawrence and Wishart, 1993); Gillian Rose, *Feminism and Geography: The Limits of Geographical Knowledge* (Minneapolis: University of Minnesota Press, 1993); Doreen B. Massey, *Space, Place and Gender* (Minneapolis: University of Minnesota Press, 1994); Women and Geography Study Group, *Feminist Geographies: Explorations in Diversity and Difference* (Harlow: Longman, 1997); Rosa Ainley, ed., *New Frontiers of Space, Bodies and Gender* (New York: Routledge, 1998); Elizabeth Kenworthy Teather, *Embodied Geographies: Space, Bodies and Rites of Passage* (New York: Routledge, 1999).

42 Susan Hanson and Geraldine Pratt, *Gender, Work, and Space* (New York: Routledge, 1995).

43 Sheila Gill, review of *Mind and Body Spaces: Geographies of Illness, Impairment and Disability*, edited by Ruth Butler and Hester Parr, *Revue Canadienne Droit et Société/Canadian Journal of Law and Society* 15,2 (2000), pp.228–34.

44 Ruth Fincher and Jane M. Jacobs, "Introduction," Ruth Fincher and Jane M. Jacobs, eds., *Cities of Difference* (London: The Guilford Press, 1998), p.2.

45 Jane M. Jacobs, *Edge of Empire: Postcolonialism and the City* (New York: Routledge, 1996), pp.33–4.

46 Mohanram, *Black Body*, p.3.

47 Goldberg, *Racist Culture*, p.185.

Chapter 1: Rewriting Histories of the Land

1 I have used a number of terms interchangeably to describe the subjects of this article. Generally, I use the term "Indigenous peoples," as it is the international term most commonly selected by Indigenous peoples to describe themselves. However, Indigenous peoples in Canada often use the term "Aboriginal" or "Native" to describe themselves; as a result, I have included these terms as well, particularly when focusing on the local context. Occasionally, the term "Indian" is included when popularly used by Native people (such as the term "American Indians").

2 Emma LaRocque, "Preface—or 'Here Are Our Voices—Who Will Hear?'" in Jeanne Perrault and Sylvia Vance, eds., *Writing the Circle: Native Women of Western Canada* (Edmonton: NeWest Publishers, 1993).

3 Linda Tuhiwai Smith, *Decolonizing Methodologies: Research and Indigenous Peoples* (London: Zed Books, 1999), p.38.

4 Winona Stevenson, "Colonialism and First Nations Women in Canada," in Enakshi Dua and Angela Robertson, eds., *Scratching the Surface: Canadian Anti-Racist Feminist Thought* (Toronto: The Women's Press, 1999), p.49.

5 Losing access to the European trade appears to have been devastating for many communities. In *The Ojibwa of Southern Ontario* (Toronto: University of Toronto Press, 1991), Peter S. Schmalz recounts how Captain St. Pierre arrived at Madeline Island in 1718 to find an isolated community of Ojibway who had, over the past twenty-two years, lost access to the fur trade as a result of geographic isolation, war with the Iroquois, and the deadly trading competition between the French and the English, which involved continuously cutting off each others' markets. After a century of growing dependence on European technology, the community no longer had the endurance to hunt without guns or the skills to make stone, bone, and wood tools and utensils to replace the metal ones they had become dependent on using. The women had lost many of the skills of treating skins (when they were able to obtain them) for clothing. St. Pierre found a ragged and starving community, desperate to enter into trade relationships again. It is not a matter, after all, simply of individuals "roughing it" and re-adapting to Indigenous forms of technology. Indigenous communities had to be able to live off the land on a scale that would keep whole communities viable.

6 James (Sakej) Youngblood Henderson, *The Mi'kmaw Concordat* (Halifax: Fernwood Publishing, 1997), p.80.

7 Olivia Patricia Dickason, *Canada's First Nations: A History of Founding Peoples from Earliest Times* (Toronto: Oxford University Press, 1992), pp.103–7.

8 Between Jacques Cartier's first visit to the Montreal region in 1534 and Samuel de Champlain's establishing of a colony in 1608—a matter of seventy years—

disease and warfare with the Haudeno-saunee Confederacy resulted in the disappearance of the extensive St. Lawrence Iroquoian communities (each village numbering up to two thousand people), which had populated what is now the Montreal region. The highly strategic nature of this location for control over the St. Lawrence trade route cannot be discounted as the reason for such continuous warfare. However, it is also the case that many of the former residents of these communities were then incorporated into the Mohawk nation, as a means of repopulating communities weakened by disease—and in this respect, the St. Lawrence Iroquoians did not become extinct but were incorporated into the Six Nations Iroquois Confederacy. See Bruce G. Trigger, *Natives and Newcomers: Canada's "Heroic Age" Reconsidered* (Montreal: McGill-Queen's University Press,1985), p.147; and James V. Wright, "Before European Contact," in Edward S. Rogers and Donald B. Smith, eds., *Aboriginal Ontario: Historical Perspectives on the First Nations* (Toronto: Dundurn Press, 1994), p.35.

9 Schmalz, *The Ojibwa of Southern Ontario*, p.16.

10 Contemporary attacks on Aboriginal harvesting, as well as the distrust that many environmentalists apparently hold for Native communities' abilities to maintain ecological relationships with the environment, have only been accelerated by the interest on the part of some historians in "debunking" notions of the viability of Aboriginal ecological relationships in the past. Calvin Martin, for example, has advanced theories that suggest Aboriginal peoples lost their respect for animals during the fur trade because of the breakdown of their spiritual framework, which was caused by illness contracted from Europeans.

11 Georges E. Sioui, "Why We Should Have Inclusivity and Why We Cannot Have It," *Ayaangwaamizin: The International Journal of Indigenous Philosophy* 1,2 (1997), p.56.

12 The Doctrine of Discovery was the formal code of juridical standards in international law that had been created by papel edict to control the different interests of European powers in the different lands they were acquiring. For its primary tenets, see Ward Churchill, *Struggle for the Land: Indigenous Resistance to Genocide, Ecocide and Expropriation in Contemporary North America* (Toronto: Between the Lines, 1992), p.36.

13 Georges E. Sioui, *Huron Wendat: The Heritage of the Circle* (Vancouver: University of British Columbia Press, 1999), pp.84–5.

14 Bruce G. Trigger, "The Original Iroquoians: Huron, Petun, and Neutral," in Rogers and Smith, eds., *Aboriginal Ontario*, p.51.

15 Sioui, *Huron Wendat*, p.86.

16 Trigger, "The Original Iroquoians," p.54.

17 Ibid., pp.55–61.

18 Sioui, *Huron Wendat*, p.153.

19 Georges E. Sioui, *For an Amerindian Autohistory* (Montreal: McGill-Queen's University Press, 1992), p.22.

20 Donald Marshall, Sr. (Grand Chief), Grand Captain Alexander Denny, and Putus Simon Marshall of the Executive of the Grand Council of the Mi'kmaw Nation, "The Covenant Chain," in Boyce Richardson, ed., *Drumbeat: Anger and Renewal in Indian Country* (Toronto: Summerhill Press and the Assembly of First Nations, 1989), p.78.

21 Gail Boyd, "Struggle for Aboriginal Mobility Rights Continues," *The First Perspective* (March 6, 1998), p.6; "Wabanaki Confederacy Conference at Odenak—1998," *Micmac Maliseet Nations News*, Aug. 3, 1998, p.3.

22 Henderson, *The Mi'kmaw Concordat*, pp.80–1.

23 Mi'kmaq people generally wish to be referred to in the terms of their own language, rather than through the generic term "Micmac," which had been applied to them. My limited understanding of the Mi'kmaq language suggests to me that individuals and family groups are referred to as "Mi'kmaw," while the nation and its language is referred to as "Mi'kmaq." My apologies to those who are better language speakers, for whom my use of terminology may not be accurate enough.

24 Henderson, *The Mi'kmaw Concordat*, p.37.

25 The independence enjoyed by the Mi'kmaq under the Concordat did not sit well with the Jesuits who came to Acadia to minister to both Acadian colonists and Mi'kmaqs. The Mi'kmaq rejected the Jesuits' authoritarian ways, after which the Jesuits attended only to the Catholics of New France. Mi'kmaki continued a relatively anomalous independence from French missionaries and colonists for most of the period of French ascendancy in North America and indeed, for the most part considered themselves, and were considered as, allies with the French Crown in its escalating war with the British in North America. Ibid., pp.82–4, 85–93.

26 David E. Stannard, *American Holocaust: The Conquest of the New World* (Toronto: Oxford University Press, 1992), p.238; Ward Churchill, *Indians Are Us? Culture and Genocide in Native North America* (Toronto: Between the Lines, 1994), pp.34–5; Jack D. Forbes, *Black Africans and Native Americans: Color, Race and Caste in the Evolution of Red-Black Peoples* (Oxford: Basil Blackwell, 1988), pp.54–8; and Dickason, *Canada's First Nations*, p.108.

27 Dickason, *Canada's First Nations*, p.159; Daniel N. Paul, *We Were Not the Savages: A Mi'kmaq Perspective on the Collision between European and Native American Civilizations* (Halifax: Fernwood Books, 2000), pp.181–2.

28 Paul, *We Were Not the Savages*, p.207.

29 Theresa Redmond, "'We Cannot Work Without Food': Nova Scotia Indian Policy and Mi'kmaq Agriculture, 1783–1867," in David T. McNab, ed., *Earth, Water, Air and Fire: Studies in Canadian Ethnohistory* (Waterloo: Wilfrid Laurier University Press, 1998), p.116–17.

30 Dickason, *Canada's First Nations*, p.110. Britain violated a number of Doctrine of Discovery tenets by including the notion of the "Norman Yoke," which stipulated that land rights would rest upon the extent to which the owners of the land demonstrated a willingness and ability to "develop" their territories in accordance with a scriptural obligation to exercise dominion over nature. By this means, Britain claimed to be abiding by existing international law, while waging warfare for control of North American colonies with the French who had no interest in "developing" the land. See Churchill, *Struggle for the Land*, p.37.

31 Marshall, Denny, and Marshall, "The Covenant Chain," p.101.

32 Henderson, *The Mi'kmaw Concordat*, p.104.

33 Stevenson, "Colonialism and First Nations Women," p.53.

34 Many of the Indigenous nations affected by this warfare appeared to have fought strategically to ensure that a balance of power between competing Europeans was maintained. It is significant that as the French and British became locked in a death struggle, the Ojibway appear to have signed a pact of non-aggression with the Iroquois. In general, as the extent of European interference in their

affairs became crucial, many of the Great Lakes nations appear to have resisted fighting each other by the mid-eighteenth century. See Schmalz, *The Ojibwa of Southern Ontario*, p.58.

35 John S. Milloy, "The Early Indian Acts: Developmental Strategy and Constitutional Change," in I.A. Getty and A.S. Lussier, eds., *As Long as the Sun Shines and the Water Flows: A Reader in Canadian Native History* (Vancouver: University of British Columbia Press, 1983), pp.56–63.

36 Dickason, *Canada's First Nations*, pp.182–4.

37 Schmalz, *The Ojibwa of Southern Ontario*, has suggested that during the Pontiac uprising, the Ojibway and other nations were too divided by their dependence on European trade goods and by the inroads that alcohol was making in the communities to successfully rout the British from the Great Lakes region, as they might have been capable of doing in earlier years. Although driving the British out of the region was undoubtedly the wish of some of the Ojibway communities, there were other communities situated far away from encroaching British settlement, but equally dependent on European technology, that were less certain of the threat the British ultimately posed.

38 Churchill, *Indians Are Us?* p.35.

39 E. Wagner and E. Stearn, *The Effects of Smallpox on the Destiny of the Amerindian* (Boston: Bruce Humphries, 1945), pp.44–5.

40 Schmalz, *The Ojibwa of Southern Ontario*, p.87.

41 J.R. Miller, *Skyscrapers Hide the Heavens: A History of Indian-White Relations in Canada* (Toronto: University of Toronto Press, 1989), p.92.

42 Schmalz, *The Ojibwa of Southern Ontario*, p.13.

43 Excluding Native women from the process was central to its success. In eastern Canada, Native women's voices were in many cases considered extremely authoritative in matters of land use. Excluding them from the signing process made land theft that much easier, by allowing those who did not control the land to sign it over. See Kim Anderson, *A Recognition of Being: Reconstructing Native Womanhood* (Toronto: Sumach Press, 2001).

44 Schmalz, *The Ojibwa of Southern Ontario*, p.123.

45 Ibid., pp.124–5.

46 Peter Russell, *The Correspondence of the Honourable Peter Russell*, eds. G.A. Cruikshank and A.F. Hunter (Toronto, 1935); J.L. Morris, *Indians of Ontario* (Toronto, 1943), as cited in Schmalz, *The Ojibwa of Southern Ontario*, p.126.

47 Schmalz, *The Ojibwa of Southern Ontario*, p.126.

48 Ibid., pp.136, 138–9.

49 Ibid., pp.116, 141, 146.

50 The traditional territory of the Caldwell band is Point Pelee, which is now a national park. The Caldwell band were involved in the War of 1812 as allies to the British Crown, where they were known as the Caldwell Rangers. After the war in 1815, the British Crown acknowledged their efforts and their loyal service and awarded them their traditional territory "for ever more." But it wasn't classified as a reserve, and meanwhile, British soldiers who retired after the war were awarded most of the land. By the 1860s the few remaining members of the Caldwell band that were still living on their traditional territories were beaten out of the new park by the RCMP with bullwhips. By the 1970s, the Caldwell band members dispersed throughout southern Ontario began to take part in ritual occupation of the park to protest their land

claim. A settlement process is currently in effect. (Anonymous Caldwell band member, interview with author, 1999.)

51 After a series of struggles towards resolving historic land claims, the Chippewas of Nawash, one of two remaining Saugeen Ojibway bands, were recognized in 1992 as having a historic right to fish in their traditional waters. This decision led to three years of racist assaults by local whites and organized fishing interests, including the sinking of their fishing boats, the destruction of thousands of dollars of nets and other equipment, assaults on local Native people selling fish, the stabbing of two Native men in Owen Sound and the beating of two others. No charges were laid by the Owen Sound Police or the OPP for any of this violence until the band called for a federal inquiry into the attacks ("Nawash Calls for Fed Inquiry into Attacks," *Anishinabek News*, June 1996, p.14).

Meanwhile, the Ontario Ministry of Natural Resources, in open defiance of the ruling recognizing the band's rights, declared a fishing free-for-all for two consecutive years, allowing anglers licence-free access to the waters around the Bruce Peninsula for specific weekends throughout the summer ("Fishing Free-for-all Condemned by Natives," *Anishinabek News*, July 1995, p.1).

In 1996, despite considerable opposition, the band took over the fishery using an *Indian Act* regulation that severed their community from the jurisdiction of the provincial government (Roberta Avery, "Chippewas Take Over Management of Fishery," *Windspeaker*, July 1996, p.3). The other Saugeen Ojibway band on the peninsula, the Saugeen First Nation, announced the formation of the Saugeen Fishing Authority and claimed formal jurisdiction of the waters of their traditional territory. They demanded

that sports fishermen and boaters would have to buy a licence from them to use their waters. The provincial government recognized the claims of neither bands, instead demanding they limit their catch and purchase licences from the provincial government in order to be able to fish at all (Roberta Avery, "Fishery in Jeopardy, Says University Researcher," *Windspeaker*, Aug. 1996, p.16).

By 1997, a government study into fish stocks in Lake Huron revealed that certain fish stocks were severely impaired. While the report was supposed to be for the whole Lake Huron area, it in fact zeroed in on the Bruce Peninsula area a number of times, feeding the attitudes of non-Natives about Native mismanagement of the fishery (Rob McKinley, "Fight Over Fish Continues for Nawash," *Windspeaker*, Sept. 1997, p.14). To add to the difficulties, in 1997, Atomic Energy of Canada announced their desire to bury 20,000 tonnes of nuclear waste in the Canadian shield. This brought to the band's attention the extent to which the fishery was already affected by nuclear contamination from the Bruce Nuclear Power Development on Lake Huron, 30 km south of the reserve (Roberta Avery, "No Nuclear Waste on Indian Land," *Windspeaker*, April 1997, p.4).

52 Dickason, *Canada's First Nations*, p.253.

53 James Morrison, "Colonization, Resource Extraction and Hydroelectric Development in the Moose River Basin: A Preliminary History of the Implications for Aboriginal People." Report prepared for the Moose River/James Bay Coalition, for presentation to the Environmental Assessment Board Hearings, Ontario Hydro Demand/Supply Plan, November 1992, p.4.

54 Bruce W. Hodgins and Jamie Benidickson, *The Temagami Experience: Recreation, Resources and Aboriginal Rights in*

the Northern Ontario Wilderness (Toronto: University of Toronto Press, 1989), pp.88–9.

55 Roy M. Longo, *Historical Highlights in Canadian Mining* (Toronto: Pitt Publishing Co., 1973), pp.66–107.

56 John M. Guilbert and Charles F. Park, Jr., "Porcupine-Timmins Gold Deposits," in *The Geology of Ore Deposits* (New York: W. H. Freeman and Company, 1986), p.863.

57 Howard Ferguson, then minister of Lands and Forests, had so consistently awarded timber and pulpwood concessions without advertisement, public tenders, or even formal agreements on price to individuals like Frank Anson who founded the powerful Abitibi Power and Paper Company, that he was found guilty in 1922 of violating the *Crown Timber Act*—one of the few whites to ever be prosecuted for disobeying federal legislation concerning Indigenous land. See Morrison, "Colonization, Resource Extraction and Hydroelectric Development."

58 Henderson, *The Mi'kmaw Concordat*, p.17.

59 Basil Johnston, *The Manitous: The Spiritual World of the Ojibway* (Toronto: Key Porter, 1995).

Chapter 2: In Between and Out of Place

An earlier version of this paper was presented at the Laws Grounds Conference at the Marshall School of Law, Cleveland State University, Cleveland, Ohio, April 2000. For their insightful comments and suggestions, my thanks go out to Douglas Harris, Carolyn Strange, Mariana Valverde, and Barrington Walker.

1 I have adapted the phrase "racial order of things" from the title of Ann Laura Stoler's excellent book, *Race and the Education of Desire: Foucault's History of Sexuality and the Colonial Order of Things* (Durham, NC: Duke University Press, 1995).

2 On Canadian nation-building, see Carolyn Strange and Tina Loo, *Making Good* (Toronto: University of Toronto Press, 1997); Mariana Valverde, *The Age of Light, Soap, and Water: Moral Reform in English Canada, 1885–1925* (Toronto: McClelland and Stewart, 1991). The quote is from Kay Anderson, "Engendering Race Research: Unsettling the Self/Other Dichotomy," in Nancy Duncan, ed., *Body Space* (New York: Routledge, 1996), p.208.

3 Kay Anderson, *Vancouver's Chinatown: Racial Discourse in Canada, 1875–1980* (Montreal: McGill-Queen's University Press, 1991); Ann Laura Stoler, "Rethinking Colonial Categories," *Comparative Studies in Society and History* 13 (1989), p.134; Ann Laura Stoler, "Making Empire Respectable: The Politics of Race and Sexual Morality in Twentieth-Century Colonial Cultures," in Anne McClintock, Aamir Mufti, and Ella Shohat, eds., *Dangerous Liaisons: Gender, Nation, and Postcolonial Perspectives* (Minneapolis: University of Minnesota Press, 1997), p.345.

4 Despite the prevalence of inter-racial couplings between other racialized groups in this period, local and provincial concerns about miscegenation were expressed most vehemently about inter-racial sex between white men and Native women. See Renisa Mawani, "The 'Savage Indian' and the 'Foreign Plague': Mapping Racial Categories and Legal Geographies of Race in British Columbia, 1871–1925" (Ph.D. diss., University of Toronto, 2001), chap. 5.

5 Sarah Carter, "Categories and Terrains of Exclusion: Constructing the 'Indian Woman' in the Early Settlement Era in Western Canada," in Joy Parr and Mark Rosenfeld, eds., *Gender and History in Canada* (Toronto: University of Toronto Press, 1996), p.30; Adele Perry, "Gender, Race, and the Making of a Colonial Soci-

ety: British Columbia, 1858–1971" (Ph.D. diss., York University, 1997), p.173; Adele Perry, "'Fair Ones of a Purer Caste': White Women and Colonialism in Late-Nineteenth Century British Columbia," *Feminist Studies* 23 (1997), p.505.

6 Edward Said, *Culture and Imperialism* (New York: Vintage Books, 1993), p.7.

7 In British Columbia, Indian reserves were first allocated by Governor James Douglas under the colonial government and were then administered by the provincial government. Although no formal acreage formula was implemented, the size of reserves was largely determined by how much land Native peoples needed. On this point see Robin Fisher, *Contact and Conflict: Indian-European Relations in British Columbia, 1774–1890* (Vancouver: University of British Columbia Press, 1977). For a history of Indian land policies, see Paul Tennant, *Aboriginal Peoples and Politics: The Indian Land Question in British Columbia, 1849–1989* (Vancouver: University of British Columbia Press, 1990).

8 R. S. C. 1876, c. 18. All subsequent references are drawn from this Act.

9 The provincial governments passed a series of legislation prohibiting the sale of intoxicants to Native peoples. In British Columbia, the first law was enacted in 1854 and was followed by a number of other acts and amendments. After Confederation, when the federal government assumed responsibility for Native peoples, it too enacted a number of prohibitions. For a summary of provincial and federal liquor laws, see C. Backhouse, "'Your Conscience Will be Your Own Punishment': The Racially Motivated Murder of Gus Ninham, Ontario, 1902," in G. B. Baker and J. Phillips, eds., *Essays in the History of Canadian Law,* vol. 8 (Toronto: University of Toronto Press, 1999). On the enforcement of

provincial legislation, see G. Marquis, "Vancouver Vice: The Police and the Negotiation of Morality, 1904–1935," in H. Foster and J. McLaren, eds., *Essays in the History of Canadian Law: B.C. and the Yukon* (Toronto: University of Toronto Press, 1995). For more information on the generating of revenues, see M. Ajzenstadt, "Cycles of Control: Alcohol Regulation and the Construction of Gender Role, British Columbia 1870–1925," *International Journal of Canadian Studies* 11 (1995), p.103; M. Valverde, *Diseases of the Will: Alcohol and the Dilemmas of Freedom* (London: Cambridge University Press, 1998), pp.162–70.

10 Stoler, *Race and the Education of Desire.* See also C. Hall, "Missionary Stories: Gender and Ethnicity in England in the 1830s and 1840s," in L. Grossberg, C. Nelson, and P. Treichler, eds., *Cultural Studies* (New York: Routledge, 1992), p.240; Stoler, "Rethinking Colonial Categories," p.154.

11 Anderson, "Engendering Race Research," p.201.

12 Stoler, "Making Empire Respectable," p.345; Anderson, *Vancouver's Chinatown,* p.204.

13 Mary Louise Pratt defines "contact zones" as "social spaces where disparate cultures meet, clash, and grapple with each other, often in highly asymmetrical relations of domination and subordination—like colonialism, slavery, or their aftermaths as they are lived out across the globe today." See M. L. Pratt, *Imperial Eyes: Travel Writing and Transculturation* (London: Routledge, 1992). On sexual relations between Native women and white men, see Perry, "Fair Ones of a Purer Caste"; J. Barman, *The West Beyond the West: A History of British Columbia,* 2nd ed. (Toronto: University of Toronto Press, 1996); J. S. H. Brown, *Strangers in Blood: Fur Trade Company*

Families in Indian Country (Vancouver: University of British Colombia Press, 1986); S. Van Kirk, Many Tender Ties: Women in Fur Trade Society in Western Canada, 1670–1870 (Norman: University of Oklahoma Press, 1980).

14 For a discussion of the racial and gender demography of British Columbia, see Barman, The West Beyond the West, especially chap. 1; and J. Barman, "Taming Aboriginal Sexuality: Gender, Power, and Race in British Columbia, 1850–1900," British Columbia Studies 115/116 (1997/98), pp.246, 248.

15 Stoler, "Making Empire Respectable," p.360.

16 Anderson, Vancouver's Chinatown.

17 Barman, The West Beyond the West.

18 See J.I. Little, "The Foundations of Government," in H.J.M. Johnston, ed., The Pacific Province: A History of British Columbia (Vancouver: Douglas and McIntyre, 1996), p.79; D. Culhane, The Pleasure of the Crown: Anthropology, Law, and First Nations (Burnaby: Talon Books, 1998), p.26. For an elaboration of this argument, see Bonita Lawrence, "'Real' Indians and Others: Mixed-Race Urban Native People, the Indian Act, and the Rebuilding of Indigenous Nations" (Ph.D. diss., Ontario Institute for Studies in Education of the University of Toronto, 1999), and her chapter in this book, "Rewriting Histories of the Land."

19 David Goldberg, Racist Culture: Philosophy and the Politics of Meaning (Oxford: Blackwell Publishers, 1993), p.187.

20 J.L. Tobias, "Protection, Civilization, Assimilation: An Outline History of Canada's Indian Policy," Western Canadian Journal of Anthropology 6 (1976), p.14; D. Roediger, Toward the Abolition of Whiteness (London: Verso, 1994), p.13.

21 Toni Morrison, Playing in the Dark: Whiteness and the Literary Imagination (New York: Vintage Books, 1993), p.6. For an excellent discussion of how whiteness was constructed in American jurisprudence through decisions about who was not white, see I. Haney-Lopez, White By Law: The Legal Construction of Race (New York: New York University Press, 1996). For a similar argument in the Canadian context, see Sherene Razack, "Making Canada White: Law and the Policing of Bodies of Colour in the 1990s," Canadian Journal of Law and Society 14,1 (1999), p.161.

22 R. Shields, Places on the Margin: Alternative Geographies of Modernity (New York: Routledge, 1991), p.165.

23 For a discussion of the government's confusion over legally defining "Eskimo," see C. Backhouse, Colour Coded: A Legal History of Racism in Canada, 1900–1950 (Toronto: University of Toronto Press, 1999), especially chap. 1.

24 Ibid., p.21.

25 Treaties and Historical Research Centre, PRE Group, Indian and Northern Affairs, The Historical Development of the Indian Act (August 1978), pp.53, 54.

26 D. Stasiulis and R. Jhappan, "The Fractious Politics of a Settler Society: Canada," in D. Stasiulis and N. Yuval-Davis, eds., Unsettling Settler Societies: Articulations of Gender, Race, Ethnicity and Class (London: Sage, 1995), p.114.

27 J.W. St. G. Walker, "Race," Rights and the Law in the Supreme Court of Canada: Historical Case Studies (Toronto: Osgoode Society for Legal History and Wilfrid Laurier University Press, 1997), p.18.

28 On racism and patriarchy under the Indian Act, see Lawrence, "'Real' Indians and Others," and Patricia Monture-Angus, Thunder in My Soul: A Mohawk Woman Speaks (Halifax: Fernwood Publishing, 1995). On racism and patriarchy generally, see bell hooks, Feminist Theory: From Margin to Centre (Boston:

South End Press, 1984); Sherene Razack, *Looking White People in the Eye: Gender, Race, and Culture in Courtrooms and Classrooms* (Toronto: University of Toronto Press, 1998), especially chap. 3; and A. K. Wing, ed., *Critical Race Feminism: A Reader* (New York: New York University Press, 1997).

29 Lawrence, "'Real' Indians and Others," p.115.

30 Ann Laura Stoler, "Sexual Affronts and Racial Frontiers: European Identities and the Cultural Politics of Exclusion in Colonial Southeast Asia," *Comparative Studies in Society and History* 34 (1992), pp.532–3. See also B. Bush, *Imperialism, Race, and Resistance: Africa and Britain, 1919–1945* (New York: Routledge, 1999). Bush points out that mixed-bloods from French Indo-China and the French West Indies were often sent to help in the "civilizing missions" in French West Africa.

31 Robert Young, *Colonial Desire: Hybridity in Theory, Culture, and Race* (New York: Routledge, 1995), p.76. Young notes an ambivalence about constructions of hybridity throughout history. On the one hand, he suggests that mixed-race people were symbols of degeneracy and, on the other hand, that they were often evoked as the most beautiful human beings in the world. In British Columbia, the former images of the "half-breed" as criminogenic and degenerate were most common.

32 Earl of Kimberley Report to His Majesty (1871). British Columbia Archives and Records Service, GR-0419, box 10, file 1871/23.

33 On this point, see R. A. J. McDonald, *Making Vancouver, 1863–1913* (Vancouver: University of British Columbia Press, 1996), p.25.

34 Department of Justice (26 March 1874) National Archives of Canada, RG 10, reel c10104, vol. 3599, file 1520.

35 There is series of correspondence addressing the large numbers of mixed-race people living on reserves between 1892 and 1913. See NAC, RG 10, reel c11063, vol. 3867, file 87,125.

36 From Loring to Vowell (25 February 1892) NAC, RG 10, reel c11063, v. 3867, file 87,125.

37 Anderson, *Vancouver's Chinatown*, p.82.

38 C. Harris, *The Resettlement of British Columbia: Essays on Colonialism and Geographical Change* (Vancouver: University of British Columbia Press, 1997), pp.83, 97.

39 Parr, "Fair Ones of a Purer Caste," p.503.

40 Ajzenstadt, "Cycles of Control," p.103.

41 For a list of statutes prohibiting liquor consumption among the Native population, see note 9 above. McDonald, *Making Vancouver*, p.30.

42 Robert Campbell's research on public drinking in Vancouver beer parlors suggests that in the 1940s, even when inter-racial drinking was tolerated, mixed-race couples (especially when the woman was white) were the targets of social censure from patrons, owners, and operators of establishments, the latter two refusing to serve them. See R.A. Campbell, "Hotel Beer Parlors: Regulating Public Drinking and Decency in Vancouver, British Columbia 1925–1954" (Ph.D. diss., Simon Fraser University, 1998), especially chap. 4.

43 R.A. Campbell, *Demon Rum or Easy Money: Government Control of Liquor in British Columbia from Prohibition to Privatization* (Ottawa: Carleton University Press, 1991), p.9; J. Noel, *Canada Dry: Temperance Crusades before Confederation* (Toronto: University of Toronto Press, 1995), pp.183–90; and D. Clayton, "Geographies of the Lower Skeena," *British Columbia Studies* 94 (1992), p.42.

44 W.J. Knott, "The Nanaimo Indian" (3 June 1912) United Church Archives,

Victoria College, Toronto, T.E. Eggerton Shore papers. Accession #78.093c, box 7, file 126.

45 Report to Eggerton from G.H. Haley (30 July 1910) UCA, T.E. Eggerton Shore papers. Accession #78.093c, box 7, file 106.

46 J.S. Hussey to McLean (20 October 1904) BCARS, GR 0429, box 10, file 4; Deasy to Vowell (1 August 1904) BCARS, GR 0429, box 11, file 4.

47 My exploration of British Columbia Provincial Court Records between 1890 and 1924 reveals that thirty-eight people were charged with supplying liquor to Indians. Although this number appears insignificant, it is important to note that many liquor offences were dealt with informally or in lower-level courts. In addition, securing convictions for this offence was often difficult due to lack of evidence or questions about whether or not the person to whom the alcohol was given was indeed an Indian by law. BCARS, GR-0605 (1890–1924) vol. 1.

48 Vowell to Attorney General (29 August 1892) BCARS, GR 0429, box 2, file 5.

49 McKay to Vowell (24 September 1892) NAC, RG 10, reel c11063, vol. 3867, file 87, 125.

50 From Methodist Missionaries to Attorney General of B.C. (21 January 1895) BCARS, GR 0429, box 2, file 5.

51 Ibid.

52 A. McClintock, *Imperial Leather: Race, Gender and Sexuality in the Colonial Contest* (New York: Routledge, 1995), p.61. On the idea of a pass system, see Carter, "Categories and Terrains of Exclusion," pp.40–1.

53 Perry, "Fair Ones of a Purer Caste."

54 From McKay to Vowell (22 August 1892) BCARS, GR 0429, box 2, file 5.

55 *Indian Liquor Ordinance* (1867) BCARS, GR 1459, box 1, file 18.

56 From Vowell to various Indian Agents (17 March 1892) NAC, RG 10, reel c11063, vol. 3867, file 87, 125.

57 Methodist Missionaries to Attorney General of B.C.

58 Vowell to unknown (9 November 1892) NAC, RG 10, reel c11063, vol. 3867, file 87, 125.

59 Phillips to Vowell (11 April 1892) NAC, RG 10, reel c11063, vol. 3867, file 87, 125.

60 B.C. Police Court, Savona's Ferry, BCARS, R-0589, vol. 1.

61 "Report on the Half-breeds residing on certain reserves." Loring to Vowell (no date) NAC, RG 10, reel c11063, vol. 3867, file 87, 125.

62 McLean to unknown (6 May 1913) NAC, RG 10, reel c11063, vol. 3867, file 87, 125.

63 Ditchum to Department of Indian Affairs Ottawa (19 February 1912) NAC, RG 10, reel c11063, vol. 3867, file 87, 125.

64 McLean to Ditchum (29 February 1912) NAC, RG 10, reel c11063, vol. 3867, file 87, 125.

65 C.J. South to Superintendent General of Indian Affairs (20 September 1905) NAC, RG 10, vol. 3816, file 57, 045-I.

66 Stoler, *Race and the Education of Desire*.

67 Stoler uses this term to describe the large numbers of illegitimate mixed-race children in the colonies. See "Making Empire Respectable," p.361.

68 David Goldberg, *Racial Subjects: Writing on Race in America* (New York: Routledge, 1997), p.68.

69 Young, *Colonial Desire*, p.174.

70 Lawrence, "'Real' Indians and Others." See also *R. v. Powley & Powley*, [1998] O.J. No. 2 (Ont. P.C.).

Chapter 3: Cartographies of Violence

1 Mona Oikawa, "Cartographies of Violence: Women, Memory, and the Subject(s) of the 'Internment'" (Ph.D. diss., University of Toronto, 1999), p.300. Pseudonyms are used for the women

cited from the interviews and their places of residence are not disclosed for reasons of privacy. The excerpts from the women's interviews that are used in this chapter are taken from the dissertation.

2   The term Internment is a composite metonym for the events of the 1940s. Informed by a community discourse, I use it in place of euphemisms such as "evacuation." I acknowledge, however, that its use is a contested one. In this chapter, I use the term internment camp to describe the B.C.-interior camps. See also K. Adachi, *The Enemy That Never Was* (Toronto: McClelland and Stewart, 1976); T.U. Nakano and L. Nakano, *Within the Barbed Wire Fence: A Japanese Man's Account of His Internment in Canada* (Toronto: University of Toronto Press, 1980); R.K. Okazaki, *The Nisei Mass Evacuation Group and P.O.W. Camp 101, Angler Ontario*, trans. J.M. Okazaki and C.T. Okazaki (Toronto, 1996); Y. Shimizu, *The Exiles: An Archival History of the World War II Japanese Road Camps in British Columbia and Ontario* (Wallaceburg, ON: Shimizu Consulting and Publishing, 1993); and Ann Sunahara, *The Politics of Racism* (Toronto: James Lorimer, 1981).

3   *War Measures Act*, [1914] c. 2, s. 4. All other references refer to this Act.

4   Michel Foucault uses the term carceral to describe various spaces where people are punished, disciplined, and monitored. Michel Foucault, *Discipline and Punish: The Birth of the Prison*, trans. A. Sheridan (New York: Random House, Vintage Books, 1995), p.299. A.M. Alonso also uses this term in "The Politics of Space, Time and Substance: State Formation, Nationalism, and Ethnicity," *Annual Review of Anthropology* 23 (1994), p.394.

5   I use the term "national violence" rather than political violence to indicate how this violence was perpetrated to further

nation-building. I also wish to emphasize the aspect of complicity through this term, as the violence of the Internment was enacted by politicians and the state, but also involved the participation of a nation of citizens.

6   Robert Shields, *Places on the Margin: Alternative Geographies of Modernity* (London: Routledge, 1991), p.18.

7   Edward Soja, *Postmodern Geographies: The Reassertion of Space in Critical Social Theory* (London: Verso, 1989), p.7.

8   Foucault, *Discipline and Punish*, p.141.

9   Soja, *Postmodern Geographies*, p.120.

10 David Goldberg, *Racist Culture* (Oxford: Blackwell, 1993), p.188.

11 Audrey Kobayashi, "The Historical Context for Japanese Canadian Uprooting," in L. Müller-Wille, ed., *Social Change and Space* (Montreal: McGill-Queen's University Press, 1990), p.70.

12 For a description of the use of the *War Measures Act*, see A. Sunahara, "Legislative Roots of Injustice," in R. Miki and S. McFarlane, eds., *In Justice: Canada, Minorities, and Human Rights* (Winnipeg: National Association of Japanese Canadians, 1996), pp.7–22.

13 Adachi, *The Enemy that Never Was*, pp.216, 232.

14 Ibid., p.232.

15 Ibid., p.200.

16 T. Watada, *Bukkyo Tozen: A History of Jodo Shinshu Buddhism in Canada* (Toronto: HpF Press and Toronto Buddhist Church, 1996), p.107.

17 Adachi, *The Enemy that Never Was*, p.209.

18 "The Case for Redress Information" (Toronto: National Association of Japanese Canadians, n.d.), p.2.

19 Sunahara, *The Politics of Racism*, pp.28, 218, 233.

20 See, for example, art critic Christopher Hume's review of Andrew Danson's photographic exhibit "Face Kao: Portraits of

Japanese Canadians Interned During World War II," *The Toronto Star*, April 11, 1996, p.66. Hume writes, "In 1941 . . . Pearl Harbor had just been attacked and if you were a Canadian of Japanese descent, you suddenly found yourself in a prison camp." While Hume does add that Japanese Canadians were "interned in isolated sites where they lived in hardship," he does not specify where these sites were, not even mentioning British Columbia as a geographical location. In addition, Hume makes an error of number in stating, "4,000 Japanese Canadians [were] forced into exile." The Danson photographic exhibit itself warrants further analysis, which cannot be attempted here.

21 I am often confronted by people who ask me various questions on different aspects of the Internment. Their questions usually follow their admissions that they know nothing or very little about the incarcerations. The reiterative appeal for factual evidence and "proving" the existence of these numerous carceral sites goes to the heart of the processes of forgetting. What was done to dematerialize these spaces? Who is held responsible for remembering them and proving their existence?

22 For an analysis of how the "respectability" of bourgeois subjects depends upon their discursive and material construction of pathologized spaces, see Sherene Razack, "Race, Space and Prostitution: The Making of the Bourgeois Subject," *Canadian Journal of Women and the Law* 10 (1998), p.341. Razack also emphasizes that the assertion of dominance over the subjects in pathologized spaces is a violent process.

23 Numbers cited herein are from the National Archives of Canada, Records of the British Columbia Security Commission, RG 36/27, vol. 42, file 2505, part 1,

Canada, *Report on the Administration of Japanese Affairs in Canada: 1942–1944* (Ottawa: Department of Labour, 1944), p.8 (hereinafter referred to as *Japanese Affairs*).

24 NAC, BCSC, RG 36/27, vol. 42, file 2505, part 1, *Removal of Japanese from Protected Areas* (Vancouver, 1942), p.2 (hereinafter referred to as *Removal of Japanese*).

25 Sunahara, *The Politics of Racism*, pp.66–70. See also Takeo Ujo Nakano's account of being incarcerated at the Angler POW camp, *Within the Barbed Wire Fence*; and Okazaki, *The Nisei Mass Evacuation Group*.

26 According to Sunahara, 296 Issei (first generation) men and 470 Nisei (second generation) men were interned in prisoner-of-war camps. *The Politics of Racism*, pp.66, 70.

27 Adachi, *The Enemy that Never Was*, p.232; Sunahara, *The Politics of Racism*, pp.59, 65–76; and *Japanese Affairs*, p.5.

28 Numbers are calculated from the 1941 Census. *Eighth Census of Canada* 1941, vol. 3 (Ottawa: Dominion Bureau of Statistics, 1946), p.164.

29 Adachi, *The Enemy that Never Was*, p.246. Approximately 14,000 people were sent directly to other sites.

30 Sunahara, *The Politics of Racism*, p.55.

31 *Removal of Japanese*, p.8. Emphasis added. The notion of modern Western "civilization" is a critical discourse in the legitimization of the incarceration of Japanese Canadians. Similar to the representation used in the colonial project to represent the colonized as "uncivilized" and "backward," white Canadian officials continually referred to the need to "Canadianize" Japanese Canadians. Spatially segregating Japanese Canadians created the pathologized spaces needed as "proof" of "degeneracy." In this way, white Canadians created

colonies to be conquered *within* the nation, separate and largely inaccessible spaces to which they could travel physically and through the imaginary in order to reconstitute their own entitlements to nationhood.

32 Meyda Yeğenoğlus, *Colonial Fantasies* (Cambridge: Cambridge University Press, 1998), p.6. While arguing against a conflation of European colonial practices outside North America as identical to practices mobilized by white settlers in Canada, I would emphasize that the genocide committed against Aboriginal peoples in Canada underpin the spatial structuring of the nation and its denotation of citizenship.

33 Ibid., p.96.

34 Sunahara, *The Politics of Racism*, p.57.

35 *Removal of Japanese*, p.8.

36 The Canadian-born "males" were listed as numbering 3,590, and the "women and children" as 2,994. NAC, RG 36/27, vol.1, file "Distribution of Japanese." "Memorandum Covering Japanese Movement Pacific Coast" (18 July 1942).

37 For an analysis of the relationship between space and constructions of disability, see R. Kitchin, "'Out of Place,' 'Knowing One's Place': Space, Power and the Exclusion of Disabled People," *Disability and Society* 13,3 (1998), pp.343–56.

38 *Removal of Japanese*, p.11.

39 For a description of Japanese-Canadian women and domestic work, see Mona Oikawa, "'Driven to Scatter Far and Wide': The Forced Resettlement of Japanese Canadians to Southern Ontario, 1944–1949" (M.A. thesis, University of Toronto, 1986), pp.54–8, and "Cartographies of Violence," pp.227–37.

40 Oikawa, "Cartographies of Violence," p.212.

41 See, for example, R.H. Webb, Lieutenant-Colonel of National Defence who, in 1942, argued that using the abandoned buildings in Greenwood, Slocan, New Denver, Sandon, and Kaslo would be the "best and most economic" plan. He also argued that this method would "cut down the cost of feeding [Japanese Canadians] by what they produce themselves." Ibid., p.105.

42 See Sunahara's conclusion that the proceeds from the confiscation and sale of people's property and possessions were used to pay for the incarcerations. *The Politics of Racism*, p.105. In addition, I would argue that the labour of Japanese Canadians was used both to support the war effort and to pay for the incarcerations.

43 Foucault writes that "forced labour is a form of incarceration." *Discipline and Punish*, p.115.

44 Oikawa, "'Driven to Scatter Far and Wide,'" chap. 2.

45 Sunahara, *The Politics of Racism*, p.82. The repatriation survey is described by Sunahara as having two objectives: "to repatriate or deport as many Japanese Canadians as possible, and to disperse the rest across Canada" (p.118). As Sunahara illustrates, the survey was fundamentally coercive and was conducted under conditions of duress. The term "repatriation" is also a misnomer as most of the incarcerated were Canadian citizens and had never lived in Japan.

46 Sunahara uses this term to describe the specific events of 1946 and the pressure exerted by the government to force people to leave the camps at that time. She is not alone in the use of this term to describe the process of leaving the camps.

47 Sunahara, *The Politics of Racism*, p.143. Sunahara also describes the fight against deportation in chap. 7.

48 Adachi, *The Enemy that Never Was*, p.317.

49 For a discussion of the "distancing" process involved in the expelling of

racialized peoples from the nation, see Goldberg, *Racist Culture*, pp.81, 98, 137.

50 *Removal of Japanese*, p.20.

51 The first three commissioners of the BCSC were industrialist Austin C. Taylor; John Shirras, the assistant commissioner of the B.C. Provincial Police; and RCMP Asst. Comnr. Frederick J. Mead. Sunahara, *The Politics of Racism*, p.53. The BCSC was established through Order-in-Council P.C. 1665 of 4 March 1942 under the authority of the Federal Minister of Labour, Humphrey Mitchell, and the supervision of the Deputy Minister, A.J. MacNamara. The BCSC was dissolved by Order-in-Council P.C. 946 of 5 February 1943. The Commission was replaced by the Japanese Division and was maintained under the authority of the federal Minister and Deputy Minister of Labour. See *Japanese Affairs*, p.8; and Oikawa, "'Driven to Scatter Far and Wide,'" p.34.

52 *Removal of Japanese*, pp.11, 25, 26.

53 Ibid., p.24.

54 Kay Anderson describes "Shaughnessy" as "Vancouver's British-origin neighbourhood," emphasizing its elite spatial positioning. K. Anderson, *Vancouver's Chinatown* (Montreal: McGill-Queen's University Press, 1991), p.30. While it is important to recognize how Doukhobors as a group were historically marginalized in Canada—their very existence in the "ghost town" areas marked their spatial exclusion—it is necessary to also acknowledge the hierarchical arrangement of subordinated communities within periphractic spaces.

55 *Japanese Affairs*, p.23.; NAC, Records of the Department of External Affairs, RG 25, Volume 2937, file 2997-40, part 1, "Japanese Population in the Dominion of Canada as of June 30, 1943," p.1.

56 W. Benjamin, *Illuminations*, edited by Hannah Arendt (New York: Harcourt, Brace and World, 1955), p.257.

57 For a description of the term *shikata ga nai*, see for example, Adachi, *The Enemy that Never Was*, pp.355–6. For an analysis of this representation, see Oikawa, "Cartographies of Violence," pp.32–3.

58 I. Grewal and C. Kaplan, "Introduction: Transnational Feminist Practices and Questions of Postmodernity," in I. Grewal and C. Kaplan, eds., *Scattered Hegemonies: Postmodernity and Transnational Feminist Practices* (Minneapolis: University of Minnesota Press, 1994), p.7.

Chapter 4: Keeping the Ivory Tower White

1 See Margaret Wetherell and Jonathan Potter, *Mapping the Language of Racism: Discourse and the Legitimation of Exploitation* (New York: Columbia University Press, 1992).

2 See Sherene Razack, "Race, Space, and Prostitution: The Making of the Bourgeois Subject," *Canadian Journal of Women and the Law* 10, 2 (1998), p.338.

3 The Subcommittee on Multicultural Teacher Education, *Multicultural Teacher Education: A Proposal for a Multicultural Teacher Education Component for the Incorporation into the Program* (Saskatoon, SK: University of Saskatchewan College of Education, 1988), p.5.

4 Ibid., pp.9, 13.

5 Ibid., p.9.

6 See M.L. Fellows and Sherene Razack, "The Race to Innocence: Confronting Hierarchical Relations Among Women," *Iowa Law Review* 1,2 (1998), p.335.

7 Kim, interview with author, November 10, 1995. All names of interviewees are pseudonyms.

8 Wetherell and Potter, *Mapping the Language of Racism*, p.189.

9 Responses are drawn from interviews with participants in November 1995.

10 Lenore Keeshig-Tobias, "O Canada (bear v)," in C. Fife, ed., *The Colour of Resistance: A Contemporary Collection of Writ-*

ing by Aboriginal Women (Toronto: Sister Vision Press, 1993), pp.69–70.

11 C. Harris, "Whiteness as Property," *Harvard Law Review* 106,8 (1993), p.1707.

12 The Subcommittee on Multicultural Education, *Multicultural Teacher Education,* p.10.

13 Ibid., p5.

14 David Sibley, *Geographies of Exclusion: Society and Difference in the West* (London: Routledge, 1995), p.116.

15 See David Goldberg, *Racist Culture: Philosophy and the Politics of Meaning* (Oxford: Blackwell, 1993).

16 See Wetherell and Potter, *Mapping the Language of Racism.*

17 Drawn from interviews with participants in November 1995.

18 Ibid.

19 Chris, interview with author, November 12, 1995.

20 Ibid. Emphasis added.

21 Pat, interview with author, November 15, 1995. Emphasis added.

22 Ibid. Emphasis added.

23 Aída Hurtado, *The Color of Privilege: Three Blasphemies on Race and Feminism* (Ann Arbor: University of Michigan Press, 1996), p.149.

24 See Harris, "Whiteness as Property."

25 See M.L. Pratt, *Imperial Eyes: Travel Writing and Transculturation* (London: Routledge, 1992).

26 Chris, interview with author, November 4, 1995. Emphasis added.

27 Bev, interview with author, November 4, 1995. Emphasis added.

28 Jan, interview with author, November 12, 1995. Emphasis added.

29 Pat, interview with author, November 15, 1995.

30 See Michel Foucault, *The History of Sexuality: An Introduction,* trans. R. Hurley, vol. 1 (New York: Vintage Books, 1990).

31 Ann Laura Stoler, *Race and the Education of Desire: Foucault's History of Sexuality*
and the Colonial Order of Things (Durham, NC: Duke University Press, 1995), p.110. Emphasis added.

32 See Toni Morrison, *Playing in the Dark: Whiteness and the Literary Imagination* (New York: Vintage, 1993).

33 Stoler, *Race and the Education of Desire,* p.53.

34 Ibid., p.54.

35 Ibid., p.69. Emphasis added.

36 Ibid.

37 See Rick Hesch, "Cultural Production and Cultural Reproduction in Aboriginal Preservice Teacher Education," in L. Erwin and D. MacLennan, eds., *Sociology of Education in Canada: Critical Perspectives on Theory, Research and Practice* (Toronto: Copp Clark Longman, 1994), pp.200, 210.

Chapter 5: Gendered Racial Violence and Spatialized Justice

1 *R. v. Kummerfield and Ternowetsky,* "Transcript of 12–15, 18–22, 25–28 November, and 2–5, 9–12, and 17–20 December 1996" [1997] (Regina, Sask. Prov. Ct. [Crim. Div.]), 3469, 4755 (hereinafter "Transcript").

2 B. Pacholik, "Relief, and Anger. Aboriginal Spokesman Demands Appeal," *Leader Post* (Regina), December 21, 1996, p.A1.

3 Barb Pacholik, "Ternowetsky in Ontario Jail, Facing New Charges," *Leader Post,* October 3, 2001, p.A1.

4 *R. v. Kummerfield,* [1998] 9 W.W.R. 619; *R. v. Kummerfield (S.T.) & Ternowetsky (A.D.),* [1998] 163 Sask. R. 257.

5 See, for example, B. Balos and M.L. Fellows, "A Matter of Prostitution: Becoming Respectable," *New York University Law Review* 74 (1999). The authors write: "The unstated assumption is that if a woman enjoyed a benefit, she 'assumed the risk' and therefore bears responsibility for the violence, leaving the alleged perpetrator less accountable for his behavior" (p.1231).

6 I use the term "degeneracy" in this article to denote those groups Foucault describes as the "internal enemies" of the bourgeois state—women, racial Others, the working class, people with disabilities—in short, all those who would weaken the vigorous bourgeois body and state. For a discussion of the concepts of respectability and degeneracy, see Sherene Razack, "Race, Space and Prostitution: The Making of the Bourgeois Subject," *Canadian Journal of Women and the Law* 10,2 (1998), pp.335–52.

7 For a general argument of this kind, made with respect to Aboriginal people in the inner city, see C. La Prairie, *Seen But Not Heard: Native People in the Inner City* (Ottawa: Minister of Justice and Attorney General of Canada, 1994). La Prairie writes: "Overall, the research suggests that social stratification and the experience people have in their families dictate the role they play in cities. It is the ill-equipped who are mostly seen on the streets of the inner city" (p.19). Similar to the deficit model in educational theory, this view places the problems Aboriginal peoples have in cities squarely on their own shoulders, leaving little room for the ongoing effects of colonial practices emphasized in this article.

8 R. Phillips, *Mapping Men and Empire: A Geography of Adventure* (New York: Routledge, 1997), p.338.

9 Quoted in "The Victims: Life and Death on the Edge of Nowhere," *Star Phoenix* (Saskatoon), June 8, 1996, p.c3. Denise McConney cites this article and I am grateful to her for bringing it to my attention. Denise McConney, "Differences for Our Daughters: Racialized Sexism in Art, Mass Media, and the Law," *Canadian Woman Studies* 19, 1 and 2 (1999), p.213.

10 D. Goldberg, *Racist Culture: Philosophy and the Politics of Meaning* (Cambridge, MA: Blackwell Publishers, 1993), pp.185–205.

11 *Canada, Profile of Census Tracts in Regina and Saskatoon* (Ottawa: Statistics Canada, 1999). Regina's total population for 1996 was 193,652. Of that total 14,565 persons identified as Aboriginal. On the problems associated with Aboriginal census data, see J. Saku, "Aboriginal Census Data in Canada: A Research Note," *Canadian Journal of Native Studies* 19,2 (1999). In coming years Saskatchewan is expected to have a greater proportion of population with Aboriginal identity: 13 per cent by 2016. See M.J. Norris, D. Kerr, and F. Nault, *Projections of the Population with Aboriginal Identity, Canada, 1991–2016* (Ottawa: Statistics Canada and Population Projections Section, Demography Division, 1996).

12 D. Anaquod and V. Khaladkar, "Case Study: The First Nations Economy in the City of Regina," in *For Seven Generations: An Information Legacy of The Royal Commission on Aboriginal Peoples*, CD-ROM (Ottawa: Libraxus, 1997), p.6.

13 J.W. Brennan, *Regina: An Illustrated History* (Toronto: James Lorimer and Company and the Canadian Museum of Civilization with the Secretary of State, 1989), p.37; Sarah Carter, *Capturing Women: The Manipulation of Cultural Imagery in Canada's Prairie West* (Montreal: McGill-Queen's Press, 1997), pp.20–1. The brutality of the NWMP and the RCMP towards Aboriginal peoples and their sexual brutality towards Aboriginal women is described in L. Brown and C. Brown, *An Unauthorized History of the RCMP* (Toronto: James Lewis and Samuel, 1973), pp.143–81.

14 Carter, *Capturing Women*, pp.179–82, 187. In 1894, amendments to the *Indian Act* racially encoded the suspect morality of the Aboriginal woman, as well as the suspect obedience to spatial confinement

of the Aboriginal man. That year Indian agents regained their criminal law authority over certain sexual offences committed by Aboriginal persons (first articulated in 1890), and two additional offences became law: Indian prostitution and Indian vagrancy. Canada, *Report of the Royal Commission on Aboriginal Peoples: Looking Forward, Looking Back*, vol. 1 (Ottawa: Supply and Services Canada, 1996), p.289.

15 Carter, *Capturing Women*, p.181.

16 Ibid, pp.189–90.

17 Jim Harding, "Presentation to the Royal Commission on Aboriginal Peoples," May 11, 1993, Regina, Saskatchewan, in *For Seven Generations*, p.321.

18 Brennan, *Regina*, p.165.

19 R.L. Barsh, "Aboriginal People in an Urban Housing Market: Lethbridge, Alberta," *Canadian Journal of Native Studies* 17,2 (1997), pp.203, 212.

20 A.M. Williams, "Canadian Urban Aboriginals: A Focus on Aboriginal Women in Toronto," *Canadian Journal of Native Studies* 17,1 (1997), p.75.

21 Canada, *Report of the Royal Commission on Aboriginal Peoples: Perspectives and Realities*, vol. 4 (Ottawa: Supply and Services Canada, 1996), p.603.

22 "Qu'Appelle Valley Indian Development Authority Inquiry Report on: Flooding Claim Cowessess First Nation, Muscowpetung First Nation, Ochapowace First Nation, Pasqua First Nation, Sakimay First Nation, Standing Buffalo First Nation." *Indian Claims Commission*. <http://www.indianclaims.ca/ english/claimsmap/prov_sask.htm>. May 2000.

23 Canada, *Report of the Royal Commission on Aboriginal Peoples: Perspectives and Realities*, p.602.

24 Ibid., p.520.

25 Anaquad and Khaladkar, "Case Study: The First Nations Economy," pp.1–2;

Canada, *Royal Commission on Aboriginal Peoples, Aboriginal Peoples in the Urban Centres: Report of the National Round Table on Aboriginal Urban Issues* (Ottawa: Supply and Services Canada, 1993), pp.77, 91; Canada, *Report of the Royal Commission on Aboriginal Peoples: Perspectives and Realities*, p.603.

26 Canada, *Report of the Royal Commission on Aboriginal Peoples: Perspectives and Realities*, p.518. The authors of the *Report of the Royal Commission on Aboriginal Peoples* are quoting the Native Council of Canada, *Decision 1992: Background and Discussion Points for the First Peoples Forum* (Ottawa: Native Council of Canada 1992), p.10.

27 Robin Bellamy, "Saskatoon Friendship Inn, 'Discussion Paper C,'" May 13, 1992, Saskatoon, Saskatchewan, *For Seven Generations*, p.366. For more general Aboriginal commentary on the pervasive quality of racism in urban life, see Canada, *Report of the Royal Commission on Aboriginal Peoples: Perspectives and Realities*, pp.367, 426–8.

28 Harding, "Presentation to the Royal Commission on Aboriginal Peoples"; Brennan, *Regina*, p.165; J. Hylton cited in *Royal Commission on Aboriginal Peoples, Bridging the Cultural Divide: A Report on Aboriginal People and Criminal Justice in Canada* (Ottawa: Supply and Services Canada, 1996), p.31n 41.

29 A. Finn et al., "Female Inmates, Aboriginal Inmates, and Inmates Serving Life Sentences: A One Day Snapshot," *Juristat* 19,5 (Ottawa: Canadian Centre for Justice Statistics /Statistics Canada, 1999), p.9. In addition, "at the provincial/territorial level, a larger proportion of Aboriginal than non-Aboriginal inmates were segregated from the rest of the inmate population (11 percent versus 4 percent)."

30 Patricia Monture-Angus, "Women and Risk: Aboriginal Women, Colonialism,

and Correctional Practice," *Canadian Woman Studies* 19, 1 and 2 (1999), p.28 n 3; Manitoba, *Report of the Aboriginal Justice Inquiry of Manitoba: The Justice System and Aboriginal People,* vol. 1 (Winnipeg: Queen's Printer, 1991), p.498 In describing the Saskatchewan situation, Manitoba's commissioners were highlighting the fact that the disproportionate rate of Aboriginal women represented in Manitoba's Portage Correctional Institution (at that time 70 per cent) was by no means unique, particularly when considered within the prairie regional context; Harding, "Presentation to the Royal Commission on Aboriginal Peoples," p.323; Hylton cited in *Royal Commission on Aboriginal Peoples, Bridging the Cultural Divide,* pp.31–2 (notes omitted).

31 "Fact Sheets: Alternatives to Incarceration." *Elizabeth Fry Society.* <http://www.elizabethfry.ca/facts1_e.htm.> July 21, 2000. According to the Society, in 1998 "41 percent of federally sentenced women who are classified as maximum security women are Aboriginal, whereas Aboriginal women represent only 18.7 percent of the total population of federally sentenced women, and less than 2 percent of the population of Canada." See "Position of the Canadian Association of Elizabeth Fry Societies (CAEFS) Regarding the Classification and Carceral Placement of Women Classified as Maximum Security Prisoners." *Elizabeth Fry Society.* <http://www.elizabethfry.ca/maxe.htm>. July 21, 2000.

32 Harding, "Presentation to the Royal Commission on Aboriginal Peoples," pp.324–6.

33 Ibid., pp.327–8, 333–5; Canada, *Report of the Royal Commission on Aboriginal Peoples: Perspectives and Realities,* p.577.

34 Canada, *Royal Commission on Aboriginal Peoples, Choosing Life: Special Report on Suicide Among Aboriginal People* (Ottawa: Supply and Services Canada, 1995), pp.33–4.

35 Of course Aboriginal women also endure considerable violence from the men of their own communities. I would argue that such violence is of a different order than the violence discussed here, although the obvious link is that both emerge out of conditions of colonization. As Emma LaRocque so insightfully commented in her testimony to the Aboriginal Justice Inquiry of Manitoba, the squaw stereotype regulates relations between Aboriginal men and women as it does between Aboriginal women and white society. Emma LaRocque, "Written Presentation to Aboriginal Justice Inquiry Hearings, 5 February 1990," cited in Manitoba, *Report of the Aboriginal Justice Inquiry,* p.479. See also Sherene Razack, *Looking White People in the Eye: Gender, Race and Culture in Courtrooms and Classrooms* (Toronto: University of Toronto Press, 1998), p.69.

36 Manitoba, *Report of the Aboriginal Justice Inquiry of Manitoba: The Deaths of Helen Betty Osborne and John Joseph Harper,* vol. 2 (Winnipeg: Queen's Printer, 1991), p.52.

37 J.L. Sheane, "Life and Death on the Edge of Nowhere," *Star Phoenix* (Saskatoon), June 8, 1996, p.c3.

38 McConney, "Differences for Our Daughters," p.212.

39 Razack, "Race, Space and Prostitution."

40 Malek Alloula, *The Colonial Harem* (Minneapolis: University of Minnesota Press, 1986) cited in R. Bishop and L. S. Robinson, *Night Market: Sexual Cultures and the Thai Economic Miracle* (London: Routledge, 1998), p.151.

41 Laura Robinson, *Crossing the Line: Violence and Sexual Assault in Canada's National Sport* (Toronto: McClelland and Stewart, 1998), pp.39, 120, 151–2.

42 S.P. Schacht, "Misogyny On and Off the 'Pitch': The Gendered World of Male Rugby Players," *Gender and Sociology* 10,5 (1996), p.555. See also A.A. Boswell and J.Z. Spade, "Fraternities and Collegiate Rape Culture: Why Are Some Fraternities More Dangerous Places for Women?" *Gender and Sociology* 10, 2 (1996).

43 P. Donnelly and K. Young, "The Construction and Confirmation of Identity in Sport Subcultures," *Sociology of Sport Journal* 5 (1988), p.235.

44 L.A. Wenner, "In Search of the Sports Bar: Masculinity, Alcohol, Sports, and the Mediation of Public Space," in G. Rail, ed., *Sport and Postmodern Times* (Albany: Suny Press, 1998), p.301.

45 "Transcript," p.3515.

46 *R. v. Kummerfield and Ternowetsky*, "Transcript of Sentencing 30 January 1997" [1997] (Regina, Sask. Prov. Ct. [Crim. Div.]), p.49 (hereinafter "Transcript of Sentencing").

47 "Transcript," p.3811.

48 Ibid., pp.3818, 3821, 3824.

49 Ibid., pp.315–24, 852, 1009, 1394, 3829.

50 Although few scholars of sports masculinity discuss the role that race plays in the making of the white male athlete in the contemporary context, several scholars have noted the connections between sport masculinities and empire. See, for example, R. Morrell, "Forging a Ruling Race: Rugby and Masculinity in Colonial Natal, c.1870–1910," in J. Navright and T.J.L. Chandler, eds., *Making Men: Rugby and Masculine Identity* (London: Frank Cass, 1996), p.91; J. Rutherford, *Forever England: Reflections on Masculinity and Empire* (London: Lawrence and Wishart, 1997). Related Canadian work on sport and national identity has not been explicitly about race and the forging of identities in a white settler society. See, for example, K.B. Wamsley, "The Public Importance of

Men and the Importance of Public Men," and A. Bélanger, "The Last Game? Hockey and the Experience of Masculinity in Quebec," in P. White and K. Young, eds., *Sport and Gender in Canada* (Don Mills, ON: Oxford University Press, 1999).

51 "Transcript," pp.315–24, 457, 595–615.

52 Ibid., pp.846–910.

53 Ibid., pp.463–4, 574–88, 869, 3588.

54 Ibid., pp.3757, 3843.

55 Ibid., pp.470–95, 3494.

56 Ibid., pp.892, 3760.

57 Ibid., p.3933.

58 At Public Hearings in Saskatoon for RCAP, Robin Bellamy contrasted this fear typical of (white) suburbanites ("people say that they are concerned about coming down there on a Saturday night at midnight") with Aboriginal citizens' fear of entering the "better areas of Saskatoon." Bellamy, "Saskatoon Friendship Inn."

59 "Transcript," p.3933. Recall Harding's assertion that the typical victim of violent crime in racialized urban space is young, female, and Aboriginal, not white and male. In 1990–91, Aboriginal persons comprised 31 per cent of the victims of reported crime in Regina, while they represented approximately 5 percent of the population. Harding, "Presentation to the Royal Commission," p.331.

60 This interpretation was suggested to me by Carol Schick.

61 "Transcript," pp.262, 304.

62 Ibid., pp.262, 280–2, 304, 1729–30, 4710.

63 Following press coverage of this incident, the Assembly of First Nations for the prairie region received nearly six hundred calls from Aboriginal men and women describing similar acts of violence towards them. M. O'Hanlon, "RCMP Investigate Deaths of Saskatoon Aboriginal's" *The Toronto Star*, February 17, 2000, p.A3.

64 "Transcript," pp.3574, 3888.

65 For example, Sander Gilman shows how prostitutes in nineteenth-century Europe were depicted with African features even though they were nearly all white. Sander Gilman, "Black Bodies, White Bodies: Toward an Iconography of Female Sexuality in Late Nineteenth-Century Art, Medicine and Literature," in J. Donald and A. Rattansi, eds., *"Race," Culture and Difference* (London: The Open University Press, 1992), p.171. Similarly, McClintock discusses the racialization of the Irish poor, routinely depicted with Black skin in nineteenth-century England. A. McClintock, *Imperial Leather* (New York: Routledge, 1995), pp.52–3.

66 "Transcript," pp.3281–2. Emphasis added.

67 Ibid., p.2922.

68 Ibid., pp.119–21, 2844–9.

69 Ibid., p.2883.

70 Hall is in this instance being read as his nineteenth-century counterpart would have been, that is, as a "squaw man." Carter notes that white lower-class men labelled in this way were often blamed by the police for crimes such as liquor offences. Carter, *Capturing Women*, p.184.

71 "Transcript," p.3008.

72 K. O'Connor, "Issac Felt Police Would Frame Him," *Leader Post* (Regina), December 23, 1996, p.A1.

73 "Transcript," pp.444, 846, 2114–16.

74 T. Sutter, "'She Was My Baby,'" *Leader Post* (Regina), May 13, 1995, p.1.

75 "Transcript," pp.33, 132, 2619, 2993, 3562, 4248.

76 Ibid., pp.457, 3763.

77 Robinson, *Crossing the Line*, p.44.

78 "Transcript," p.2139.

79 "Transcript of Sentencing," p.37.

80 "Transcript," p.3480.

81 "Transcript," pp.4632–3, 4525–7.

82 Ibid., p.4449.

83 Cynthia Lee speculates that this may be the case in cases where provocation is the defence used by men who kill unfaithful wives. Cynthia Lee, "She Made Me Do It! Killings in Response to Infidelity." Unpublished paper in author's possession.

84 "Transcript of Sentencing," p.69.

85 "Transcript," p.4755.

86 Ibid., p.4825.

87 Ibid., pp.4344, 4809, 4824, 4795.

88 Ibid., pp.406, 1409, 3205.

89 "Transcript of Sentencing," p.47.

90 Justice Malone, "Response to the Honourable Chief Justice Allan McEachern to Complaints by Ms. Sharon Ferguson-Hood and Ms. Ailsa Watkinson and Others, February 6, 1997" [1997] (Regina, Sask. Prov. Ct. [Crim. Div.]).

91 Robinson, *Crossing the Line*, p.44.

92 "Transcript," p.2550.

93 Ibid., p.2173.

94 "Transcript of Sentencing," p.50.

95 That Aboriginal peoples are stereotyped as drunk and criminal is acknowledged by the court in *R. v. Williams*, [1998] 1 S.C.R. 1158 at para. 58.

96 "Transcript of Sentencing," p.40.

97 Justice Malone, "Response to the Honourable Chief Justice Allan McEachern. Emphasis added.

98 "Transcript," p.5023.

99 Ibid., p.60. While I do not take a position on the value of long prison terms, I note here that they have been traditionally understood by society as an indicator of the severity of the crime.

Chapter 6: The Unspeakability of Racism

1 Manitoba, Legislative Assembly, *Debates and Proceedings* (30 May 1995), p.235 (G. Filmon) (hereinafter *Debates*).

2 *Debates* (1 November 1995), p.4449 (O. Lathlin).

3 I use the concept of "performance" here to describe the way in which the seemingly stable identities of subjects and of places (i.e., "Canadian," "Canada," "Man-

itoban," "Manitoba") are in fact *consti-tuted by*, and thus their meanings are dependent upon, what Judith Butler calls "a stylized repetition of acts." Judith Butler, *Gender Trouble: Feminism and the Sub-version of Identity*, 2nd ed. (New York: Routledge, 1999), p.179. We can think about the production and reproduction of national identities as Butler does in the case of gender identity, where gender is understood as a project that has *cultural survival* as its end. Gender, in this formu-lation, is "a corporeal style, an 'act' . . . which is both intentional and performa-tive, where 'performative' suggests a dra-matic and contingent construction of meaning" (p.177). In this essay I empha-size the affects and effects of speech ("discursive" or "narrative"), acts whose *performance* reactivates and remains highly contingent upon a racialized legal, political, economic, social, and spatial order. Thus, to perform an identity (and by implication, a history), is to repeatedly act out a story about oneself through time. (The need for repetition is wherein lies the tenuous and unstable nature of identity.) To perform a geography (i.e., a "racism-free" Manitoba) is to mobilize a story about place: the dramatization of a spatial narrative that in turn limns out the nature and the location of the subject doing the telling. Geography, after all, is a story told from a particular point of view, about a space that only becomes a "place" through someone's authoritative telling ("mapping") of it, and by people's continued production (or "performance") of it within the authorized terms of refer-ence. In the argument that follows my primary interest is in the way the law constrains and enables particular kinds of tellings, of both the spatial and the onto-logical variety.

4   Recall that in 1990 the seventy-eight-day standoff at Kanesatake (Oka) between Mohawks, police, and the Canadian mili-tary pushed Aboriginal affairs to the forefront of media attention. In 1991 the Royal Commission on Aboriginal Peoples was mounted, and that year Innu fami-lies were encamped in protest of military installations in Labrador. In 1995, Kettle and Stony Point First Nation protesters blockaded Ipperwash Provincial Park in Ontario, and the police killed protester Dudley George. Also making national headlines in 1995 was a standoff between the Shuswap Ts'peten Defend-ers and the RCMP, at Gustafsen Lake in British Columbia.

5   Jane Jacobs writes: "Imaginary and material geographies are not incommen-surate, nor is one simply the product, a disempowered surplus of the other. They are complexly intertwined and mutually constitutive. . . . Together they have cre-ated the most painfully uneven geogra-phies of advantage and disadvantage. The social construction of space is part of the very machinery of imperialism. . . . [These spatial events] established the beginnings [and I add, the ongoing pro-duction] of that most permanent legacy of imperialism: the contest between that which, through space itself, has been 'naturalised' and that which has been made 'illegitimate.'" Jane M. Jacobs, *Edge of Empire: Postcolonialism and the City* (New York: Routledge, 1996), pp.158–9.

6   *An Act Respecting the Manitoba Hydro-Electric Board*, 1961, R.S.M. 1970 (2nd Sess.), c. H190. All subsequent references are from this Act. For historical reasons I work with the version passed in 1961 and re-enacted in 1970, reflecting revisions up to and including those of 1969 (2nd Sess.). A subsequent version of the *The Hydro Act* was published in 1987, while an *Amendment Act* was published in 1998. The specific articles that I examine

undergo no significant change in these later versions. *The Manitoba Hydro Act* R.S.M. 1987 vol.3 c. H190; *The Manitoba Hydro Amendment Act,* 1997 S.M. 1998 (3rd. Sess.) c. 55.

7   Manitoba, *Report of the Aboriginal Justice Inquiry of Manitoba: The Justice System and Aboriginal People,* vol.1 (Winnipeg: Queen's Printer, 1991) (Commissioners: A. C. Hamilton & C.M. Sinclair); Manitoba, *Report of the Aboriginal Justice Inquiry of Manitoba: The Deaths of Helen Betty Osborne and John Joseph Harper,* vol.2 (Winnipeg: Queen's Printer, 1991) (Commissioners: A. C. Hamilton & C.M. Sinclair) (hereinafter *Report*).

8   Premier Filmon's Conservatives first took power in 1988 after the fall of Howard Pawley's New Democrat government. In September of 1999 (following a year replete with Tory scandal related to the 1995 election), the Filmon team lost to the New Democrats, led by current Premier Gary Doer.

9   *Debates* (29 May 1995), p.212 (O. Lathlin).

10 Ibid., pp.215–17. Emphasis added.

11 *Debates* (29 May 1995), p.222 (G. Filmon).

12 Ibid. On a Point of Order, Opposition House Leader Steve Ashton, Member for Thompson, made this allegation regarding the Premier's conduct. Mr. Lathlin also restated the charge when he rose on a Matter of Privilege the following day.

13 *Debates* (29 May 1995), p.222 (L. Dacquay).

14 *Debates* (7 June 1995), p.953 (L. Dacquay).

15 *Debates* (7 June 1995) at 954 (O. Lathlin). "MLA" refers to "Member of the Legislative Assembly."

16 *Debates* (11 October 1995), p.3789 (O. Lathlin, A Driedger, S. Ashton).

17 *Debates* (1 November 1995), p.4447 (L. Dacquay).

18 *Debates* (1 November 1995), p.4449 (O. Lathlin). A Member of the Opposition alleged that while Lathlin delivered these remarks, a member of the government "was heard to say from his seat, 'this is bullshit.'" Ibid., p.4449 (G. Mackintosh).

19 The following brief description of processes of self- and Other-making in liberal democratic thought and practice draws considerably on the detailed discussion in M. L. Fellows and S. Razack, "The Race to Innocence: Confronting Hierarchical Relations among Women," *The Journal of Gender, Race and Justice* 1 (1998), pp.341–4.

20 L. M. Alcoff, "Philosophy and Racial Identity," *Radical Philosophy* 75 (1996), p.5.

21 *Debates* (30 May 1995), p.235 (G. Filmon).

22 *Debates* (29 May 1995), p.222 (G. Filmon).

23 R. Mohanram, *Black Body: Women, Colonialism, and Space* (Minneapolis: University of Minnesota Press, 1999), p.3.

24 Alcoff, "Philosophy and Racial Identity." Footnotes omitted.

25 *Report,* vol. 1, p.162.

26 Edward Said, *Culture and Imperialism* (New York: Vintage Books, 1993), pp.xii–xiii.

27 *Report,* vol. 1, p.6.

28 Mohanram, *Black Body,* p.183.

29 Report, vol. 1, p.162.

30 *Debates,* (29 May 1995), p.220 (G. Filmon).

31 Ibid. Reductive "marvelling" at Aboriginal peoples' skills is a common feature of imperial travel discourse. See M. L. Pratt, *Imperial Eyes: Travel Writing and Transculturation* (London: Routledge, 1992), especially chap. 3, "Narrating the Anti-Conquest."

32 *Debates,* (29 May 1995), p.220 (G. Filmon).

33 Ibid., p.221–2.

34 "Electrical Power in Canada" (1995). *Canadian Electricity Association.* <http://www.canelect.ca/media/directory.html>. February 15, 1999.

35 "Land" is defined in the Act as "real property of whatsoever nature or kind and included tenements, hereditaments, and appurtenances, leaseholds, and any estate, term, easement, right or interest in, to, over, under or affecting land, including rights-of- way, and waters, water rights, water powers, and water privileges. . . ."

36 "Electrical Power in Canada" (1995). *Canadian Electricity Association.*

37 "The Hydro Province" (1999). *Manitoba Hydro.* <http://www.hydro.mb.ca/all_about_us/the_hydro_province.html>. September 9, 1999.

38 "Canada" (1999). *Canadian Electricity Association.* <http://www.canelect.ca/connections_online/this_week/canada/canada.html>. September 9, 1999.

39 *Report,* vol. 1, pp.172–5. The commissioners recommended that both the provincial and federal governments recognize the *Northern Flood Agreement* as a treaty, honouring and implementing its terms; that equivalent rights be granted by agreement to other Aboriginal people affected by the flooding, but not signatory to the NFA; and that a moratorium be placed on major natural resource development projects "unless, and until, agreements or treaties are reached with the Aboriginal people in the region who might be negatively affected by such projects in order to respect their Aboriginal or treaty rights in the territory concerned" (p.175).

40 John Lyons, "Fox Lake Band Members Refuse to Accept Federal Treaty Payment," *The Winnipeg Free Press,* July 3, 1999, p.A7.

41 Doug Nairne, "Newman goes on the attack at Cross Lake," *The Winnipeg Free Press,* June 26, 1999, p.A3. Nairne reported that members of a church-led inquiry into issues of flooding compensation were "taken aback by the apparent hostility" of the provincial Minister of Northern Affairs, David Newman, when he addressed the hearing at Cross Lake. To the credit of the provincial government, it did send a representative, while no federal officials were even in attendance.

42 For insightful discussion regarding "dreams" of Canadian innocence, see Sherene Razack, "Making Canada White: Law and the Policing of Bodies of Colour in the 1990s," *Canadian Journal of Law and Society* 14, 1 (1999), p.159.

43 *Debates* (30 May 1995), p.234 (O. Lathlin).

44 Randy Fred contends that "[t]he elimination of language has always been a primary stage in the process of cultural genocide. This was the primary function of the residential school." Randy Fred, "Introduction," in C. Haig-Brown, *Resistance and Renewal: Surviving the Indian Residential School* (Vancouver: Tillacum Library, 1988), p.15.

45 *Debates* (30 May 1995), p.233 (O. Lathlin).

46 *Debates* (30 May 1995), p.235 (G. Filmon).

47 *Report,* vol. 2. Section one of this volume focuses exclusively on matters relating to Osborne's death, while section two (separately paginated) deals with the death of J.J. Harper. Harper died from a gunshot wound caused by the firearm of Constable Robert Andrew Cross of the Winnipeg Police Department. A member of the Wasagamack Indian band, Harper was known as a leader in Manitoba's Aboriginal community. At the time of his death he was

married, had three children, and was thirty-seven years old.

48 *Report*, vol. 1, pp.2–3.

49 Ibid., p.5. In contrast with the Inquiry's more general work regarding the justice system, the nature of the Osborne and Harper matters, compounded by a number of legal challenges launched by the Winnipeg Police Association, obliged the commissioners to proceed in these instances "in a formal way, ensuring that all interested parties were represented by counsel, that all witnesses could be cross-examined, that their rights would be respected and that all testimony was given under oath."

50 Ibid., pp.765–7.

51 Ibid., p.6.

52 Ibid., pp.9–10. More recent statistics attest to the worsening of this trend. On a national scale where Aboriginal people represent 2 per cent of the adult population in Canada, this same demographic accounted for 11 per cent of admissions to federal penitentiaries in 1991–92; 15 per cent in 1996–97; and 17 per cent in 1997–98. M. Reed and J. Roberts, "Adult Correctional Services in Canada, 1997–1998," *Juristat* 19,4 (Ottawa: Canadian Centre for Justice Statistics/Statistics Canada, 1999), p.1.

53 *Report*, vol. 1, p.561.

54 Ibid., p.101. Reed and Roberts report that the combined figure rose to 61 per cent in 1997–98.

55 Ibid., p.8. Reed and Roberts compare prison statistics with welfare rates for Manitoba's Aboriginal population, rates which rank among the highest in Canada at close to 85 per cent for reserve residents. Note as well that 63 per cent of Status Indians in Manitoba live on reserves, which is "one of the highest proportions of on-reserve residencies in Canada."

56 *Report*, vol. 1, p.102 (footnotes omitted); "Fact Sheets: Alternatives To Incarceration." *Elizabeth Fry Society* <http://www.elizabethfry.ca/facts1_e.htm>. July 21, 2000. This same source notes that in 1997 First Nations women represented 19 per cent of federally sentenced women, while they make up 1–2 per cent of the Canadian population.

57 *Report*, vol. 1, p.12.

58 *Debates* (30 May 1995), p.234 (O. Lathlin).

59 Manitoba Bureau of Statistics, *Manitoba Provincial Electoral Divisions: Detailed Statistical Profiles* (Winnipeg: MBS, 1990), p.23.

60 Manitoba Bureau of Statistics, *Manitoba Provincial Electoral Divisions*, p.22.

61 Carol LaPrairie, *Examining Aboriginal Corrections in Canada* (Ottawa: Aboriginal Corrections, Ministry of the Solicitor General, 1996), p.64.

62 John Loxley, "Aboriginal People in the Winnipeg Economy," *For Seven Generations: An Information Legacy of The Royal Commission on Aboriginal Peoples*, CD-ROM (Ottawa: Libraxus, 1997).

63 In October of 1986 charges of murder were laid against Lee Colgan and Dwayne Archie Johnston. In March 1987 Lee Colgan was granted immunity from prosecution in exchange for his testimony. James Houghton was arrested and charged on July 5, 1987, on the strength of evidence provided by Colgan. Both Houghton and Johnston were committed to stand trial at a preliminary hearing later that month, and the case came to trial in December 1987. An exclusively non-Aboriginal jury found Johnston guilty of the murder of Helen Betty Osborne. Johnston was sentenced to life imprisonment without parole eligibility for ten years. The jury acquitted Houghton. Following his acquittal, the

Crown gave no consideration to charging him with other offences. Lee Colgan was acquitted. Evidence against Norman Manger had been deemed insufficient to support a charge: "[I]n addition, all the evidence suggested that Manger was too drunk to form the requisite criminal intent." Johnston's appeal of his conviction was dismissed by the Manitoba Court of Appeal on September 14, 1988. On March 13, 1989, his application for leave to appeal to the Supreme Court of Canada was also denied. *Report*, vol. 2.

64 Michael Smith, "Tent City Preferable to Living in Poor Housing," *Windspeaker* (December 1995), p.3.

65 Tracy Lindberg, "What Do You Call an Indian Woman with a Law Degree? Nine Aboriginal Women at the University of Saskatchewan College of Law Speak Out," *Canadian Journal of Women and the Law* 9,2 (1997), p.318.

66 Goldberg, *Racist Culture*, p.204.

67 *Report*, vol. 1, p.49.

68 Kathleen Kirby, "Re: Mapping Subjectivity: Cartographic Vision and the Limits of Politics," in N. Duncan, ed., *Body Space: Destabilizing Geographies of Gender and Sexuality* (New York: Routledge, 1996), p.48.

69 Toni Morrison, *Playing in the Dark: Whiteness and the Literary Imagination* (Cambridge, MA: Harvard University Press, 1992), p.xiii.

Chapter 7: Making Space for Mosques

We would like to thank Stacy Clark and Shaheen Ramputh for their superb assistance in conducting various aspects of this research. Many thanks to Zak Ghanim for providing the photographs. We are also grateful to Evelyn Ruppert, Patricia Wood, Jon Caulfield, Ali Bolbol, and Kenise Kilbride who read and commented on earlier drafts of this chapter.

1 Phinjo Gombu, "Muslims Get Their Mosque," *The Toronto Star,* July 11, 1995, p.A6.

2 Abdur Ingar, interview conducted by Shaheen Ramputh, Toronto, Ontario, June 18, 1998.

3 Talim-Ul-Islam, *Document Book* (Toronto, 1996).

4 Gombu, "Muslims Get Their Mosque," p.A3.

5 David Lewis Stein, "Better to Abolish East York than to Block Mosque," *The Toronto Star*, October 4, 1995, p.A23.

6 East York Council, *Regulatory and Development Committee Report*, February 12, 1996.

7 Stein, "Better to Abolish East York," p.A23.

8 Jane M. Jacobs, *Edge of Empire: Postcolonialism and the City* (London: Routledge, 1996), p.9.

9 Statistics Canada, *The Daily: 1996 Census Immigration and Citizenship* (Ottawa: Statistics Canada, November 4, 1998).

10 Sheila L. Croucher, "Constructing the Image of Ethnic Harmony in Toronto, Canada: The Politics of Problem Definition and Nondefinition," *Urban Affairs Review* 32, 3 (1997), pp.319–47.

11 Michael Ornstein, *Ethno-Racial Inequality in the City of Toronto: An Analysis of the 1996 Census* (Toronto: City of Toronto. Access and Equity Unit, Strategic and Corporate Policy Division, Chief Administrator's Office, 2000), p.122.

12 Myer Siemiatycki, Time Rees, Roxana Ng, and Khan Rahi, *Integrating Community Diversity in Toronto: On Whose Terms?* Working Paper 14 (Toronto: Centre of Excellence for Research on Immigration and Settlement, 2001).

13 Myer Siemiatycki, and Engin F. Isin, "Immigration, Diversity and Urban Citizenship in Toronto," *Canadian Journal of Regional Science* 20, 1 and 2 (1998), pp.73–102.

14 Engin F. Isin, "Cities and Citizenship,"
    Citizenship Studies 3, 2 (1999),
    pp.165–283; Engin F. Isin, ed., *Democ-
    racy, Citizenship and the Global City, Innis
    Centenary Series* (London: Routledge,
    2000); Soledad Garcia, "Cities and Citi-
    zenship," *International Journal of Urban
    and Regional Research* 20, 1 (1996),
    pp.7–21; and James Holston, ed., *Cities
    and Citizenship* (Durham, NC: Duke Uni-
    versity Press, 1999).

15 Engin F. Isin and Patricia K. Wood,
    Citizenship and Identity (London: Sage,
    1999).

16 Edward S. Said, *Culture and Imperialism*
    (New York: Vintage Books, 1993), p.301.

17 Sophie Body-Gendrot, "Migration and
    the Racialization of the Postmodern City
    in France," in M. Cross and M. Keith,
    eds., *Racism, the City and the State* (Lon-
    don: Routledge, 1993), p.80. See also
    Gilles Kepel, "Islamic Groups in Europe:
    Between Community Affirmation and
    Social Crisis, " in S. Vertovec and C.
    Peach, eds., *Islam in Europe: The Politics
    of Religion and Community* (New York:
    St Martin's Press, 1997), pp.48–55; and
    Michael E. Salla, "Political Islam and the
    West: A New Cold War or Convergence?"
    Third World Quarterly 18, 4 (1997),
    pp.729–42.

18 John L. Esposito, *The Islamic Threat:
    Myth or Reality?* 3rd ed. (New York:
    Oxford University Press, 1999), p.233;
    Aziz Al-Azmeh, *Islams and Modernities*,
    2nd ed. (London: Verso, 1996); and
    David Marquand and Ronald L. Nettler,
    Religion and Democracy (Oxford: Black-
    well, 2000).

19 Esposito, *The Islamic Threat: Myth or
    Reality?* p.234.

20 Ibid., p.237.

21 Carolyn Gallaher, "Identity Politics and
    the Religious Right: Hiding Hate in the
    Landscape," *Antipode* 29, 3 (1997),
    pp.256–77.

22 Will Kymlicka, *Multicultural Citizenship*
    (Oxford: Oxford University Press, 1995);
    Iris Marion Young, "Polity and Group
    Difference: A Critique of the Ideal of Uni-
    versal Citizenship," *Ethics* 99 (January
    1989), pp.250–74; Nira Yuval-Davis, "The
    'Multi-Layered Citizen': Citizenship in
    the Age of 'Glocalization,'" *International
    Feminist Journal of Politics* 1, 1 (1999),
    pp.119–36.

23 Regula Burckhardt Qureshi, "Transcend-
    ing Space: Recitation and Community
    among South Asian Muslims in Canada,"
    in B. D. Metcalf, ed., *Making Muslim
    Space in North America and Europe*
    (Berkeley: University of California Press,
    1996), pp.47, 48.

24 Barbara Daly Metcalf, "Introduction:
    Sacred Words, Sanctioned Practice, New
    Communities," in Metcalf, ed., *Making
    Muslim Space in North America and
    Europe*, p.6.

25 John Eade, "Nationalism, Community,
    and the Islamization of Space in Lon-
    don," in Metcalf, ed., *Making Muslim
    Space in North America and Europe*, p.217.

26 Ibid., p.277.

27 Gulzar Haider, "Muslim Space and the
    Practice of Architecture," in Metcalf, ed.,
    *Making Muslim Space in North America
    and Europe*, p.41.

28 David Goldberg, *Racist Culture: Philoso-
    phy and the Politics of Meaning* (Oxford:
    Blackwell, 1993), pp.95, 185.

29 Jacobs, *Edge of Empire*, p.3.

30 Leonie Sandercock, *Towards Cosmopolis:
    Planning for Multicultural Cities* (New
    York: Wiley, 1998), p.3.

31 Saskia Sassen, *Guests and Aliens* (New
    York: New Press, 1999); Saskia
    Sassen, "The Global City: Strategic
    Site/New Frontier, " in Isin, ed., *Democ-
    racy, Citizenship and the Global City*; E.F.
    Isin, "Introduction: Democracy, Citizen-
    ship and the City," in Isin, ed., *Democ-
    racy, Citizenship and the Global City*.

32 Mohammad Quadeer, "Pluralistic Planning for Multicultural Cities: The Canadian Practice," *Journal of the American Planning Association* 63, 4 (1997), p.491.

33 Sandercock, *Towards Cosmopolis*, p.101.

34 Abdur Ingar, interview conducted by Shaheen Ramputh, Toronto, Ontario, June 18, 1998; Hassan Yussuf, interview conducted by Shaheen Ramputh, Toronto, Ontario, July 10, 1998.

35 Quadeer, "Pluralistic Planning for Multicultural Cities," p.491.

36 Muhammad Ashraf, interview conducted by Shaheen Ramputh, Toronto, Ontario, July 14, 1998; Yussuf, interview.

37 Muhammad Ibrahim, interview conducted by Shaheen Ramputh, Toronto, Ontario, July 3, 1998.

38 Talim-Ul-Islam, *Document Book*.

39 Ibrahim interview.

40 Talim-Ul-Islam, *Document Book*, p.7.

41 Ontario Municipal Board, *Talim-Ul-Islam Ontario V. Toronto (City) Committee of Adjustment*, August 5, 1998, p.8.

42 Ibid., p.1.

43 Siemiatycki and Isin, "Immigration, Diversity and Urban Citizenship in Toronto."

44 Ontario Municipal Board, *Canadian Islamic Trust Foundation V. Mississauga (City)*, March 4, 1998, p.4.

45 Anonymous Planner, interview conducted by Stacy Clark, Toronto, Ontario, August 2, 1998.

46 Rick Gosling, interview conducted by Myer Siemiatycki, Toronto, Ontario, July 11, 1998.

47 Anonymous Planner, interview.

48 Ontario Municipal Board, *Talim-Ul-Islam Ontario V. Toronto (City) Committee of Adjustment*.

49 Ibid., pp.21, 24.

50 John Stewart, "Ratepayers, Councillor Fear the Mosque," *Mississauga News*, March 11, 1998, p.1.

51 Ashraf, interview.

52 Ibid.

53 Ontario Municipal Board, *Araujo V. York (City) Committee of Adjustment*, August 8, 1997, p.1.

54 Ibid., p.12.

55 Rocco DeLellis, interview conducted by Shaheen Ramputh, Toronto, Ontario, August 11, 1998.

56 Ontario Municipal Board, *Araujo V. York (City) Committee of Adjustment*, August 8, 1997, p.1. Emphasis in original.

57 Fred Lindsay, interview conducted by Shaheen Ramputh, Toronto, Ontario, August 11, 1998.

58 Enzo Di Matteo, "Mosque's New Roof Sets off Storm in York," *Now* (Toronto), December 26, 1996–January 2, 1997, p.25.

59 Ontario Municipal Board, *Araujo V. York (City) Committee of Adjustment*, August 8, 1997, p.35.

60 Lindsay interview; Sayed Sheik, interview conducted by Shaheen Ramputh, Toronto, Ontario, July 29, 1998.

61 Sandercock, *Towards Cosmopolis*, p.219.

62 Ontario Municipal Board, *Araujo V. York (City) Committee of Adjustment*, August 8, 1997.

63 Bilal Abdullah, Letter to the Editor, *NOW* (Toronto), January 9–January 15, 1996.

64 Bonnie Honig, "How Foreignness 'Solves' Democracy's Problems," *Social Text* 16, 3 (1998), p.16.

65 Ruth Fincher and Jane M. Jacobs, eds., *Cities of Difference* (New York: Guilford, 1998), p.2.

Chapter 8: The Space of Africville

1 G. Stephenson, *A Redevelopment Study of Halifax, Nova Scotia* (Halifax: Corporation of the City of Halifax, 1957), pp.27–8.

2 L. Johnson, "Occupying the Suburban Frontier: Accommodating Difference on Melbourne's Urban Fringe," in A. Blunt and G. Rose, eds., *Writing Women and*

Space: Colonial and Postcolonial Geographies (New York: Guilford Press, 1994), p.146.

3   For early historical information, I have relied on: Africville Genealogical Society, eds., *The Spirit of Africville* (Halifax: Formac, 1992); D. H. Clairmont and D.W. Magill, *Africville Relocation Report* (Halifax: Institute of Public Affairs, Dalhousie University, 1971); D. H. Clairmont and D.W. Magill, *Africville: The Life and Death of a Canadian Black Community,* 1st and 3rd editions (Toronto: McClelland and Stewart, 1974, 1999); F. Henry, *Forgotten Canadians: The Blacks of Nova Scotia* (Don Mills, ON: Longman Canada Limited, 1973).

4   For documentation of relocation, see Clairmont and Magill, *Africville,* and the Africville Genealogical Society, eds., *The Spirit of Africville.*

5   The letter of R.J. Britton, Director of Social Planning for the City of Halifax, to Halifax City Council can be found in "Letter to Halifax City: Re: Africville Genealogy Society," in the Halifax Public Library: Africville File, October 28, 1994. Housing purchase prices are listed in this letter. The amounts city council claims to have paid are seen as inaccurate by some Africville activists with whom I have spoken. There have been accusations of bribery, in which city officials are alleged to have offered residents suitcases of cash in exchange for their eviction. See J. Robson, "Last Africville Resident," *The Mail Star* (Halifax), January 12, 1970, p.5.

6   David Goldberg, *Racist Culture* (Oxford: Blackwell, 1993), pp.191–2.

7   Henri Lefebvre, "The Production of Space (Extracts)," in N. Leach, ed., *Rethinking Architecture: A Reader in Cultural Theory* (London: Routledge, 1997), p.140.

8   Barnor Hesse, "Black to Front and Black Again," in M. Keith and S. Pile, *Place and the Politics of Identity* (London: Routledge, 1993), p.175.

9   Henri Lefebvre, "Reflections on the Politics of Space," *Antipode* 8 (1876), p.31.

10 C. R. Saunders et al., "A Visit to Africville," in Africville Genealogical Society, eds., *The Spirit of Africville,* p.33.

11 See Goldberg, *Racist Culture,* p.7; David Sibley, "Racism and Settlement Policy: The State's Response to a Semi-Nomadic Minority," in P. Jackson, ed., *Race and Racism: Essays in Social Geography* (London: Allen and Unwin, 1987), p.74; David Sibley, *Geographies of Exclusion* (London: Routledge, 1995); P. Stallybrass and A. White, *The Politics and Poetics of Transgression* (Ithaca: Cornell University Press, 1986); E. Said, *Culture and Imperialism* (New York: Vintage, 1993).

12 P. Marcuse, "Not Chaos, but Walls: Postmodernism and the Partitioned City," in S. Watson and K. Gibson, eds., *Postmodern Cities and Spaces* (Cambridge: Blackwell, 1995), p.243.

13 Sherene Razack, "Race, Space and Prostitution," *Canadian Journal of Women and the Law* 10,2 (1998), p.338.

14 Reports of some bootlegging in Africville are cited in Clairmont and Magill, *Africville Relocation Report.*

15 David Sibley, *Outsiders in Urban Societies* (Oxford: Blackwell, 1981).

16 Samira Kawash, "The Homeless Body," *Public Culture* 10 (1998), p.319.

17 Goldberg, *Racist Culture,* p.190.

18 Ibid., p.198. See also K. Anderson, *Vancouver's Chinatown: Racial Discourse in Canada, 1875–1980* (Montreal: McGill-Queen's University Press, 1991).

19 Stephenson, *A Redevelopment Study of Halifax, Nova Scotia.* The Stephenson Report focuses most intensely on the downtown region of Halifax and what might be done about the poor and over-crowded living conditions of its resi-

dents, the majority of whom would have been white.

20 Ibid.

21 Sibley, *Outsiders in Urban Societies*.

22 C. R. Saunders, "Relocation and Its Aftermath: A Journey Behind the Headlines," in Africville Genealogical Society et al., eds., *Africville: A Spirit that Lives On* (Halifax: The Art Gallery, Mount Saint Vincent University, 1989), p.17.

23 Many references to the city's intended desegregation are cited in Clairmont and Magill, *Africville Relocation Report,* and Clairmont and D.W. Magill, *Africville: The Life and Death of a Canadian Black Community*; see also Britton, "Letter to Halifax City: Re: Africville Genealogy Society," note 5 above.

24 R. Simon, "The Touch of the Past: The Pedagogical Significance of a Transactional Sphere of Public Memory," in P. Trifonas, ed., *Revolutionary Pedagogies: Cultural Politics, Education, and the Discourse of Theory* (New York: Routledge, 2000), p.61.

25 Goldberg, *Racist Culture*, p.204.

26 Sherene Razack, "Gendered Racial Violence and Spatialized Justice: The Murder of Pamela George," chap. 5 in this volume.

27 Sherene Razack, *Looking White People in the Eye: Gender, Race and Culture in Courtrooms and Classrooms* (Toronto: University of Toronto Press, 1998), p.40.

28 Britton, "Letter to Halifax City: Re: Africville Genealogy Society," note 5 above.

29 Ibid.

30 R. Thompson Ford, "The Boundaries of Race: Political Geography in Legal Analysis," *Harvard Law Review* 107 (1994), p.1843.

31 Goldberg, *Racist Culture*.

32 Clairmont and Magill, *Africville Relocation Report*.

33 Goldberg, *Racist Culture,* pp.204–5.

34 D. Harvey, *Justice, Nature and the Geography of Difference* (Cambridge: Blackwell, 1996).

35 Kathleen Kirby, "Re: Mapping Subjectivity: Cartographic Vision and the Limits of Politics," in N. Duncan, ed., *Bodyspace: Destabilizing Geographies of Gender and Sexuality* (London: Routledge, 1996), p.45.

36 L. MacLean, "Seaview Officially Opens" *The Mail Star* (Halifax), June 24, 1985, p.1.

37 Jane Jacobs, "Resisting Reconciliation: The Secret Geographies of (Post)colonial Australia," in S. Pile. and M. Keith, eds., *Geographies of Resistance* (London: Routledge, 1997), pp.206–8.

38 Lefebvre, "The Production of Space Extracts," p.140.

39 M. Lightstone, "Africville Showdown Brewing," *The Halifax Daily News*, February 12, 1995.

40 C. MacKeen, "City Responds to Protest over Seaview Park Land," *The Halifax Chronicle-Herald*, May 12, 1995.

41 T.L. Paynter, "City Gives Carverys the Boot," *North End News*, March 24, 1995; M. Lightstone, "Mayor: 'No Racism in This,'" *The Halifax Daily News*, March 25, 1995; C. McKeen, "Get Out, Protesters Warned," *The Halifax Chronicle-Herald*, May 17, 1995, p.A1.

42 Charles Saunders, "Scenes from Africville Reunion," *Halifax Daily News*, August 8, 1999, p.20.

43 Sibley, *Geographies of Exclusion*.

44 See Bonita Lawrence, "'Real' Indians and Others: Mixed-Race Urban Native People, the Indian Act, and the Rebuilding of Indigenous Nations" (Ph.D. diss., Ontario Institute of Studies in Education of the University of Toronto, 1999).

Chapter 9: Delivering Subjects

1 D. L. Martin, "The Midwives Tale: Old Wisdom and a New Challenge to the

Control of Reproduction," *Columbia Journal of Gender and Law* 3,1 (1992), p.417. See especially V. Van Wagner, "Women Organizing for Midwifery in Ontario," *Resources for Feminist Research* 17,3 (1988), p.136.

2   See R. E. Davis Floyd, *Birth as an American Rite of Passage* (Berkeley: University of California Press, 1992); A. Oakley, *The Captured Womb: A History of the Medical Care of Pregnant Women* (Oxford: Basil Blackwell, 1984); B. K. Rothman, *In Labor: Women and Power in the Birthplace* (New York: Norton, 1991); and D. Scully, *Men Who Control Women's Health: The Miseducation of Obstetrician Gynecologists* (New York: Teachers College Press, 1994).

3   Bill 56, *An Act Respecting the Regulation of the Profession of Midwifery*, 1st Sess., 35th Leg., Ontario, 1991 (assented to 25 November 1991. S.O.1991, c. 31). All subsequent references are from this Act.

4   The number of midwives of colour expressing an interest in having their credentials recognized in the province has, since 1986, outstripped their proportion in the population at large, accounting for nearly half of those who, by 1994, had sought information from the College of Midwives and its predecessors about credentials assessment. Relatively few of these women, however, have succeeded in becoming registered as midwives. The College of Midwives of Ontario has not collected statistics on the ethnic/racial group identification of its members. Consequently, any claims about the numbers of racialized minority women who are registered midwives represent estimates. In June 2000, I asked four individuals who are intimately involved with midwifery in Ontario to review the most recent lists of registered midwives issued by both the Association of Ontario Midwives and the College of Midwives of Ontario. These women were able to identify seventeen women of colour and two Aboriginal women, who, in total, represented just over 10 per cent of the approximately 180 midwives listed as registered in the province. Three of the women of colour identified were known not to be practising. While I must emphasize that this is not an official accounting, this estimate is likely highly accurate.

5   P. Essed, *Understanding Everyday Racism* (Newbury Park, NJ: Sage, 1991).

6   The use of the term "Third World" continues to demand explication on the parts of those who use it. While acknowledging the assertion of David Goldberg that "Third World" is one of three "conceptual schemata hegemonic in the production of contemporary racialized knowledge that now define and order popular conceptions of people racially conceived" and that of Ella Shohat and Robert Stam that "First World"/ "Third World" struggles take place not only *between* nations but also *within* them, I will adopt this term here as a provisional one. Ella Shohat and Robert Stam, *Unthinking Eurocentrism: Multiculturalism and the Media* (London: Routledge, 1994), p.26; and David Goldberg, *Racist Culture: Philosophy and the Politics of Meaning* (Oxford: Blackwell, 1993), p.155.

7   See especially, in the Canadian context, A. Bakan and D. Stasiulis, "Making the Match: Domestic Placement Agencies and the Racialization of Women's Household Work," *Signs* 20,2 (1995), p.303.

8   See E. Said, *Culture and Imperialism* (New York: Alfred A. Knopf, 1993), and A. L. Stoler, *Race and the Education of Desire: Foucault's History of Sexuality and the Colonial Order of Things* (Durham, NC: Duke University Press, 1995).

9   R. J. Johnston et al., *The Dictionary of Human Geography* (Oxford: Blackwell, 2000), p.546.

10 A. Burton, *Burdens of History: British Feminists, Indian Women and Imperial Culture, 1865–1915* (Chapel Hill: University of North Carolina Press, 1994), p.1.

11 See E. Soja, *Thirdspace: Journeys to Los Angeles and Other Real-and-Imagined Places* (Cambridge: Blackwell, 1996).

12 I wish to thank Margot Francis for suggesting the use of the term "midwifery tourism."

13 In identifying myself and other women here as "white," I am signalling our positionality as the beneficiaries of numerous social privileges that accrue to those whose appearance, comportment, habits, and behaviours are construed as white in the wake of specific historical processes. Whiteness is not an essential, immutable identity, but rather a relational one. Its privileged status can be compromised and its attendant privileges diminished when its bearer transgresses the boundaries of gender, class, sexual, religious, or bodily normativity. It is nearly impossible, however, to divest oneself of white privilege in an environment highly structured by racial meanings and hierarchies. See A. Bailey, "Despising an Identity They Taught Me to Claim," in C.J. Cuomo ans K.Q. Hall, eds, *Whiteness: Feminist Philosophical Reflections* (Lanham: Rowan and Littlefield, 1999), p.85.

14 Sheryl Nestel, "Obstructed Labour: Race and Gender in the Re-emergence of Midwifery in Ontario" (Ph.D. diss., Ontario Institute for Studies in Education of the University of Toronto, 2000).

15 See M. Enkin et al., eds., *A Guide to Effective Care in Pregnancy and Childbirth* (New York: Oxford University Press, 1995), and J. Kaczorowski et al., "A National Survey of Use of Obstetric Procedures and Technologies in Canadian Hospitals: Routine or Based on Existing Evidence," *Birth* 25,1 (1998), p.11.

16 The terminology surrounding the classification of midwives is complex and shifts, depending on geographical and temporal location. The use of the term "lay midwife" here is meant to invoke the context during which that term was current. It is meant to identify midwives who may have been trained in formal training programs and through empirical means, but who are not affiliated with nurse-midwifery or direct-entry midwifery training in medical institutions. For a discussion of the different usages of classificatory terms for midwives, see J. P. Rooks, *Midwifery and Childbirth in America* (Philadelphia: Temple University Press, 1997), p.8.

17 For a discussion of the early midwifery movement in Ontario, see M. T. Fynes, "The Legitimation of Midwifery in Ontario 1960–1987" (M.A. thesis, Graduate Department of Community Health, University of Toronto, 1994).

18 For critical perspectives on traditional women's health movements, see D. Gorham and F. K. Andrews, "The La Leche League: A Feminist Perspective," in K. Arnup, A. Lévesque, and R. R. Pierson, eds., *Delivering Motherhood* (London: Routledge, 1990), and J. D. Ward, *La Leche League: At the Crossroads of Medicine, Feminism, and Religion* (Chapel Hill: University of North Carolina Press, 2000). On feminist women's health movements in Canada see N. Kleiber and L. Light, *Caring for Ourselves: An Alternative Structure for Health Care* (Vancouver, BC: School of Nursing, University of British Columbia, 1978), and E. Dua et al., eds., *On Women Healthsharing* (Toronto: Women's Press, 1994). On the 1960s counterculture's effects on the childbirth reform movement, see L. Umansky, *Motherhood Reconceived: Feminism and the Legacies of the Sixties* (New York: NYU Press, 1996). For an examination of 1970s

and early 1980s childbirth reform in Canada, see S. Romalis, "Struggle Between Providers and Recipients: The Case of Birth Practices," in V. Oleson and E. Lewin, eds., *Women Health and Healing* (New York: Tavistock, 1985), p.74.

19 While the Canadian Medical Association announced its official position opposing the licensing of midwives in 1987, Ontario physicians did not endorse this stance. They were, however, unequivocally opposed to home birth, a practice that Ontario midwives considered to be the foundation of alternative childbirth and one which they categorically refused to abandon in the struggle for legalization. See H. A. Davidson, "Territoriality Among Health Care Workers: Opinions of Nurses and Doctors Towards Midwives" (Ed.D. diss., University of Toronto, 1997).

20 For discussions of racialized images in the campaign to eliminate midwifery in the U.S. at the beginning of the last century, see B. Ehrenreich and D. English, *For Her Own Good: 125 Years of Experts' Advice to Women* (New York: Doubleday, 1978), p.96, and R. D. Wertz and D. Wertz, *Lying-In: A History of Childbirth in America* (New Haven: Yale University Press, 1989), p.216. As recently as 1995, physicians in Sudbury, Ontario, published an advertisement in which they denounced proposed midwife-run birth centres. Using a discursive strategy with unmistakably racist overtones, the ad claimed that "the only model for this is Somalia (no doctors or nurses there anyway)." *Northern Life* (Spring 1995), p.5.

21 J. Winkup, "Reluctant Redefinition: Medical Dominance and the Representation of Midwifery in the *Canadian Medical Association Journal 1967–1997*" (M.A. thesis, University of Guelph, 1998), p.122.

22 While I use the term "Ontario midwives" to designate the predominantly white group that practised midwifery outside of the medical system and organized the profession's legalization campaign, I acknowledge the contradictory nature of the term. I would argue that midwives trained outside of the province who wish to practise but who are not registered, also need to be regarded as Ontario midwives (although legally proscribed from using that term) inasmuch as they have undergone formal training and are residents of the province.

23 H. Tyson, "Outcomes of 1001 Midwife-Attended Home Births in Toronto, 1983–1988," *Birth* 18,1 (1991), p.14.

24 It must be stressed that this number is merely an average. In fact, some midwives attended thirty or forty births per year in this period while others attended relatively few. Also, owing to family responsibilities, travel or study, midwives would often withdraw from practice for an extended period, during which other practitioners would take on larger case loads (personal communication with Christine Sternberg, RM, May 25, 2000).

25 The practice of midwifery was never proscribed by law during its re-emergence in Ontario. Unlike in other provinces, where midwives had faced charges of criminal negligence causing bodily harm, in Ontario no midwife had been charged with a criminal act related to the practice of midwifery. See B. Burch, *Trials of Labour: The Re-emergence of Midwifery* (Montreal: McGill-Queen's University Press, 1994).

26 M. Eberts et al., *Report of the Task Force on the Implementation of Midwifery in Ontario* (Toronto: Government of Ontario, 1987).

27 See, for example, *Issue: Newsletter of the Ontario Association of Midwives* (1981–1983), and *The Association of Ontario Midwives Newsletter* (1985–1993).

28 For a discussion of the North American childbirth reform movement's engagement with racist discourses of "Third World" women's bodies, see S. Nestel, "'Other Mothers': Race and Representation in Natural Childbirth Discourse," *Resources for Feminist Research* 23,4 (1995), p.4; Norma Alarcon, "Anzaldua's Frontera: Inscribing Gynetics," in S. Lavie and T. Swedenburg, eds., *Displacement, Diaspora and Geographies of Identity* (Durham, NC: Duke University Press, 1996), p.45.

29 Candidates for the Michener Institute Pre-Registration program, which assessed midwives practising in the province prior to legislation and "grandparented" into practice those whose assessments were deemed adequate, required that midwives had attended sixty births, thirty of which could have taken place outside of Ontario and twenty of which could have been attended in the capacity of observer/assistant. D.M. Schatz, *Report on the Admission Process, Pre-Registration Program Midwifery* (Toronto: The Michener Institute, November 30, 1992), p.2.

30 Lata Mani, *Contentious Traditions: The Debate on Sati in Colonial India* (Berkeley: University of California Press, 1998), p.3.

31 For examples of this literature, see M. L. Pratt, *Imperial Eyes: Travel Writing and Transculturation* (London: Routledge, 1992); N. Chaudhuri and M. Stroebel, eds., *Western Women and Imperialism: Complicity and Resistance* (Bloomington: University of Indiana Press, 1992); I. Grewal, *Home and Harem: Nation, Gender, Empire and the Cultures of Travel* (Durham, NC: Duke University Press, 1996); and V. Ware, *Beyond the Pale: White Women, Racism and History* (London: Verso, 1992).

32 Sherene Razack, "Race, Space and Prostitution: The Making of the Bourgeois Subject," *Canadian Journal of Women and the Law* 10,2 (1998), p.338.

33 Barbara Heron, "Desire for Development: The Education of White Women as Development Workers" (Ph.D diss., Ontario Institute for Studies in Education of the University of Toronto, 1999), pp.186, 189.

34 Grewal, *Home and Harem,* p.2.

35 Jane Jacobs, *Edge of Empire: Postcolonialism and the City* (New York: Routledge, 1996), p.142.

36 Griselda Pollock, "Territories of Desire: Reconsiderations of an African Childhood," in George Robertson et al., eds. *Traveller's Tales: Narratives of Home and Displacement* (New York: Routledge, 1994), p.72.

37 Caren Kaplan, *Questions of Travel: Postmodern Discourses of Displacement* (Durham, NC: Duke University Press, 1996), p.35.

38 Quoted in A. McClintock, *Imperial Leather: Race, Gender and Sexuality in the Colonial Contest* (New York: Routledge, 1995), p.130.

39 See Margaret Mead, *Male and Female: A Study of the Sexes in a Changing World* (1949; reprint, New York: William Morrow, 1967), and Sheila Kitzinger, *Ourselves as Mothers* (London: Doubleday, 1992).

40 Bridget Jordan, *Birth in Four Cultures* (Montreal: Eden Press, 1983), p.3, and Bridget Jordan, "Preface to the 4th edition of Birth in Four Cultures," quoted in "Introduction: The Anthropology of Birth," in R. E. Davis-Floyd and C. F. Sargent, eds., *Childbirth and Authoritative Knowledge: Cross Cultural Perspectives*, (Berkeley: University of California Press, 1997), p.1.

41 The film, *Birth in the Squatting Position*, was produced in 1979 by Brazilian physicians Moyses and Claudio Paciornik in their hospital in Curitiba, Brazil. In the

summer of 1982, the Paciorniks published an article that describes how the patients in their clinic follow the example of "our teachers, the Indian women out of the woods." Moyses and Claudio Paciornik, "Rooming-in: Lessons Learned from the Forest Indians of Brazil," *Birth* (1982).

42 G. C. Spivak, *A Critique of Postcolonial Reason: Toward a History of the Vanishing Present* (Cambridge, MA: Harvard University Press, 1999), p.60.

43 Gloria Anzaldúa, *Borderlands/La Frontera: The New Mestiza* (San Francisco: Spinsters/Aunt Lute, 1987), pp.2–3.

44 L. Salzinger, "From High Heels to Swathed Bodies: Gendered Meanings Under Production in Mexico's Export-Processing Industry," *Feminist Studies* 23, 4 (1997), p.569.

45 D. Nathan, "Death Comes to the Maquilas: A Border Story," in R. Kamel and A. Hoffman, eds, *The Maquiladora Reader: Cross-border Organizing since NAFTA* (Philadelphia: American Friend Service Committee, 1999), p.27.

46 R. Moure-Eraso et al., "Back to the Future: Sweatshop Conditions on the Mexico/U.S. Border," *American Journal of Industrial Medicine* 31 (1995), p.597.

47 Salzinger, "From High Heels to Swathed Bodies," p.569.

48 V. S. Mills, "Gender and Work in the Maquiladoras of Ciudad Juarez, Mexico" (M.A. thesis, McGill University, 1991).

49 For a discussion of border surveillance see M. Kearney, "Borders and Boundaries of State and Self at the End of Empire," *Journal of History and Sociology* 4,1 (1991), p.52. See also Linda Diebel, "Fatal Journeys," *The Toronto Star*, August 26, 2001, pp.B1–B3.

50 T. C. Brown, "The Fourth Member of NAFTA: The U.S.–Mexico Border," *The Annals of the American Academy of Politics and Social Science* 55 (1997), pp.105, 108.

51 N. Rodriguez, "The Battle for the Border: Notes on Autonomous Migration, Transnational Communities and the State," *Social Justice* 23,3 (1996), p.21.

52 S. Guendelmann and M. Jasis, "Giving Birth Across the Border: The San Diego Tijuana Connection," *Social Science and Medicine* 34,4 (1992), p.419. See also, H. Ortega, "Crossing the Border for Bargain Medicine: Findings of the Primary Health Care Review in Ambos Nogales," *Carnegie Quarterly* 35 (1991), p.1.

53 Rooks, *Midwifery and Childbirth in America*, p.153.

54 "Maternidad La Luz Direct-Entry Midwifery Program," mimeo, n.d. Received by author 1997. For one of the few early accounts of a highly influential border midwifery, see W. T. McCallum, "The Maternity Center at El Paso," *Birth and the Family Journal* 6, 4 (1979), p.259.

55 Rooks, *Midwifery and Childbirth in America*, p.150.

56 Ibid., p.268.

57 "Jamaica Clinical Trip Information Sheet," International School of Midwifery, Miami Beach, Florida, 1997.

58 Ortega, "Crossing the Border for Bargain Medicine," p.2.

59 "Maternidad La Luz Direct-Entry Midwifery Program."

60 Ibid., p.16.

61 See J. Seabrook, *Travels in the Skin Trade: Tourism and the Sex Industry* (London: Pluto Press, 1996).

62 R. Bishop and L. Robinson, *Night Market: Sexual Cultures and the Thai Economic Miracle* (New York: Routledge, 1998), p.10.

63 Letter from Linda Arnold Milligan, Administrative/Clinical Director of Casa de Nacimiento, El Paso, Texas, to prospective interns, n.d. Received by author in 1997.

64 Trinh, Minh-ha T., *When the Moon Waxes Red: Representation, Gender and Cultural*

Politics (New York: Routledge, 1991), p.22.

65 Bishop and Robinson, *Night Market*, p.126.

66 Van Wagner, "Women Organizing for Midwifery in Ontario," p.137.

67 Teresa de Lauretis, *Alice Doesn't: Feminism, Semiotics, Cinema* (Bloomington: Indiana University Press, 1984), p.159.

68 Hayden White, "The Value of Narrativity in the Representation of Reality," in W.J.T. Mitchell, ed., *On Narrative* (Chicago: University of Chicago Press, 1981).

69 College of Midwives of Ontario, *Philosophy of Midwifery Care in Ontario* (January 1994).

70 "Maternidad La Luz Direct-Entry Midwifery Program"; Casa de Nacimiento pamphlet for prospective students, El Paso, Texas. Received by author in 1997.

71 B. Curtis and C. Pajaczkowska, "'Getting There': Travel, Time and Narrative," in G Robertson et al., eds., *Traveller's Tales: Narratives of Home and Displacement* (New York: Routledge, 1994).

72 O. Schutte, "Cultural Alterity: Cross-Cultural Communication and Feminist Theory in North-South Contexts," *Hypatia* 13,2 (1998), p.53.

73 C. F. Sargent and G. Bascope, "Ways of Knowing about Birth in Three Cultures," in R. E. Davis-Floyd and C. F. Sargent, eds., *Childbirth and Authoritative Knowledge* (Berkeley: University of California Press, 1997), p.193.

74 B. A. Daviss, "From Social Movement to Professional Project: Are We Throwing the Baby Out with the Bathwater?" (M.A. thesis, Carleton University, 1999), p.107.

75 Brian Goldman, "Home Birth: 'We Did It, All of Us,'" *Canadian Medical Association Journal* 139 (1988), p.773.

76 M. J. Alexander, "Imperial Desire/Sexual Utopias: White Gay Capital and Transnational Tourism," in E. Shohat, ed., *Talking Visions: Multicultural Feminism in a Transnational Age* (Cambridge, MA: The MIT Press, 1998), p.300.

77 I. Grewal, "'Women's Rights as Human Rights': Feminist Practices, Global Feminism, and Human Rights Regimes in Transnationality," *Citizenship Studies* 3,3 (1999), p.348.

Selected Bibliography

Alcoff, Linda Martin. "Philosophy and Racial Identity." *Radical Philosophy* 75 (Jan./Feb. 1996), pp.5-14.

Anderson, Kay. *Vancouver's Chinatown: Racial Discourse in Canada, 1875–1980*. Montreal: McGill-Queen's Press, 1991.

Anderson, Kim. *A Recognition of Being: Reconstructing Native Womanhood*. Toronto: Sumach Press, 2001.

Backhouse, Constance. *Colour Coded: A Legal History of Racism in Canada, 1900–1950*. Toronto: University of Toronto Press, 1999.

Berger, Carl. *The True North Strong and Free*. In Peter Russell, ed. *Nationalism in Canada*. Toronto: McGraw-Hill, 1966.

Bishop, Ryan, and Lillian Robinson. *Night Market: Sexual Cultures and the Thai Economic Miracle*. London: Routledge, 1998.

Blunt, Alison, and Gillian Rose, eds. *Writing Women and Space: Colonial and Postcolonial Geographies*. New York: Guilford Press, 1994.

Butler, Judith. *Gender Trouble: Feminism and the Subversion of Identity*. 2nd ed. New York: Routledge, 1999.

Carter, Erica, James Donald, and Judith Squires, eds. *Space and Place: Theories of Identity and Location*. London: Lawrence and Wishart, 1993.

Carter, Sarah. *Capturing Women: The Manipulation of Cultural Imagery in Canada's Prairie West*. Montreal: McGill-Queen's Press, 1997.

Churchill, Ward. *Struggle for the Land: Indigenous Resistance to Genocide, Ecocide and Expropriation in Contemporary North America*. Toronto: Between the Lines, 1992.

—. *Indians Are Us? Culture and Genocide in Native North America*. Toronto: Between the Lines, 1994.

Cross, Michael, and Michael Keith, eds. *Racism, the City and the State*. London: Routledge, 1993.

Culhane, Dara. *The Pleasure of the Crown: Anthropology, Law and First Nations*. Burnaby, B.C.: Talonbooks, 1998.

Dickason, Olivia Patricia. *Canada's First Nations: A History of Founding Peoples from Earliest Times*. Toronto: Oxford University Press, 1992.

Donald, James, and Ali Rattansi, eds. *"Race," Culture and Difference*. London: The Open University Press, 1992.

Dua, Enakshi, and Angela Robertson. *Scratching the Surface: Canadian Anti-Racist Feminist Thought*. Toronto: University of Toronto Press, 1999.

Duncan, Nancy, ed. *Body Space*. New York: Routledge, 1996.

Esposito, John L. *The Islamic Threat: Myth or Reality?* 3rd ed. New York: Oxford University Press, 1999.

Fellows, Mary Louise, and Sherene Razack. "The Race to Innocence: Confronting Hierarchical Relations among Women." *The Journal of Gender, Race and Justice* 1 (1998), pp.335-52.

Fincher, Ruth, and Jane M. Jacobs, eds. *Cities of Difference*. London: The Guilford Press, 1998.

Foucault, Michel. *Discipline and Punish: The Birth of the Prison*. Trans. A. Sheridan. New York: Random House, Vintage Books, 1995.

—. *The History of Sexuality: An Introduction*. Trans. R. Hurley. New York: Vintage Books, 1990.

Goldberg, David. *Racist Culture: Philosophy and the Politics of Meaning*. Oxford: Blackwell Publishers, 1993.

Grewal, Inderpal. *Home and Harem: Nation, Gender, Empire and the Cultures of Travel*. Durham, NC: Duke University Press, 1996.

Grewal, Inderpal, and Caren Kaplan, eds. *Scattered Hegemonies: Postmodernity and Transnational Feminist Practices*. Minneapolis: University of Minnesota Press, 1994.

Haney-Lopez, Ian. *White by Law: The Legal Construction of Race*. New York: New York University Press, 1996.

Harvey, David. *Justice, Nature and the Geography of Difference*. Cambridge: Blackwell, 1996.

Heron, Barbara. "Desire for Development: The Education of White Women as Development Workers." Ph.D. Dissertation, The Ontario Institute for Studies in Education of University of Toronto, 1999.

Hurtado, Aída. *The Color of Privilege: Three Blasphemies on Race and Feminism*. Ann Arbor: University of Michigan Press, 1996.

Isin, Engin F., and Patricia K. Wood. *Citizenship and Identity*. London: Sage, 1999.

Jacobs, Jane M. *Edge of Empire: Postcolonialism and the City*. New York: Routledge, 1996.

Kawash, Samira. "The Homeless Body." *Public Culture* 10,2 (1998).

Kirby, Kathleen. "Re-Mapping Subjectivity: Cartographic Vision and the Limits of Politics." In Nancy Duncan, ed. *Body Space: Destabilizing Geographies of Gender and Sexuality*. New York: Routledge, 1996.

Lefebvre, Henri. *The Production of Space*. Trans. Donald Nicholson-Smith. Oxford: Blackwell Publishers, 1991.

Manitoba. *Report of the Aboriginal Justice Inquiry of Manitoba*. Winnipeg: Queen's Printer, 1991.

McCann, Eugene J. "Race, Protest, and Public Space: Contextualizing Lefebvre in the U.S. City." *Antipode* 31,2 (1999), pp.163-84.

McClintock, Anne. *Imperial Leather: Race, Gender and Sexuality in the Colonial Contest*. New York: Routledge, 1995.

Mohanram, Radhika. *Black Body: Women, Colonialism, and Space*. Minneapolis: University of Minnesota Press, 1999.

Monture-Angus, Patricia. *Thunder in My Soul: A Mohawk Woman Speaks*. Halifax: Fernwood Publishing, 1995.

—. *Journeying Forward: Dreaming First Nations' Independence*. Halifax: Fernwood Publishing, 1999.

Morrison, Toni. *Playing in the Dark: Whiteness and the Literary Imagination*. New York: Vintage Books, 1993. Original edition, Cambridge, MA: Harvard University Press, 1992.

Parr, Joy, and Mark Rosenfeld, eds. *Gender and History in Canada*. Toronto: University of Toronto Press, 1996.

Paul, Daniel N. *We Were Not the Savages: A Mi'kmaq Perspective on the Collision between European and Native American Civilization*. Halifax: Fernwood Books, 2000.

Phillips, Richard. *Mapping Men and Empire: A Geography of Adventure*. New York: Routledge, 1997.

Pile, Steve, and Michael Keith, eds. *Geographies of Resistance*. New York: Routledge, 1997.

Pratt, Mary Louise. *Imperial Eyes: Travel Writing and Transculturation*. London: Routledge, 1992.

Rabinow, Paul, ed. *The Foucault Reader*. New York: Pantheon, 1984.

Razack, Sherene. *Looking White People in the Eye: Gender, Race, and Culture in Courtrooms and Classrooms*. Toronto: University of Toronto Press, 1998.

—. "Race, Space, and Prostitution: The Making of the Bourgeois Subject." *Canadian Journal of Women and the Law* 10,2 (1998), pp.338-76.

—. "Making Canada White: Law and the Policing of Bodies of Colour in the 1990s." *Canadian Journal of Law and Society* 14,1 (1999), pp.159-84.

—. "From the 'Clean Snows of Petawawa': The Violence of Canadian Peacekeepers in Somalia." *Cultural Anthropology* 15,1 (2000), pp.127-63.

—. "'Simple Logic': Race, the Identity Documents Rule and the Story of a Nation Besieged and Betrayed." *Journal of Law and Social Policy* 15 (2000), pp.181-209.

Roediger, David. *Toward the Abolition of Whiteness*. London: Verso, 1994.

Rose, Gillian. *Feminism and Geography: The Limits of Geographical Knowledge*. Minneapolis: University of Minnesota Press, 1993.

Said, Edward. *Culture and Imperialism*. New York: Vintage Books, 1993.

Shields, Robert. *Places on the Margins: Alternative Geographies of Modernity*. New York: Routledge, 1991.

Shohat, Ella, ed. *Talking Visions: Multicultural Feminism in a Transnational Age*. Cambridge, MA: The MIT Press, 1998.

Sibley, David. *Geographies of Exclusion: Society and Difference in the West*. London: Routledge, 1995.

Sioui, Georges E. *For an Amerindian Autohistory*. Montreal: McGill-Queen's University Press, 1992.

—. "Why We Should Have Inclusivity and Why We Cannot Have It." *Ayaangwaamizin: The International Journal of Indigenous Philosophy* 1,2 (1997).

Smith, Linda Tuhiwai. *Decolonizing Methodologies: Research and Indigenous Peoples*. London: Zed Books, 1999.

Soja, Edward W. *Postmodern Geographies: The Reassertion of Space in Critical Social Theory*. London: Verso Press, 1989.

Spivak, Gayatri Chakravorty. *A Critique of Postcolonial Reason: Toward a History of the Vanishing Present*. Cambridge, MA: Harvard University Press, 1999.

Stasiulis, Daiva, and Nira, Yuval-Davis., eds. *Unsettling Settler Societies: Articulations of Gender, Race, Ethnicity and Class*. London: Sage, 1995.

Stoler, Ann Laura. *Race and the Education of Desire: Foucault's History of Sexuality and the Colonial Order of Things*. Durham, NC: Duke University Press, 1995.

Sunahara, Ann. *The Politics of Racism*. Toronto: James Lorimer, 1981.

Ware, Vron. *Beyond the Pale: White Women, Racism and History*. London: Verso, 1992.

Wetherell, Margaret, and Jonathan Potter. *Mapping the Language of Racism: Discourse and the Legitimation of Exploitation*. New York: Columbia University Press, 1992.

Wing, Adrien Katherine, ed. *Critical Race Feminism: A Reader*. New York: New York University Press, 1997.

Contributors

SHEILA GILL is a Ph.D. candidate in the Department of Sociology and Equity Studies in Education at the Ontario Institute for Studies in Education of the University of Toronto. "The Unspeakability of Racism" is drawn from her master's thesis, which she completed in September 1999. Her current work examines relationships between the law, race/racism, late colonial culture, and the gendered social locations of Aboriginal youth on the Canadian Prairies.

ENGIN F. ISIN is Canada Research Chair and associate professor in the Division of Social Sciences at York University. He is the author of *Cities Without Citizens: Modernity of the City as a Corporation;* with P.K. Wood, *Citizenship and Identity and Being Political: Genealogies of Citizenship;* editor of *Democracy, Citizenship and the Global City;* co-editor (with Bryan S. Turner) of *Handbook of Citizenship Studies;* and currently co-editing (with Gerald Delanty) *Handbook of Historical Sociology* (forthcoming).

BONITA LAWRENCE, a non-status Mi'kmaw, is assistant professor at the Institute of Women's Studies, Queen's University. Her research and publications focus on urban, non-status and Métis identities and histories of colonization. She is the author of *"Real" Indians and Others: Mixed-Blood Urban*

Native People, the Indian Act, and the Rebuilding of Indigenous Nations (forthcoming) and co-editor (with Kim Anderson) of *Reclaiming Our Authority: Aboriginal Women and Community Survival* (forthcoming). She is vice-president of the board of Anduhyaun, an Aboriginal women's shelter, and serves on the board of Katorokwi Native Friendship Centre in Kingston. She teaches traditional women's singing and hand-drumming at Four Directions Aboriginal Students Centre at Queen's.

RENISA MAWANI is assistant professor, Department of Sociology at Brock University. Her research interests are in the areas of race, racism, and the law; postcolonial legal studies/critical race theory; and race, space and the law. She has published several articles and book chapters on prostitution, the legal construction of race, and the making of bourgeois subjects through public health education. Her current research explores the interface between medical and penal practices of exclusion through D'Arcy Island, a Chinese leper colony that was established off the coast of Vancouver Island and in operation between 1891 and 1924.

JENNIFER J. NELSON is a post-doctoral researcher in the Department of Sociology and Equity Studies in Education at the

Ontario Institute for Studies in Education of the University of Toronto. "The Space of Africville" is drawn from her dissertation entitled "The Operation of Whiteness and Forgetting in Africville: A Geography of Racism" completed in 2001. She has also published articles on the spatial politics of working-class identity and on the Canadian men's movement. She is currently beginning work on the spatial underpinnings of reparations for African Canadians.

SHERYL NESTEL teaches in the Department of Sociology and Equity Studies in Education at the Ontario Institute for Studies in Education of the University of Toronto, and is a research fellow at the Institute for Women's and Gender Studies, New College, University of Toronto. She has published extensively on race and racism in women's health movements, and is currently working on issues of race in the undergraduate nursing curriculum.

MONA OIKAWA is the Margaret Lawrence Post-Doctoral Fellow in Women's Studies, University of Manitoba. She researches and writes on the internment of Japanese Canadians and the historical construction of racialized identities and sexualities. She is the co-editor of *Resist!: Essays Against A Homophobic Culture* and *Out Rage,* and co-author of a collection of poetry and short stories, *All Names Spoken.*

SHERENE H. RAZACK is professor of Sociology and Equity Studies in Education at the Ontario Institute for Studies in Education of the University of Toronto. Her books include *Looking White People in the Eye: Gender, Race, and Culture in Courtrooms and Classrooms* and *Canadian Feminism and the Law: The Women's Legal and Education Fund and the Pursuit of Equality.* She has published articles on Canadian national mythologies and immigration policies of the 1990s; race,

space and prostitution; racial violence and the law; and gendered racism. Her current work explores the role of racial violence in the constitution of white settler societies and law's response to it, a theme she pursues in the context of the violence of Canadian peacekeepers in Somalia and police violence in Canada.

CAROL SCHICK is assistant professor in the Faculty of Education at the University of Regina. She is involved in the theory and practice of anti-oppression pedagogy, especially as it addresses race and gender. Her research and publishing focus on the construction of whiteness in sites of identity formation in Canada, such as teacher-education programs and narratives of settler history. Her most recent work examines the question of who can be called a Canadian with respect to normative claims about whose religious practices can be performed in public space.

MYER SIEMIATYCKI is professor in the Department of Politics and School Administration at Ryerson Polytechnic University. His publications have intersected with labour studies, urban studies, and immigration studies. The interplay of dominance and resistance has been a recurring theme in his work.